INTERSECTIONAL PEDAGOGY

Intersectional Pedagogy is the first academic text to extend intersectional theory into the domain of pedagogical praxis. Editor Kim A. Case brings together works from a variety of fields, including social work, higher education, Afro-American Studies, psychology, sociology, American studies, and gender studies, to advance an educational agenda that dismantles the dominant categorical approach which treats social identities as mutually exclusive. Case's pedagogical model for teaching intersectionality and the additional contributors' groundbreaking essays lay the theoretical foundation for intersections of identity pedagogy and provide scholarship and practical applications to aid faculty in promoting complex critical dialogues about systems of privilege and oppression. With its range of disciplinary perspectives and evidence-based strategies, *Intersectional Pedagogy* is a much needed resource for any student or educator who wishes to bring social justice into the classroom.

Kim A. Case, PhD, is Professor of Psychology, Director of the Applied Social Issues graduate program, Director of Undergraduate Psychology, and the Faculty Mentoring Program Chair at the University of Houston-Clear Lake, Houston, Texas, USA. She is a Fellow of the American Psychological Association and of the Society for the Psychological Study of Social Issues.

INTERSECTIONAL PEDAGOGY

Complicating Identity and Social Justice

Edited by Kim A. Case

Routledge
Taylor & Francis Group

NEW YORK AND LONDON

First published 2017
by Routledge
711 Third Avenue, New York, NY 10017

and by Routledge
2 Park Square, Milton Park, Abingdon, Oxon, OX14 4RN

Routledge is an imprint of the Taylor & Francis Group, an informa business

Library of Congress Cataloging in Publication Data
A catalogue record for this book has been requested

ISBN: 978-1-138-94296-7 (hbk)
ISBN: 978-1-138-94297-4 (pbk)
ISBN: 978-1-315-67279-3 (ebk)

Typeset in Bembo
by Swales & Willis Ltd, Exeter, Devon, UK

Dedicated to educators committed to teaching social justice and taking on-the-ground action for pedagogical advancement toward ally development and peace.

CONTENTS

FOREWORD

Teaching Intersectionality for Our Times

Although the concept of intersectionality was, to a large extent, foreshadowed in the writings of many generations of African American scholar activists (Hancock, 2005), since being coined by Kimberlé Crenshaw (1989), it has been hailed, variously, as the signal contribution of women's studies (McCall, 2005), a mantra (Puar, 2007), and a buzzword (Davis, 2008). Indeed, the term intersectionality was not clearly defined in Crenshaw's early work, and consequently it has been taken up and invoked widely and flexibly, often in ways that are not recognizable to those close to the primary sources. Today the word, if not always the concept, has traveled so far and become so frequently invoked that some now claim we have reached a moment of post-intersectional theorizing (Carbado, 2013). Thus, it is worth considering why the concept of intersectionality is still relevant today, and more to the point, why it is vitally important for educated citizens to have more than a passing familiarity with how to use an intersectionality framework to understand how historical and contemporary manifestations of identity, difference, and disadvantage continue to shape life chances and outcomes.

Today we often see the concept of intersectionality used to convey the obvious fact that every individual simultaneously occupies multiple social locations with respect to race, gender, social class, sexuality, etc. While it is true that sometimes the obvious needs to be stated, this characterization flattens intersectionality, rendering it as simply descriptive. In fact, the concept of intersectionality was originally identified and developed as a *mechanism*, a way to think about how these distinctions are socially constructed such that they depend on one another for meaning, which almost paradoxically can create vulnerabilities, erasures and gaps, particularly for members of groups defined by multiple axes of disadvantage. For example, Crenshaw (1989) famously observed how African American women, who should have been protected by laws against both racial and gender discrimination in workplaces, were not protected *as Black women* because the law was premised on the experiences of those who are disadvantaged by race but not by gender, or by gender but not by race. Those who were doubly disadvantaged were essentially invisible to the law and thus had no access to redress.

Crenshaw's initial, very generative publications appeared in 1989 and 1993, an era of very public and contested conversations about Black women's vulnerability and their credibility as witnesses. For example, in 1991–1992, former heavyweight boxing champion Mike Tyson was accused, tried, and eventually convicted of raping a young Black woman in his hotel room. Much of the public conversation surrounding the Tyson case sought to portray the victim, Desiree Washington, as either inviting her rape or being a liar. When Tyson was released from prison in 1995, he was honored at a rally in Harlem billed as a "Day of Redemption." In 1991, we also saw the televised confirmation hearings of U.S. Supreme Court Justice Clarence Thomas, during which Anita Hill, a Black woman civil rights attorney, testified that Thomas had sexually harassed her when they were coworkers at the Equal Employment Opportunity Commission (EEOC) a decade earlier. The eventual confirmation of Thomas suggests that the Senate found Hill's allegations lacking in either credibility or importance.

These events, and others of the era (e.g., the 1990 acquittal of the rap group 2 Live Crew for obscenity based on their lyrics that degraded and portrayed violence against Black women, the Nation of Islam's patriarchal Million Man March in Washington DC in 1995) share features that beg for intersectional analysis. First, much of the contemporary public discussion of these events tended to privilege analyses based on either race or gender. For example, Thomas' characterization of the scrutiny he received during the hearings as a "high-tech lynching," in which he framed himself as an African American man as the victim in the scenario, was widely quoted. Second, the experiences of Black women were essentially negated or silenced by the outcomes of these controversies, whether it was Thomas' confirmation or Tyson's light sentence and warm reception by the community upon release. And third, as Barbara Ransby (2000) described, African American women responded to these issues with leadership, activism, and scholarship that refused single-axis analyses in favor of those that centered Black women, building dynamic coalitions that demonstrated Audre Lorde's (1984) axiom, "There is no such thing as a single-issue struggle because we do not live single-issue lives" (p. 138).

This third point highlights the hallmarks of intersectional analysis. As Vivian May (2015) observed, intersectionality is animated by the desire to fully understand and challenge inequality and exclusion. It is fundamentally a theory of anti-subordination. Characterization of intersectionality simply as descriptive of multiple identities, rather than as a mechanism explaining inequality, does violence to the central idea that animates the concept. Moreover, because intersectional analyses aim to reveal connections across different forms of sub-ordination without prioritizing them or hierarchically ordering them, these analyses are innately coalitional (Cole, 2008). As Ransby (2000) noted, "Instead of policing boundaries, racial or otherwise, Black feminists have more often than not penetrated these barriers, expanding the meaning of 'we' and 'community' in the process" (p. 1219).

For these reasons, I argue that not only have we not come to a "post-intersectional" moment, our students need to be able to nimbly employ an intersectional analysis to make sense of the complexity and diversity of human experience as well as the processes that create and maintain inequality. If Kimberlé Crenshaw named intersectionality at a moment that begged for the concept in order to make sense of the issues of the day, today we face a moment that is not dissimilar. Notably, today Crenshaw is among the leaders of the #SayHerName movement which brings an intersectional lens to police brutality against African Americans and other communities of color. They aim toward inclusion of Black women's experiences of police brutality in media coverage, policy formation, and popular awareness. I watched Crenshaw (2015) ask a standing-room-only crowd at the meeting of the National Women's Studies Association to raise their hands while she read a list of names of African Americans who had been killed by police and keep them raised until they heard a name they did not recognize. She began with a list of men, many of them tragically young, whose stories were familiar to all: Michael Brown; Freddie Gray; Tamir Rice. The list went on at length and most hands stayed raised. Then she moved to another set of names beginning with Sandra Bland. By the time she reached the third woman's name, I could easily count the raised hands in the room on the fingers of one hand because both of my own were in my lap. By highlighting the role of gender in racialized state violence, the work of #SayHerName simultaneously raises the question of whose lives are deemed worth organizing to protect.

The lens of intersectionality makes questions like this legible and gives us the framework to answer it . . . and to change the answer. These are not new questions (e.g., Malveaux's 2002 essay on teaching intersectionality), but inter-sectionality offers students new ways to understand persistent patterns of inequity that reflect and respect complexity and diversity. The catch is that these are dif-ficult lessons, both because the theory is complex and because an intersectional analysis compels us to fundamentally challenge many ideas, usually taken-for-granted: that racism, sexism, and homophobia are primarily attitudes; categories like *woman* and *African American* are best defined by the experiences of the most advantaged members of those categories; and the experiences of members of multiply marginalized groups are exceptional special cases and therefore not that important to consider. Any instructor who wants to take on this material has set the bar high.

In this volume, Case offers a model of intersectional pedagogy that directly addresses these challenges. The model succeeds on three levels by: (1) giving sustained attention to oppression without shying away from recognition of privilege and power; (2) making visible the erasures of single-axis analyses; and (3) most significantly, consistently connecting the theoretical construct of intersectionality and the goals of social justice that motivate it. The pedagogical model and chapters throughout the collection accomplish this through both attention to the history and theory of intersectionality and by providing college instructors with practical tools to engage students in the practice and praxis of intersectionality.

Elizabeth R. Cole, Ph.D.

Professor of Women's Studies, Psychology, and
AfroAmerican & African Studies
Associate Dean for Social Science in the College
of Literature, Science, and the Arts
University of Michigan
Ann Arbor, Michigan

References

Carbado, D. W. (2013). Colorblind intersectionality. *Signs, 38*, 811–845. doi:10.1086/ 669666

Cole, E. R. (2008). Coalitions as a model for intersectionality: From practice to theory. *Sex Roles, 59*, 443–453.

Crenshaw, K. (1989). Demarginalizing the intersection of race and sex: A Black feminist critique of antidiscrimination doctrine, feminist theory, and antiracist politics. *University of Chicago Legal Forum, 1989*, 139–167.

Crenshaw, K. W. (1993). Mapping the margins: Intersectionality, identity politics, and violence against women. In M. A. Fineman & R. Mykitiuk (Eds.), *The public nature of private violence* (pp. 93–120). New York, NY: Routledge.

Crenshaw, K. W. (2015, November). *Presidential session: Contesting precarity, engaging intersectionality*. Presentation at the 36th Annual Conference of the National Women's Studies Association, Milwaukee, WI.

Davis, K. (2008). Intersectionality as buzzword: A sociology of science perspective on what makes a feminist theory successful. *Feminist Theory, 9*, 67–85. doi:10.1177/ 1464700108086364

Hancock, A. (2005). W.E.B. Du Bois: Intellectual forefather of intersectionality? *Souls, 7*(3–4), 74–84.

Lorde, A. (1984). *Sister outsider*. Trumansburg, NY: Crossing Press.

Malveaux, J. (2002). Intersectionality – Big word for small lives. *Black Issues in Higher Education, 19*(12), 27.

May, V. M. (2015). *Pursuing intersectionality, unsettling dominant imaginaries*. New York, NY: Routledge.

McCall, L. (2005). The complexity of intersectionality. *Signs, 30*, 1771–1800.

Puar, J. (2007). *Terrorist assemblages: Homonationalism in queer times*. Durham, NC: Duke University Press.

Ransby, B. (2000). Black feminism at twenty-one: Reflections on the evolution of a national community. *Signs, 25*, 1215–1221.

ACKNOWLEDGMENTS

Those close to me who supposedly love me know that after editing my first book, I asked them all to stop me if I ever hinted at planning another book. None, zero, nada, not one among you lifted a finger or indicated even the slightest effort to block me when I started preparing the proposal for this edited collection. You were supposed to stop me, host an intervention, kick off a hunger strike, or do something! I blame each and every one of you. Here we are again. Therefore, I am committing in print this time – No more!

As those of you who know him will attest, my life partner and soulmate, Kent, is hands down the most patient, generous, and calming force in all the universes. Gracias, mi media naranja, for lifting me up, keeping me laughing every day, and taking delicate care of me with such selflessness. Thank you for all you do for our past, present, and future feline sons Shaggy, Rusty, and Guster. Also, stop me next time.

Mom, as my first and greatest friend, thank you for teaching me to always go for it, learn something new, give more than I take, and focus on authenticity, loyalty, and communal values. Without your guidance in life and promoting my education all the way through the doctoral level, I would be nowhere. Thank you for my life and for my career.

To my local, national, and global feminist friends and colleagues, thank you for valuing integrity, truth, honesty, inclusion of marginalized voices even when they challenge your views or behaviors, and advancing scholarly debate rather than the easy road of polite passivity. I am particularly grateful for years of inspiration, friendship, support, encouragement, professional mentoring, and advice from Elizabeth Cole, Abby Stewart, Allen Omoto, Michelle Fine, Peggy McIntosh, Desdamona Rios, Lillian Benavente-McEnery, Jeannetta Williams, and Sandra Neumann. I would never have jumped into editing a second book without your generosity and guidance (so I mostly blame you for this torture).

My deepest thanks to the chapter authors for patience, cooperation, speedy revisions, resisting the urge to physically hurt me, and unique contributions that will serve educators developing intersectional pedagogies. In addition, the following volunteers gave their time to provide thoughtful feedback and suggestions as reviewers: Lillian Benavente-McEnery, Santiba Campbell, Elizabeth Cole, Danielle Dickens, Stephen Arch Erich, Adam Fingerhut, Ronni Greenwood, Laura Groves, Beth Hentges, Phia Salter, Stacey Williams, Annemarie Vaccaro. This book would literally not exist without the support of Catherine Bernard, Senior Publisher at Routledge, who took another chance on me and this new edited volume. Both Catherine and Matthew Friberg showed infinite kindness that kept me grounded and (almost) sane as I worked through the final stages of this project.

And last but not least, gracias to the kind, social justice allies and activists otherwise known as my graduate student assistants. Many extra special thanks to Whitley Louvier, Gabriella Vargas, and Kelsey Braun for their detailed and exceptional work on this collection catching errors, calming me down, pushing me along, and telling me I would survive this. Thank you to all of my students in the Applied Social Issues graduate concentration and the broader research lab for being supremely committed to social justice, ally action for change, public policy, and community organizing.

1

TOWARD AN INTERSECTIONAL PEDAGOGY MODEL

Engaged Learning for Social Justice

Kim A. Case

The first time I taught Psychology of Women as a University of Cincinnati graduate student, the textbook was extremely narrow in focus, lacking any hint of inclusion outside normative and privileged identities within the vastly diverse group called women. Due to this shortcoming, I created a supplemental packet with readings to address race, sexual diversity, poverty, and non-Western women's experiences. This "solution" felt like a legitimate approach at the time to correct for the main book's reinforcement of defining women via only white[1] heterosexual middle-class perspectives. On the first day of class, a brave student raised her hand to point out that the textbook did not represent her as an African American woman and seemed focused exclusively on White women. She was right. My co-instructor immediately defended the text saying "no one book can cover everything." I then agreed with the student and pointed to the packet as one way to include diverse viewpoints and avoid the idea that all women are White, middle-class, heterosexual, U.S. citizens.

Over 15 years later, I view our supplemental packet and our response to the student as an insufficient, dismissive, and insulting Band-Aid that essentially perpetuated the marginalization of women outside the mythical norm as described by Lorde (1984). Just as Bowleg (2008) critiqued her previous research as additive in nature and lacking intersectionality, my original approach to teaching gender from a multicultural perspective served as a lesson in what not to do. At the same time, adding the packet allowed us to pat ourselves on the back as two White women instructors who believed we were acting as exceptional anti-racist allies. Not only was the packet an add-on afterthought residing outside the centralized (read: important; legitimate) textbook, but it also treated various social identity categories and their associated structural oppressions as separate considerations. That moment when the student expressed her own marginalization due to the course readings made a distinct impression on me as someone who feels professionally and ethically responsible for making sure students from a broad range of backgrounds feel represented in the course materials and get the message that their identities are worthy of academic study. In other words, intersectional theory translated to pedagogical practice is my professional and ethical responsibility (Grzanka, this volume).

Jones and Wijeyesinghe (2011) encouraged consideration of how teaching might be altered when instructors infuse intersectional theory. Without intersectional theory applied in the classroom, educational spaces serve to both perpetuate invisible privilege by focusing on personal oppression and construct only mythical norms as worthy of earning valuable real estate within course materials and broader curricular designs. Valid pedagogies must stop pretending, for example, that White women possess no race, Latino men are genderless, or Black and Asian women embody mutually exclusive gendered and racial social locations. Even though some privileged women in my gender courses insist race and sexuality are irrelevant to the study of women while men of color often resist the deconstruction of gender and gender identity in courses addressing race and racism, intersectional theory demands attention to the mutually constitutive nature of these interacting and intra-connected systems.

During and after graduate school as a lecturer at Northern Kentucky University, my first syllabus for a Psychology of Race and Gender course situated the two topics as isolated entities. The 15-week course included gender-focused content in the first seven weeks with race-focused content in the seven weeks following the midterm exam. Even though the course included multiple intersecting social identities, it pains me to admit that I mostly delivered them categorically (See Figure 1.1).

Similar to Naples' (this volume) early teaching experience, I taught from more of an additive model, kept social identity categories artificially separated, and struggled to incorporate multiple voices into the flawed framework. Although reading materials, lectures, and activities highlighted marginalized voices within

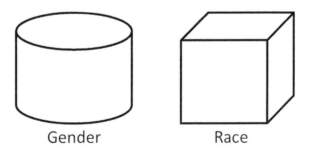

FIGURE 1.1 Categorical Teaching of Race and Gender

each section, the course schedule essentially treated race and gender as distinct and disconnected categories. As Crenshaw (1989) warned, this limiting single-axis framework problematically treats race and gender as mutually exclusive, thereby erasing women of color. Even though the readings on gender included gender identity and sexual orientation, and the readings on race included some women of color, this co-existence fell far short of intersectional analysis. In the end, the gender section of the course privileged White women's experiences while the race section privileged Black men's experiences. Crenshaw (1989) argued that scholarship must avoid centralizing and privileging White women's experiences as representative of all women and Black men's experiences as representative of Black women and all people of color. This prompted me to ask:

- How can we teach about prejudice and racism without addressing how race interacts with sexuality, ability, class, nationality, and a multitude of additional identities?
- How do I teach about women and gender systems to help students think about gender beyond the idea of "woman" as a White, middle class, able-bodied, heterosexual, Christian, gender-identity privileged U.S. citizen?

To help answer these questions, the course could and should be taught with a deep and well-planned infusion of intersectional theory, readings, activities, application, and assignments which might look like this (See Figure 1.2).

Given that no one image or metaphor could ever fully encapsulate the theoretical foundations of intersectionality (see Dessel & Cordivae, this volume, for metaphor summary table), this image nevertheless demarks a more complex pedagogy that challenges additive modes of false boundaries. The intersectionality image could represent complicated identity patterns operating within an individual person or patterns of concurrent, codependent, and interactive structural systems of oppression. Considering the image from an *individual perspective*, the concentric circles might represent various systemic aspects of the self interacting and affecting each other as the circles rotate like the gears of a clock to propel each other and even alter colors and patterns. Larger circles illustrate more salient aspects of identity in a given social context such as race or gender. Circles oriented toward the foreground could highlight privileged group memberships with marginalized and oppressed identities pushed to the back where those experiences go unnoticed and dismissed by the normative culture. Circles within circles represent complexity within each aspect of the self and invisible within-group diversity so often overlooked. Class discussions might deconstruct how some aspects of self may collide or even repel each other depending on one's viewpoint such as religion and sexuality or bicultural experiences of a middle-class professional from a working-class family.

At the same time, the image may call forth conceptions of interactions among the myriad facets of *systemic oppression and privilege*. For example, each set of

FIGURE 1.2   Intersectional Pedagogy: Individual and Structural Levels (art credit to Greg Kitzmiller)

concentric circles might represent one aspect of social identity such as ability, with privileged able-bodied groups toward the center and marginalized groups with physical and mental disabilities pushed to the outer circles. However, the ability/disability concentric circles are affected and altered by overlapping circles that represent race and social class with their respective privileged groups at the center. Several circles hidden behind others illustrate the invisible intersections and often forgotten aspects of systemic oppression such as immigrant status, global nationality, or imperialist/colonized citizenship (e.g., undocumented immigrant; born a U.S. citizen; citizen and resident of a colonized nation; see Kurtis & Adams, this volume). While certain intersections remain invisible, others occupy salient and centered spaces, such as gender, race, and sexuality, represented by larger circles at the forefront of the image.

In consideration of introducing students to the theory of intersectionality, using the Figure 1.1 image to facilitate their critique of false boundaries, additive approaches, and imagined categorical distinctions could open new spaces for analysis and set the tone for the course. Taking their analysis further, Figure 1.2 could serve as a prime for several pedagogical exercises that ask students to:

- contrast the two images using theoretical tenets of intersectionality;
- connect course readings or personal examples to the image's illustration of intersectionality; and
- suggest new improvements to the latter image that would deepen the representation of intersectional theory and lived experiences at the individual, group, cultural, institutional, and structural levels.

For a complete description of infusing intersectional pedagogy throughout an undergraduate Psychology of Women course, see Case and Rios (this volume). In addition, Grzanka (this volume) presents the case for, and a roadmap to, intersectional infusion throughout a Psychology of Gender course.

Complex Interactions: Intersectionality Theory and Pedagogy for Social Justice

Most existing books, anthologies, and articles about teaching diversity, multiculturalism, or the impact of group identities, focused on a single aspect of social identity at a time such as gender or race (e.g., Aveling, 2002; Caplan, 2010; Case & Hemmings, 2005; Dottolo, 2011; Frankenberg, 1993; Good & Moss-Racusin, 2010; Lawrence & Bunche, 1996; McIntyre, 1997; Rothenberg, 2008; Tatum, 1994). To be fair, pedagogical practice certainly benefits from these contributions, and they clearly provided insights that advance teaching approaches. Only recently have attempts to unpack pedagogical approaches to teaching intersectional theory begun permeating the literature (Pliner & Banks, 2012). This edited book examines how educators and learners can address issues of intersectionality in a diverse classroom. Over two decades ago, bell hooks (1984) and Kimberlé Crenshaw (1989) argued that individuals occupy unique and specific social locations built upon a set of simultaneous and multiple identities, such as race, sexuality, nation, class, ability, and gender. Introducing the term *intersectionality*, Crenshaw (1989) described these complex identities in opposition to categorical generalizations. Collins' (1990) matrix of domination offered a pedagogically useful conceptual structure for unravelling situated social locations that include both disadvantaged and advantaged identities. The foundational contributions of these and other Black feminist scholars (Collins, 1990; Combahee River Collective, 1977/2007; Crenshaw, 1989, 1991; Davis, 1983; hooks, 1984; Lorde, 1984; Smith, 1980) advanced intersectional theory within women's studies, law, sociology, humanities, and many additional disciplines such that use of the theory spread like wildfire in the 1990s and 2000s. During that time, the work of these Black women intersectionality scholars, Chicana lesbian activist scholars Cherrie Moraga and Gloria Anzaldua (1984, 1987), and international scholars such as Chandra Mohanty (1984) and Gayatri Spivak (1988) paved the way for institutionalization of intersectionality (Grzanka, 2014). Although less often recognized, contributions from White lesbian scholars such as Adrienne Rich (1986), transgender activists including Kate Bornstein (1994) and Leslie Feinberg (1993, 1998), and indigenous activist scholars such as Winona LaDuke (1999) and Paula Gunn Allen (1986), aided the critique of mainstream feminist theory with calls for inclusive attention to the complexity of women's identity and intersectional experiences of oppression.

Within the vast majority of disciplines, intersectionality remains marginalized, and instructors rarely incorporate intersectionality into diversity courses (Dill, 2009). Scholars also called for an intersectional focus to transform higher education (Berger & Guidroz, 2009), institutionalize intersectionality (Fitts, 2009), and imagine political interventions for social justice (May, 2015). The intersecting complexities among social identity categories and structural oppression are often neglected within courses that traditionally focus on only one aspect of identity and oppression, ultimately failing to simultaneously integrate multiple oppressions or privileges. What do these single-axis courses tell students about disciplinary perceptions of identity? What messages do the curriculum and course titles send to students about "diversity"? On the other hand, intersectional theory calls for moving beyond multiculturalism, single-axis models, and additive approaches to oppression. How do educators help themselves and students move toward an intersectional model? What questions must be asked?

Intersectionality Benefits to Student Learning

Use of an intersectional pedagogical design is supported by research that extensively examined intersectional invisibility as manifest within multiple subordinate group identities (Purdie-Vaughns & Eibach, 2008; Rios & Stewart, 2013). Social psychological research found intersectional consciousness (Greenwood, 2008) correlated with white privilege awareness and acknowledgement of blatant racism (Cole, Case, Rios, & Curtin, 2011) and also increased positive attitudes toward Muslim women (Greenwood & Christian, 2008). Curtin, Stewart, and Cole (2015) discovered intersectional awareness was positively related to openness to experience, taking the perspectives of others, intentions to create social change, and rights-based activism. In addition, intersectional awareness was negatively associated with justification for gender and race inequalities and endorsement of a powerful group's dominance over out-groups (i.e., social dominance orientation).

By implementing the framework of intersectionality, teachers may avoid over-emphasizing any single characteristic or quality in their understanding of individual realities (Dill & Zambrana, 2009) and turn the focus to examination of social locations with respect to privilege and oppression (Cole, 2009). Within this recognition of social locations, teachers must diligently facilitate student analysis of structural power to move beyond the individual level and the tendency to view intersectionality as highlighting each person's uniqueness (Rios, Bowling, & Harris, this volume). Pedagogically, the intersectional approach provides instructors and students with a critical framework for validating subjugated knowledge, unveiling power and privilege, examining the complexity of identity, and developing action strategies for empowerment (Collins, 1990; Dill & Zambrana, 2009).

As Ferber and Herrera (2013) argued, intersectional pedagogy helps prevent overlooking the invisible impact of what they call the matrix of privilege and oppression. In fact, the absence of pedagogies that take intersectionality into account may do harm by further isolating and invalidating students from marginalized backgrounds (Ferber & Herrera, 2013). Educators utilizing intersectional pedagogy not only move away from such invalidation, but also promote students' social literacy (Berger & Guidroz, 2009). As students develop this social literacy, they increase their ability to recognize internalized oppression, limitations of singular viewpoints, and the costs of dominance (Weber, 2010). Considering that learning may evoke guilt, shame, blame, frustration, and defensiveness, intersectional pedagogy offers avenues for engaging all students to participate in the process (Banks, Pliner, & Hopkins, 2013; Wise & Case, 2013). This inclusive approach helps reduce resistance because it validates various lived experiences without forcing students to ignore oppressed identities while discussing personal privilege (Wise & Case, 2013). Despite these benefits to students, the availability of techniques and strategies for teaching and learning remains drastically sparse.

Bringing Intersectional Pedagogy into Focus

Although scholarship addressing intersectional theory increased in recent decades (Berger & Guidroz, 2009; Cole, 2009; Collins, 1990; Crenshaw, 1989; Dill & Zambrana, 2009), the lack of effective pedagogical tools for teaching and learning about intersections of identity persists. Educators continue to seek out scholarship, resources, and practical advice for bringing intersectional theory into the classroom (Banks & Pliner, 2012; Ferber & Herrera, 2013). Instructors frequently lament about the struggle to locate quality teaching materials related to intersectional theory (Berger & Guidroz, 2009). Currently, there is an urgent and growing need for a model of intersectional pedagogy to address the complex lived experiences of privilege and oppression within the matrix of domination. My hope is that this book will support the development of what Grant and

Zwier (2011) labeled an "intersectionally-aware teacher identity" (p. 186). The main goals of the volume are to:

- provide an *intersectional pedagogy model* for effective teaching and learning about intersectional theory, complex intersections of identity, and the systemic consequences of those social locations;
- develop *inclusive intersectional studies* that incorporate a multiplicative analysis of both marginalized and privileged locations throughout the matrix of domination; and
- promote interdisciplinary and multidisciplinary *infusion of intersectional studies* both within a wide array of diversity-focused courses and across the broader curriculum.

This book connects theory and practice for effective teaching and learning about intersectional theory by introducing a new model for intersectional pedagogy. Both the model below and the subsequent chapters approach intersectionality with special attention to analyzing social locations within structural and institutional power, deconstructing privilege, and implementing social justice action.

Developing a Model of Intersectionality Pedagogy

Since my first encounter with student evaluations of gender-focused courses claiming "we talk about race too much in this class" (Case, Miller, & Jackson, 2012) or that the class "has an LGBT agenda," my search for pedagogical resources addressing intersectional theory has been continuous yet overwhelmingly unsuccessful. Innovative instructional resources and scholarship are essential in order for educators to make the dynamic shift from single-axis content, additive models that fail to engage with complex interactions, and "everyone is unique" identity approaches that flatten intersectional theory.

In my first book, *Deconstructing Privilege: Teaching and Learning as Allies in the Classroom* (2013), I introduced a pedagogical model emphasizing the importance of intersectionality for teaching privilege awareness. My experiences with infusing intersectionality into privilege studies reshaped my thinking and led to my current view that intersectional studies requires and deserves its own pedagogical model, with the two models complementing each other. As with any topic that gains momentum at conferences and in publications, pedagogical discussions often splinter and form into vague and imprecise conceptualizations. In the end, educators need a clear model to unite these efforts to infuse intersectionality across the curriculum. The newly developed 10-point pedagogical model below summarizes my current vision of best practices based on intersectional theory literature and data-based research. This collection calls for instructors teaching intersectional theory and application to engage in a model of intersectional pedagogy with the following main tenets.

Model of Intersectional Pedagogy

Effective intersectional pedagogy:

- *conceptualizes intersectionality* as a complex analysis of both privileged and oppressed social identities that simultaneously interact to create systemic inequalities, and therefore, alter lived experiences of prejudice and discrimination, privilege and opportunities, and perspectives from particular social locations. Intersectional theory pushes us beyond the additive model that conceptualizes identity and structural oppression as categorical and mutually exclusive;
- *teaches intersectionality across a wide variety of oppressions*, including not only gender and race, but also the long list of social identities typically neglected in the curriculum (e.g., sexuality, ability, gender identity, immigrant status);
- *aims to uncover invisible intersections*, analyzing the consequences of that invisibility for the privileged and the oppressed, and lifting the veil to make these crucial intersections more visible;
- *includes privilege* as an essential aspect of learning about intersectional theory by extending learning goals to consistently deconstruct privileged identities and how privilege operates to maintain oppression;
- *analyzes power* in teaching about intersectional theory, pushing the boundaries of teaching multiculturalism, diversity, oppression, and discrimination;
- *involves educator personal reflection on intersecting identities*, biases, assumptions, and the ways instructor social identity impacts the learning community;
- *encourages student reflection* and writing about their own intersecting identities and careful consideration of how those identities shape their own lives, psychology, perceptions, and behaviors;
- *promotes social action* to dismantle oppression through student learning that extends beyond the classroom walls via service learning, public education projects, community engagement assignments, and ally action for social change;
- *values the voices of the marginalized and oppressed* by avoiding claims of equal validity awarded to all perspectives and maintaining critical analysis of the ways power and privilege limit individual perspectives and experiences with oppression; and
- *infuses intersectional studies across the curriculum*, including a wide variety of disciplines as well as courses not typically associated with diversity content.

Conceptualizing Intersectionality

Inclusive Exploration of Invisible Intersections

Traditional intersectional practice originating with Black feminist and womanist scholars focused quite clearly on the interactions of gender and race, although not exclusively. In other words, intersectional theory centered on Black women's experiences (Collins, 1990; Combahee River Collective, 1977/2007; Crenshaw, 1989, 1991; Davis, 1983; hooks, 1984; Lorde, 1984; Smith, 1980). Alexander-Floyd (2012) rightly argued that scholars often underemphasize or completely overlook previous foundational work on intersectional theory, thus re-subjugating Black women's intellectual legitimacy and "privileging dominant modes of knowledge production" (p. 17). As Shields (2008) warns, any advancement or broadening of intersectionality must acknowledge and name the historical roots of the theory in Black women's original scholarship.

Although some have called for a return to an intersectionality focusing exclusively on women of color (Alexander-Floyd, 2012), this conceptualization risks neglecting oppressions based on sexuality, social class, immigrant status, ability, religion, age, or gender identity. Communication studies and intersectionality scholars Griffin and Chavez (2012) pointed out an over-emphasis on race and gender ultimately erased sexuality, class, and additional arenas of great import in lived experiences. Over 25 years of intersectional theory development yielded creative application to a wide variety of intersections that deserve the critical analysis that this specific theory offers. For example, intersectional theory complicates and advances examinations of White women's privilege and anti-racist identity development (Case, 2012), Latino men's feminist identity (Hurtado & Sinha, 2008), masculinity's intersections with sexuality, social class, and disability (Coston & Kimmel, 2012), and White working-class women's marginalization within upper-class contexts (Weber, 2010). I submit that intersectionality scholars and educators must maintain a vigilant connection to the history of the theory and the work of Black women scholars while continuing to expand applications to any analyses that facilitate social justice action and deconstruction of power, privilege, and oppression.

Beyond the Individual to Structural Power

Rios et al. (this volume) describe a tendency for students to embrace intersectional theory as a celebration of individual uniqueness that glosses over power differences. Michelle Fine critiqued the popular explosion of intersectionality as lacking in structural analysis, thus leaving her "concerned about a kind of 'flattening' of intersectionality, with racial disparities in health, education, or criminal justice appearing to be artifacts of culture or genetics, rather than systematic effects of cumulative oppression" (Guidroz & Berger, 2009, p. 70). In fact, May (2015) further warned that many of the widespread claims of intersectional scholarship merely co-opt the theory as a catch phrase or apo-litical descriptive device. These misconstrued and distorted treatments often undermine the very tenets of the theory with empty gestures and careless or ignorant application (May, 2015). This trend of flattening intersectional theory appears quite common with students getting stuck at the individual level. Jones and Wijeyesinghe (2011) noted students' persistent focus on personal margin-alization and lack of power analysis, such as the White male who discounts privilege due to his working-class origins, and called for educators' cultivation of structural-level intersectionality to unveil power relationships.

Pushing students beyond the individual level presents a difficult pedagogical challenge for intersectionality. The statements in the Intersectional Awareness Scale (Curtin et al., 2015) illustrated conceptualizations that could be used peda-gogically to encourage a structural analysis. For example, "Black and White women experience sexism in different ways" (Curtin et al., 2015, p. 15) could serve as a teaching tool to spark discussion and facilitate students' critical engage-ment with intersectionality beyond the individual level while avoiding additive frameworks of gender plus race. Likewise, the scale item "People don't think enough about how connections between social class, race, gender, and sexual-ity affect individuals" (Curtin et al., 2015, p. 15) provides a path for students to apply the lens of intersectional theory as they focus on the depth of meaning behind the word *connections* in this particular sentence. A successful intersec-tional approach must maintain the centrality of unveiling power via structural analysis and making visible the layered complexities of oppression (Andersen & Collins, 2010; Banks & Pliner, 2012; Dill & Zambrana, 2009; Grzanka, 2014; May, 2015).

Privilege and Power: Making Intersections Visible

As the above pedagogical model asserts, intersectionality simply must include analysis of privilege and power. The current model preserves marginalized voices as the center of the analysis while deconstructing privilege and shedding light on invisible intersections that maintain power. My original privilege studies pedagogical model offered more details for those interested in specific atten-tion to teaching privilege awareness (Case, 2013) as an important component of intersectional studies. Ferber and Herrera (2013) emphasized the necessity of privilege as part of the intersectional theory learning experience by naming their framework the matrix of privilege and oppression. As privilege and oppression happen simultaneously (Wildman, Armstrong, Davis, & Grillo, 1996), intersec-tional scholars called for clear inclusion of privilege as part of critical examination of intersections of identity and structural power (Banks & Pliner, 2012; Perrin et al., 2013; Samuels & Ross-Sheriff, 2008; Shields, 2008). By unveiling power and discussing privilege in every single course, educators make these issues vis-ible (Jones & Wijeyesinghe, 2011). To promote such reflections, the concept of intersectional invisibility (Purdie-Vaughns & Eibach, 2008) provides new paths for examining privileged identities. Without privilege analyses in the classroom, intersectionality leaves dominant groups unacknowledged, thus maintaining privileged status as the normative standard to which all others get compared and labeled as deficient (Warner, 2008).

Intersectional Pedagogy for Social Justice

As Alexander-Floyd (2012) stated, application of intersectional theory requires an emphasis on political social action. Intersectional theory's recognition of systems of power creates new possibilities for not only documenting the impact, but also imagining ways to change intersecting systems (Andersen & Collins, 2010; May, 2015). Weber (2010) asserted that intersectional awareness of oppression and "acting in pursuit of social justice are mutually reinforcing parts of the same process" (p. 220). Intersectionality reinforces teaching about social justice action with grounding in community partnerships as well as personal reflection and awareness of social location in the matrix of domination. In fact, social justice must be a core feature of the intersectional pedagogical approach (Wise & Case, 2013). My intersectionality education project required individual students to educate the general public, teaching them about intersectional theory or a particular intersectional social location (Case & Lewis, this volume). et al. Rios et al. (this volume) provide a detailed description of a class project that involved student groups utilizing intersectional theory to design and implement a social justice action plan. By implementing intersectional pedagogy focused on social justice, teachers offer students new avenues for engaging with the material in meaningful ways.

With the goal of promoting student engagement in learning about intersectionality and considering social justice connections, I often use humor and cartoons. Students typically open up to challenging messages from cartoons perhaps because they experience the cartoon characters as non-threatening. For example, Miriam Dobson's (2013) cartoon illustration of Bob the striped triangle received social media attention due to its accessibility and fun tone (See Figure 1.3). For the same reasons, I began sharing it in my courses to demonstrate intersectional theory's potential impact on forming coalitions among groups for social justice advocacy. In fact, when my undergraduate students developed intersectionality education projects, I included Bob as an example of a possible approach to their project, and some created their own intersectionality cartoon as a result. Humor and cartoons also tend to help reduce resistance to learning in these contexts.

Learning about privilege and oppression may lead to resistant behaviors (Case & Cole, 2013; Case & Hemmings, 2005; Chan & Treacy, 1996; Higginbotham, 1996; Jackson, 1999; Tatum, 1994). As course content begins to challenge long-held values, traditions, and beliefs (Lawrence & Bunche, 1996; Tatum, 1992), students may experience hopelessness, guilt, anger, frustration, defensiveness,

FIGURE 1.3 Intersectionality: A Fun Guide (art credit to Miriam Dobson, 2013)

and cognitive dissonance (Stewart, Laut, Branscombe, Phillips, & Denney, 2012; Tatum, 1992; Wise & Case, 2013). Experiential & applied learning provides students with opportunities for channeling such responses into actions to address social issues (Case & Lewis, this volume; Williams & Melchiori, 2013). Opportunities for experiential learning via social action promote student engagement in the process (Case, 2013). When introduced to the idea of experiential service learning, students may slip into thinking "they are serving people who are unable to help themselves, rather than conceptualizing their service learning as working with a community organization to bring about social change" (Williams & Melchiori, 2013, p. 176). Facilitation of applied social justice projects and service learning in the community must include careful preparation, intersectional analysis, and student reflection on empowerment models for addressing social issues.

Intersectionality Studies across the Curriculum

Over the last 20 years, Women's and Gender Studies began building an intersectional curriculum that could serve as a model for other disciplines across the higher education landscape. Although intersectional theory gained much attention as more scholars and educators named it explicitly, the time has arrived for psychology and other social sciences, education, counselor and practitioner training programs, the humanities, fine arts, physical sciences, and business to bring intersectionality into students' learning environments. Naming intersectionality in university mission statements, strategic plans, course titles, catalogue descriptions, syllabi, assignments, grading rubrics, promotion and tenure materials, and program reviews, just to name a few, sends a message of culturally shifting to intersectional studies across the curriculum. How can faculty incorporate intersectionality and social justice action into diversity courses and the broader curriculum at both undergraduate and graduate levels? For effective infusion of intersectional theory across the curriculum, diversity matters become relevant to all courses, even pedagogical spaces where faculty perceive intersectionality as irrelevant to their disciplinary content (Banks & Pliner, 2012).

To achieve these goals of intersectional infusion, what resources exist to support this work and what resources need to be created? Faculty need not only the development of innovative teaching resources in the literature, but also peer support to expand and maintain this work. Through pedagogical peer support, educators benefit from sharing resources such as books, websites, articles, or blogs that help them develop intersectional approaches customized to their own courses. These resources lend themselves to structural support in the form of discussion groups, faculty book clubs, and lending libraries where colleagues may borrow resources from each other. For example, the Feminist Teacher faculty discussion group on my campus meets monthly to address pedagogical issues. For my turn as facilitator, I chose intersectional pedagogy as our topic. We read "Intersectional Pedagogy and Transformative Learning" (Pliner, Banks, & Tapscott, 2012) for practical application along with Dill and Zambrana's (2009) exceptional theoretical review of intersectionality. This discussion, debate, and brainstorming allowed each of us to grapple with application on the ground in our disciplines across literature, communication, history, psychology, sociology, and humanities. For me, professional development in this peer learning community led me to seek out better readings for my students on the intersection of gender, disability, and access to resources.

Of course, one of the most productive ways teachers support each other manifests through sharing ideas for activities and assignments. Unfortunately, educators typically trudge along working in silos to imagine new exercises for in-class demonstrations of intersectionality or innovative papers and projects that aid student understanding. However, developing a more public scholarly community that develops and shares (publishes) pedagogical tools will enhance student learning while bringing intersectionality to a broader base of educators across disciplines. The more teachers who publish their theoretically grounded, innovative practical tools for intersectional studies, the more effective the approaches will be in reaching a wide range of students across the curriculum.

Of course, motivation to write and publish about intersectional pedagogy may be influenced by administrative culture within a given academic institution. In fact, simply incorporating intersectional theory into courses may feel risky, especially for non-tenured faculty, if department chairs, deans, and upper administrators fail to express their support for these efforts. Administrative influence in the form of hiring decisions, merit review, and promotion and tenure evaluation provide structural opportunities to express support for intersectional research and pedagogy. In fact, merit review and promotion policies, mission statements, and strategic plans that explicitly recognize the value of intersectionality encourage faculty to engage in scholarship and pedagogical endeavors. When students express their refusal to learn about oppression, privilege, and intersectionality, administrative support of faculty pedagogical approaches and academic freedom is essential. Using an example related to privilege pedagogy, a White male student at a Houston-area community college reported his frustration after reading Peggy McIntosh's (1988) essay on white privilege as an optional assignment in one of his courses. This student went directly to a local news station, and the story made the nightly news. Although the reporter merely stopped random students to ask their opinions and failed to interview any academics with expertise on the pedagogical implications, the community college released an impressive statement clearly supporting difficult dialogues and student reflection on personal biases. In this instance, the administrative response sent a strong message that placed value on learning about identity and oppression. Without such unashamed support at the highest levels of institutional authority, many educators will remain hesitant to cover intersectionality for fear of student retaliation, low evaluations and merit reviews, challenges during promotion decisions, or perhaps even being fired as a tenured professor.

Organization of *Intersectional Pedagogy*

This collection presents three sections designed to provide intersectional theoretical foundations, classroom approaches, and social justice teaching strategies. The chapter authors contributed multidisciplinary perspectives and expertise from social work, higher education, Afro-American studies, psychology, sociology, American studies, and women's studies. These scholars share theoretical analyses, practical teaching innovations, and experiential learning approaches that advance pedagogical efforts to challenge narrow additive models and individual uniqueness frameworks. Three sections of the collection address:

1. intersectional theory and foundations;
2. classroom strategies for teaching and learning about intersectionality; and
3. intersectional approaches for teaching social justice.

Part I: Intersectional Theory and Foundations

In the opening section that follows, Chapters 2 and 3 explore the theoretical origins of intersectionality and its potential applications to research, practice, educational, and activist contexts as well as feminist theory. The chapters address many of the standard critiques of intersectional theory, explore the boundaries of disciplinary utilization, and provide insights into typically invisible intersections that need more focused attention.

Recognized as one of the first social psychologists to bring intersectional theory into research practice, Greenwood (Chapter 2) reviews the history and origins of intersectionality and its deep connections to social justice organizing and activism. Using the framework of three major disciplinary applications of intersectionality, Greenwood describes: (a) health disparities in connection with nursing research and practitioner training (b) social work research, practice, and education; and (c) psychological theory, scholarship, and pedagogy. Her essay responds to various critiques of intersectional theory by outlining its effectiveness and enhancement of scholarship, pedagogy, and social action.

Calling attention to typically invisible and neglected intersections serves as a central tenet of intersectionality. Kurtis and Adams (Chapter 3) introduce intersectionality via transnational feminist perspectives, and thereby problematize assumptions of the Global North mythical norm that affect intersectional work. Their much needed critique of intersectional theory and application points out the common focus on U.S. women, Western frameworks, and Global North perspectives. Kurtis and Adams argue that this neglect of the experiences of the majority of the world's population reproduces colonialism and domination by Western feminisms. They call for a decolonial intersectionality in the classroom and conclude with a discussion of implications for decolonizing theory, research, and pedagogy.

Part II: Intersectionality and Classroom Applications

Chapters 4 to 8 provide detailed information for practical application of intersectional theory in the classroom in connection with the intersectional pedagogy model introduced above.

In this section, the authors describe effective undergraduate and graduate pedagogical strategies, course designs, readings, courses, assignments, exercises, and more. Within the comprehensive explanations, authors also include instructor reflections on social location, privilege, and biases as well as suggested alterations for improved student learning outcomes.

Teaching within the discipline of psychology which traditionally promotes positivist science, Grzanka (Chapter 4) highlights the long list of tensions between psychology and intersectional theory. In teaching his Psychology of Gender course, he outlines the challenges associated with teaching gender intersectionally. Arguing that intersectional praxis requires more than merely incorporating multiple dimensions of diversity, Grzanka presents his commitment and approach to the practice of intersectional pedagogy. Through fieldwork assignments, research critiques, and gender autobiographies, his students learn that gender never operates in a vacuum separate from race, ability, class, sexuality, and more.

With the goal of infusing intersectionality, Case and Rios (Chapter 5) present a pedagogical roadmap for teaching an undergraduate Psychology of Women course. From the syllabus framework, to readings, quizzes, activities, and assignments, we illustrate practical applications of the tenets of the intersectional pedagogical model at each level of course design. For example, using the Global Feminisms Project interviews with feminist scholars and activists from around the world, the curriculum promoted transnational feminisms and challenged normative notions applied to Western feminisms. Student assessments focusing on privilege awareness, intersectional photovoice presentations, and intersectionality final projects demonstrated learning with regard to intersectionality's complexity.

Naples (Chapter 6) shares her practice of teaching intersectionality intersectionally. To serve her graduate students in their struggles to conduct intersectional scholarship, Naples developed the Theories of Intersectionality course. With a sociological perspective on women's studies and the growing infusion of intersectional theory, she critiques additive models that simply add oppressions together and provides justification for intersectional pedagogy. After describing the course that maps the field of intersectionality, Naples calls for intersectional feminist praxis that transforms the academy and ignites social justice activism.

Teaching lesbian, gay, bisexual, and transgender (LGBT) psychology using an intersectional pedagogical approach offers several advantages to enhance student learning. In Chapter 7, Case and Lewis document the benefits and challenges of critical liberatory feminist pedagogy and the intersectional framework within two courses: (a) Black Issues in LGBT Psychology and (b) Psychology of Gender, Race, and Sexuality. Taught in the context of a historically Black university and a Hispanic-serving institution, the intersectional theoretical approach supported integration of students' privileged and marginalized identities in connection with learning about LGBT psychology. The chapter offers instructors a guide for using readings, videos, assignments, and in-class activities to enhance student engagement with LGBT psychology via intersectional theory.

With special attention to power and privilege in the classroom, Hall (Chapter 8) presents her approach to undergraduate courses at a Historically Black University. She describes recognizing early on that the lack of intersectional training as a graduate student sharply contrasted with her own life experiences and research goals. Hall infuses intersectionality into highly innovative activities and assignments that enhance student engagement, such as quote analyses, reaction blogs, autobiographical diagrams, and counter-storytelling projects. The chapter concludes with advice for navigating the challenges inherent in teaching intersectional theory within undergraduate contexts.

Part III: Intersectional Pedagogy for Social Justice

The third section of the book (Chapters 9 to 11) expands the pedagogical model's emphasis on the use of intersectional theory and application for social justice learning goals. Authors provide guidance on effective instructor reflexivity with regard to social location and the impact of intersectional identities on the learning environment. Through experiential learning, group-based projects, and intergroup dialogues, students gain insight into invisible intersections, such as the lived experiences of LGBT people of color, and making them visible to others.

Rivera (Chapter 9) recalls his graduate career taking courses that clearly emphasized race and the experiences of people of color, but rarely covered sexual or gender identities. Working from the synergistic lenses of intersectional theory, critical race theory, and queer theory, Rivera outlines his approach to teaching at the intersections of race, ethnicity, gender identity, and sexual orientation. The chapter presents pedagogical guidance for effective use of strategies including precision in language, the recursive funnel approach, prioritization of social and historical contexts, and facilitation of difficult dialogues.

Rios, Bowling, and Harris (Chapter 10) discuss intersectionality pedagogy within a graduate course, Psychology of Gender, Race, and Sexuality, which included experiential learning and self-reflexivity within a social justice context. The chapter describes the group-based project that divided a main topic chosen by the class into intersectional sub-parts for research by each small group. This project moved students from over-simplified understanding of intersectionality as a list of identities to a structural analysis of power, privilege, and oppression in the matrix of domination. The instructor and two graduate students from the course reflect on the process of teaching and learning the theory of intersectionality and invisible intersections.

The final contribution by Dessel and Cordivae (Chapter 11) conveys strategies for teaching and learning about social identity intersectionality within a graduate social work course on diversity and social justice. The pedagogical design incorporated creative activities such as metaphor analysis, personal narratives, the Take a Position exercise, and privilege fishbowls to engage students in examining intersectionality or privileged and oppressed identities as well as movement toward social action. In reflecting on their teaching experiences, the authors describe student learning about intersectionality as well as student development of skills to facilitate intergroup dialogues using this theoretical frame.

Extending the Intersectional Pedagogy Conversation

I do not intend for this volume to close the conversation or provide all solutions, but instead contribute to dialogues on effective intersectional teaching. In fact, I argue that educators attempting to teach intersectional theory are only beginning to dig into scholarly dialogues that enhance student learning. Although I thoroughly enjoy conference symposia and discussions on teaching intersectionality, more publications of innovative ideas and outcomes are essential across disciplines and within interdisciplinary spaces (e.g., journals, edited books). As these discussions develop, educators can improve individual courses and content and discover ways to incorporate intersectionality studies across the curriculum (e.g., core courses for the major, core liberal arts courses, graduate training courses).

Note

1 The word "White" will be capitalized per APA style when referring to an individual or group of people. When used in reference to a concept, theories, etc., "white" will not be capitalized.

References

Allen, P. G. (1986). *The sacred hoop: Recovering the feminine in American Indian traditions.* Boston, MA: Beacon Press.

Alexander-Floyd, N. G. (2012). Disappearing acts: Reclaiming intersectionality in the social sciences in a post-Black feminist era. *Feminist Formations, 24*(1), 1–25. doi:10.1353/ff.2012.0003

Andersen, M., & Collins, P. H. (2010). *Race, class, and gender: An anthology* (7th ed.). Belmont, CA: Wadsworth.

Anzaldua, G. (1987). *Borderlands/La frontera*. San Francisco, CA: Aunt Lute Books.

Aveling, N. (2002). Student teachers' resistance to exploring racism: Reflections on 'doing' border pedagogy. *Asia-Pacific Journal of Teacher Education, 30*(2), 119–130. doi:10. 1080/13598660220135630

Banks, C. A., & Pliner, S. M. (2012). Introduction. In S. M. Pliner & C. A. Banks (Eds.), *Teaching, learning, and intersecting identities in higher education* (pp. 1–13). New York, NY: Peter Lang.

Banks, C. A., Pliner, S. M., & Hopkins, M. B. (2013). Intersectionality and paradigms of privilege: Teaching for social change. In. K. A. Case (Ed.), *Deconstructing privilege: Teaching and learning as allies in the classroom* (pp. 102–114). New York, NY: Routledge.

Berger, M. T., & Guidroz, K. (Eds.). (2009). *The intersectional approach: Transforming the academy through race, class, and gender*. Chapel Hill, NC: University of North Carolina Press.

Bornstein, K. (1994). *Gender outlaw: Men, women, and the rest of us*. New York, NY: Routledge.

Bowleg, L. (2008). When Black + lesbian + woman ≠ Black lesbian woman: The methodological challenges of qualitative and quantitative intersectionality research. *Sex Roles, 59*(5–6), 312–325. doi:10.1007/s11199-008-9400-z

Caplan, P. J. (2010). Teaching critical thinking about psychology of sex and gender. *Psychology of Women Quarterly, 34*(4), 553–557. doi:10.1111/j.1471-6402.2010. 01586.x

Case, K. A. (2012). Discovering the privilege of whiteness: White women's reflections on anti-racist identity and ally behavior. *Journal of Social Issues, 68*(1), 78–96. doi:10.11 11/j.1540-4560.2011.01737.x

Case, K. A. (Ed.). (2013). *Deconstructing privilege: Teaching and learning as allies in the classroom*. New York, NY: Routledge.

Case, K. A., & Cole, E. R. (2013). Deconstructing privilege when students resist: The journey back into the community of engaged learners. In. K. A. Case (Ed.), *Deconstructing privilege: Teaching and learning as allies in the classroom* (pp. 34–48). New York, NY: Routledge.

Case, K. A., & Hemmings, A. (2005). Distancing strategies: White women preservice teachers and anti-racist curriculum. *Urban Education, 40*(6), 606–626. doi:10.1177/00 42085905281396

Case, K. A., & Lewis, M. (this volume). Teaching intersectional psychology in racially diverse settings. In K. A. Case (Ed.), *Intersectional pedagogy: Complicating identity and social justice* (pp. 129–149). New York, NY: Routledge.

Case, K., Miller, A., & Jackson, S.B. (2012). "We talk about race too much in this class!" Complicating the essentialized woman through intersectional pedagogy. In S. Pliner & C. Banks (Eds.), *Teaching, learning, and intersecting identities in higher education* (pp. 32–48). New York, NY: Peter Lang.

Case, K. A., & Rios, D. (this volume). Infusing intersectionality: Complicating the Psychology of Women course. In K. A. Case (Ed.), *Intersectional pedagogy: Complicating identity and social justice* (pp. 82–109). New York, NY: Routledge.

Chan, C. S., & Treacy, M. J. (1996). Resistance in multicultural courses: Student, faculty, and classroom dynamics. *American Behavioral Scientist, 40*(2), 212–221. doi:10.1177/ 000276 4296040002012

Cole, E. R. (2009). Intersectionality and research in psychology. *American Psychologist, 64*(3), 170–180. doi:10.1037/a0014564

Cole, E. R., Case, K. A., Rios, D., & Curtin, N. (2011). Understanding what students bring to the classroom: Moderators of the effects of diversity courses on student attitudes. *Cultural Diversity and Ethnic Minority Psychology, 17*(4), 397–405. doi:10.1037/a002 5433

Collins, P. H. (1990). *Black feminist thought: Knowledge, consciousness, and the politics of power.* New York, NY: Routledge.

Combahee River Collective. (2007). A Black feminist statement. In E. B. Freedman (Ed.), *The essential feminist reader* (pp. 325–330). New York, NY: Modern Library. (Original work published 1977).

Coston, B. M., & Kimmel, M. (2012). Seeing privilege where it isn't: Marginalized masculinities and the intersectionality of privilege. *Journal of Social Issues, 68*(1), 97–111. doi:10.1111/j.1540-4560.2011.01738.x

Crenshaw, K. (1989). Demarginalizing the intersection of race and sex: A Black feminist critique of antidiscrimination doctrine, feminist theory, and antiracist politics. *University of Chicago Legal Forum, 1989,* 139–167.

Crenshaw, K. W. (1991). Mapping the margins: Intersectionality, identity politics, and violence against women of color. *Stanford Law Review, 43,* 1241–1299.

Curtin, N., Stewart, A. J., & Cole, E. R. (2015). Challenging the status quo: The role of intersectional awareness in activism for social change and pro-social intergroup attitudes. *Psychology of Women Quarterly, 39,* 512–529. doi:10.1177/0361684315580439

Davis, A. Y. (1983). *Women, race, and class.* New York, NY: Vintage Books.

Dessel, A., & Corvidae, T. (this volume). Experiential activities for engaging intersectionality in social justice pedagogy. In K. A. Case (Ed.), *Intersectional pedagogy: Complicating identity and social justice* (pp. 214–231). New York, NY: Routledge.

Dill, B. T. (2009). Intersections, identities, and inequalities in higher education. In B. T. Dill & R. E. Zambrana (Eds.), *Emerging intersections: Race, class, and gender in theory, policy, and practice* (pp. 229–252). New Brunswick, NJ: Rutgers.

Dill, B. T., & Zambrana, R. E. (2009). Critical thinking about inequality: An emerging lens. In B. T. Dill & R. E. Zambrana (Eds.), *Emerging intersections: Race, class, and gender in theory, policy, and practice* (pp. 1–21). New Brunswick, NJ: Rutgers.

Dobson, M. (2013, April 24). Intersectionality: A fun guide [Weblog post]. Retrieved from beyondthesemountains.wordpress.com/

Dottolo, A. L. (2011). "I'm not a feminist, but . . . ": Introducing feminism in psychology of women courses. *Psychology of Women Quarterly, 35*(4), 632–635. doi:10.1177/03616843 11410541

Feinberg, L. (1993). *Stone butch blues.* Ithaca, NY: Firebrand Books.

Feinberg, L. (1998). *Trans liberation: Beyond the pink or blue.* Boston, MA: Beacon Press.

Ferber, A. L., & Herrera, A. O. (2013). Teaching privilege through an intersectional lens. In K. A. Case (Ed.), *Deconstructing privilege: Teaching and learning as allies in the classroom* (pp. 83–101). New York, NY: Routledge.

Fitts, M. (2009). Institutionalizing intersectionality: Reflections on the structure of women's studies departments and programs. In M. T. Berger & K. Guidroz (Eds.), *The intersectional approach: Transforming the academy through race, class, and gender* (pp. 249–257). Chapel Hill, NC: University of North Carolina Press.

Frankenberg, R. (1993). *The social construction of whiteness: White women, race matters.* Minneapolis, MN: University of Minnesota Press.

Good, J. J., & Moss-Racusin, C. A. (2010). "But, that doesn't apply to me": Teaching college students to think about gender. *Psychology of Women Quarterly, 34*(3), 418–421. doi:10.1111/j.1471-6402.2010.01586.x

Grant, C. A., & Zwier, E. (2011). Intersectionality and student outcomes: Sharpening the struggle against racism, sexism, classism, ableism, heterosexism, nationalism, and linguistic, religious, and geographical discrimination in teaching and learning. *Multicultural Perspectives, 13*(4), 181–188. doi:10.1080/15210960.2011.616813

Greenwood, R. (2008). Intersectional political consciousness: Appreciation for intra-group differences and solidarity in diverse groups. *Psychology of Women Quarterly, 32*(1), 36–47. doi:10.1111/j.1471-6402.2007.00405.x

Greenwood, R. (this volume). Intersectionality foundations and disciplinary adaptations: Highways and Byways. In K. A. Case (Ed.), *Intersectional pedagogy: Complicating identity and social justice* (pp. 27–45). New York, NY: Routledge.

Greenwood, R., & Christian, A. (2008). What happens when we unpack the invisible knapsack? Intersectional political consciousness and inter-group appraisals. *Sex Roles, 59*(5), 404–417. doi:10.1007/s11199-008-9439-x

Griffin, C. L., & Chavez, K. R. (2012). Introduction: Standing at the intersections of feminisms, intersectionality, and communication studies. In K. R. Chavez & C. L. Griffin (Eds.), *Standing at the intersection: Feminist voices, feminist practices in communication studies* (pp. 1–31). Albany, NY: SUNY Press.

Grzanka, P. (2014). *Intersectionality: A foundations and frontiers reader.* Boulder, CO: Westview Press.

Grzanka, P. (this volume). Undoing the psychology of gender: Intersectional feminism and social science. In K. A. Case (Ed.), *Intersectional pedagogy: Complicating identity and social justice* (pp. 63–81). New York, NY: Routledge.

Guidroz, K., & Berger, M. T. (2009). A conversaton with founding scholars of intersectionality Kimberlé Crenshaw, Nira Yuval-Davis, and Michelle Fine. In M. T. Berger & K. Guidroz (Eds.), *The intersectional approach: Transforming the academy through race, class, & gender* (pp. 61–78). Chapel Hill, NC: The University of North Carolina Press.

Hall, N. (this volume). Quotes, blogs, diagrams, and counter-storytelling: Teaching intersectionality at a minority-serving institution. In K. A. Case (Ed.), *Intersectional pedagogy: Complicating identity and social justice* (pp. 150–170). New York, NY: Routledge.

Higginbotham, E. (1996). Getting all students to listen: Analyzing and coping with student resistance. *American Behavioral Scientist, 40*(2), 203–211. doi:10.1177/0002764296040002011

hooks, b. (1984). *Feminist theory: From margin to center.* Boston, MA: South End Press.

Hurtado, A., & Sinha, M. (2008). More than men: Latino feminist masculinities and intersectionality. *Sex Roles, 59,* 337–349. doi:10.1007/s11199-008-9405-7

Jackson, R. L. (1999). White space, white privilege: Mapping discursive inquiry into the self. *Quarterly Journal of Speech, 85*(1), 38–54. doi:10.1080/00335639909384240

Jones, S. R., & Wijeyesinghe, C. L. (2011). The promises and challenges of teaching from an intersectional perspective: Core components and applied strategies. *New Directions for Teaching and Learning, 2011*(125), 11–20. doi:10.1002/tl.429

Kurtis, T., & Adams, G. (this volume). Deolonial intersectionality: Implications for theory, research, and pedagogy. In K. A. Case (Ed.), *Toward an intersectional pedagogy model: Engaged learning for social justice* (pp. 46–59). New York, NY: Routledge.

LaDuke, W. (1999). *All our relations: Native struggles for land and life.* Cambridge, MA: South End Press.

Lawrence, S. M., & Bunche, T. (1996). Feeling and dealing: Teaching White students about racial privilege. *Teaching and Teacher Education, 12*(5), 531–542. doi:10.1016/0742-051X(95)00054-N

Lorde, A. (1984). *Sister outsider*. Freedom, CA: Crossing Press.

May, V. (2015). *Pursuing intersectionality, unsettling dominant imaginaries*. New York, NY: Routledge.

McIntosh, P. (1988). *White privilege and male privilege: A personal account of coming to see correspondences through work in women's studies*. Working Paper No. 189. Wellesley, MA: Wellesley Centers for Women.

McIntyre, A. (1997). *Making meaning of whiteness: Exploring racial identity with White teachers*. Albany, NY: State University of New York Press.

Mohanty, C. T. (1984). Under Western eyes: Feminist scholarship and colonial discourses. *boundary 2, 12*(3), 333–358. doi:10.2307/302821

Moraga, C., & Anzaldua, G. (Eds.). (1984). *This bridge called my back: Writings by radical women of color* (2nd ed.). Cambridge, MA: Kitchen Table: Women of Color Press.

Naples, N. A. (this volume). Pedagogical practice and teaching intersectionality intersectionally. In K. A. Case (Ed.), *Intersectional pedagogy: Complicating identity and social justice* (pp. 110–128). New York, NY: Routledge.

Perrin, P. B., Bhattacharyya, S., Snipes, D. J., Hubbard, R. R., Heesacker, M., Calton, J. M., Perez, R. M., & Lee-Barber, J. (2013). Teaching social justice ally development among privileged students. In K. A. Case (Ed.), *Deconstructing privilege: Teaching and learning as allies in the classroom* (pp. 49–62). New York, NY: Routledge.

Pliner, S. M., & Banks, C. A. (Eds.). (2012). *Teaching, learning and intersecting identities in higher education*. New York, NY: Peter Lang.

Pliner, S. M., Banks, C. A., & Tapscott, A. M. (2012). Intersectional pedagogy and transformative learning. In S. M. Pliner & C. A. Banks (Eds.), *Teaching, learning and intersecting identities in higher education* (pp. 148–161). New York, NY: Peter Lang.

Purdie-Vaughns, V., & Eibach, R. P. (2008). Intersectional invisibility: The distinctive advantages and disadvantages of multiple subordinate-group identities. *Sex Roles, 59*, 377–391. doi:10.1007/s11199-008-9424-4

Rich, A. (1986). Blood, bread, and poetry: The location of the poet. In A. Rich (Ed.), *Blood, bread, and poetry: Selected prose, 1979–1985* (pp. 167–187). New York: Norton.

Rios, D., Bowling, M., & Harris, J. (this volume). Decentering student "uniqueness" in lessons about intersectionality. In K. A. Case (Ed.), *Intersectional pedagogy: Complicating identity and social justice* (pp. 194–213). New York, NY: Routledge.

Rios, D., & Stewart, A. J. (2013). Recognizing privilege by reducing invisibility: The Global Feminisms Project as a pedagogical tool. In K. A. Case (Ed.), *Deconstructing privilege: Teaching and learning as allies in the classroom* (pp. 115–131). New York, NY: Routledge.

Rivera, D. P. (this volume). Revealing hidden intersections of gender identity, sexual orientation, race, and ethnicity: Teaching about multiple oppressed identities. In K. A. Case (Ed.), *Intersectional pedagogy: Complicating identity and social justice* (pp. 173–193). New York, NY: Routledge.

Rothenberg, P. S. (Ed.). (2008). *White privilege: Essential readings on the other side of racism* (3rd ed.). New York, NY: Worth.

Samuels, G. M., & Ross-Sheriff, F. (2008). Identity, oppression, and power: Feminisms and intersectionality theory. *Journal of Women and Social Work, 23*(1), 5–9. doi:10.1177/0886109907310475

Shields, S. A. (2008). Gender: An intersectionality perspective. *Sex Roles, 59*(5–6), 301–311. doi:10.1007/s11199-008-9501-8

Smith, B. (1980). Racism and women's studies. *Frontiers: A Journal of Women's Studies, 5*(1), 48–49.

Spivak, G. C. (1988). Can the subaltern speak? In C. Nelson & L. Grossberg (Eds.), *Marxism and the interpretation of culture* (pp. 271–313). Urbana, IL: University of Illinois Press.

Stewart, T. L., Latu, I. M., Branscombe, N. R., Phillips, N. L., & Denney, H. T. (2012). White privilege awareness and efficacy to reduce racial inequality improve White Americans' attitudes toward African Americans. *Journal of Social Issues, 68*(1), 11–27. doi:10.1111/j.1540-4560.2012.01733.x

Tatum, B. D. (1992). Talking about race, learning about racism: The application of racial identity development theory in the classroom. *Harvard Educational Review, 62*(1), 1–24.

Tatum, B. D. (1994). Teaching White students about racism: The search for White allies and the restoration of hope. *Teachers College Record, 95*(4), 462–476.

Warner, L. R. (2008). A best practices guide to intersectional approaches in psychological research. *Sex Roles, 59*(5), 454–463. doi:10.1007/s11199-008-9504-5

Weber, L. (2010). *Understanding race, class, gender, and sexuality: A conceptual framework* (2nd ed.). New York, NY: Oxford University Press.

Wildman, S. M., Armstrong, M. J., Davis, A. D., & Grillo, T. (1996). *Privilege revealed: How invisible preference undermines America.* New York, NY: New York University Press.

Williams, W. R., & Melchiori, K. J. (2013). Class action: Using experiential learning to raise awareness of social class privilege. In K. A. Case (Ed.), *Deconstructing privilege: Teaching and learning as allies in the classroom* (pp. 169–187). New York, NY: Routledge.

Wise, T., & Case, K. A. (2013). Pedagogy for the privileged: Addressing inequality and injustice without shame or blame. In K. A. Case (Ed.), *Deconstructing privilege: Teaching and learning as allies in the classroom* (pp. 17–33). New York, NY: Routledge.

PART I

Intersectional Theory and Foundations

2

INTERSECTIONALITY FOUNDATIONS AND DISCIPLINARY ADAPTATIONS

Highways and Byways

Ronni Michelle Greenwood

Intersectionality, as originally conceptualized by Crenshaw (1989, 1991) within critical race theory and by Collins (1990) within feminist theory, offers an important framework for understanding macro systems of dominance and subordination such as patriarchy, classism, racism, and heteronormativity as mutually constitutive.[1] This phrase simply means that systems of power simultaneously shape and are shaped by one another. As a consequence of intersecting systems of power, one social category, such as gender, is always given meaning through other contextually relevant categories, such as race, sexual orientation, and social class. As a corollary, attempts to theorize or investigate axes of dominance or subordination either singularly or additively systematically yield misrepresentations of individuals' lived experiences (Case, 2013; Case, this volume; Greenwood, 2012).

Intersectionality's utility for exposing, describing, and theorizing the experiences of dominant and subordinate groups is repeatedly demonstrated in theory, research, and education across a wide range of academic disciplines (e.g., Anderson-Nathe, Gringeri, & Wahab, 2013; Bowleg, 2008; Collins, 1990; Crenshaw, 1989; Gibson, 2015; Hankivsky, 2012). More recently, the translational promise of intersectional theory for real-world justice concerns was shown, for example, in racial justice efforts in the United States (such as the work of the African American Policy Forum) and in European Commission investigations into discrimination (Burri & Schiek, 2009). Following a brief overview of the foundations of intersectionality, I review disciplinary implementations and real-world application. I aim to offer a taste of the many ways that intersectionality enhanced scholarship, pedagogy, and social action, and provided insights into ways that the intersectional pedagogical model (Case, this volume) can be put to use in practical applications. Below, I include examples of some techniques educators could use to infuse intersectionality into their social justice curriculum.

A Brief Overview of Intersectionality and Social Justice

Intersectionality was originally conceived to explain the experiences of race and gender in the lives of Black women, but its utility has much broader reach. Indeed, intersectionality immeasurably advanced understanding of the ways single-axis approaches to social identities simultaneously generalize the experiences of some (e.g., White women) while they elide, erase, or otherwise render invisible the experiences of other, often less powerful groups (e.g., Black women) (Bowleg, 2008; Crenshaw, 1989, 1991; Purdie-Vaughns & Eibach, 2008). As a result, single-axis modes fail to interrogate or interrupt, and thereby perpetuate, systems of domination and subordination.

Importantly, both Crenshaw (1989, 1991) and Collins (1990) use intersectionality to explain how intersecting systems are dynamic rather than static and every individual simultaneously belongs to dominant and subordinate groups, not solely to one or the other. No one individual or group is ever always and only dominant or subordinate relative to all others. Thus, a full intersectional analysis of social justice concerns must account not only for disadvantage associated with subordinate group membership, but also for privilege associated with dominant group membership and shifts in power over time, place, and context (Case, 2013; Case, this volume). Intersectionality is integral to social justice efforts because it is an effective analytical tool for illuminating the ways different oppressions are interlinked and shaped by one another.

Understanding identities as dynamic as well as intersecting is important. Although the intersection of ethnicity with gender creates a situation of greater privilege for most White women relative to most women of color, and relatively lower status of most women relative to most White men, this is not always the case. Social category memberships may confer either privilege and advantage or subordination and disadvantage at different times and in different places and contexts. Imagine a poor or working-class rural White student, the first in her family to go to university, encountering for the first time a Black woman professional who holds a position of status, authority, and power over the White female student's outcomes. We can equally easily imagine that same White female asserting her heterosexual and Christian privilege during interactions with members of her university's gay/straight alliance. This example illustrates the ways social category intersections are never statically associated with privilege, power, advantage or disadvantage within the matrix of domination and subordination (Collins, 1990). Nevertheless, some people belong to privileged social categories that smooth their way in most contexts, such as White people in the United States, while members of other social categories encounter prejudice and discrimination in many contexts, such as Latina/o people in the United States.

Because intersectionality was introduced to explain and describe experiences of Black women in America, the theory is sometimes portrayed as only relevant to minority or subordinate groups (e.g., Alexander-Floyd, 2012). This could not be further from the truth because intersectionality is also an important framework for understanding the intimate relationship of dominance to subordination and advantage to disadvantage (Case, 2013; Case, this volume). Although most researchers do continue to focus on subordinate groups in their intersectional analyses, some have begun shifting their attention to the ways that social injustice is maintained through social category intersections that produce power and privilege for some groups but not others (e.g., Case, 2013). In the following sections, I describe some of the ways intersectionality has been implemented in a selection of disciplines that share core social justice concerns.

Intersectionality across the Academy

As Carbado, Crenshaw, Mays, and Tomlinson (2013) observed, there are very few contemporary theories that have received the level of attention shone on intersectionality since the term's inception in the 1980s (Crenshaw, 1989). Since then, intersectionality has been disseminated transnationally and across widely divergent academic disciplines, including biomedical sciences, nursing and health, psychology, sociology, geography, anthropology, social work, political science, education, and philosophy. In each of these areas, scholars justified the adoption of an intersectional approach to fill in the gaps, and addressed the limitations of, existing disciplinary frameworks that use some form of a single-axis or additive approach to explain domination, subordination, power relations, and social inequality and their effects on individuals, groups, communities, and societies.

The following section describes and illustrates how intersectionality has been adopted within three academic domains: health, social work, and psychology. These three domains were selected because they have direct relevance to pressing social justice concerns and the published scholarship attends to theory, research, and pedagogy. In each example, I provide:

- an overview of the way intersectionality was used to illuminate and understand power structures as interacting to create and sustain social inequality;
- examples of empirical research in which an intersectional lens was applied; and
- examples of the incorporation of intersectionality into social justice related research, practice, and pedagogy.

Some themes may be observed across these three academic domains. First, theoretical or critical review papers often build the case for importing intersectionality into their discipline's analytic approach to theory and research. They typically pose a conceptual problem or identifying lacunae and then propose intersectionality as the solution. Second, virtually all include a brief overview of the history of intersectionality, which inevitably draws on the work of Crenshaw (1989, 1990) and Collins (1990). Third, scholars select one or more research domains from their discipline to illustrate the ways single-axis or additive models yield distorted knowledge by misrepresenting a problem or producing biased findings. Fourth, each attends to some methodological challenge or critique. Some raise concerns about the methodological limitations associated with an intersectional approach while others introduce best practice guidelines for intersectional research. I next illustrate these themes in three academic domains: health disparities, social work, and psychology.

Intersectional Approaches to Health Disparities and Nursing

Group differences in health disparities have been demonstrated on a wide range of key outcomes such as infant mortality, cancer diagnoses and treatment, cardiovascular disease, diabetes, smoking, HIV/AIDS, and immunization (Bates, Hankivsky, & Springer, 2009; Hankivsky, 2012; Weber & Parra-Medina, 2003). Traditionally, these health disparities have been investigated along a single axis that differentiates two groups, such as men and women or ethnic group majority and minority. In recent years, however, the limitations of this approach have been identified and analyzed from a number of different approaches. For example, Mullings and Schulz (2006) focused on issues of intersectionality and health. In 2012, *Social Science and Medicine* published a special issue on gender and health that included intersectional approaches. In both cases, scholars used intersectionality to critique single-axis explanations of health disparities and offer up alternative explanations (Springer, Hankivsky, & Bates, 2012).

From an intersectional perspective, single-axis approaches to health outcomes research have been criticized on several grounds. Most compelling is the observation that focusing on one dimension alone, usually gender or ethnicity, elides important differences within groups (Hankivsky, 2012). Hankivsky argued that conceiving of social categories as monolithic occludes important health disparities within groups and renders important structural influences invisible. One dimension that is often the focus of single-axis health disparities research is gender. Critics of this focus argued that "gender" is too often equated with "women," so that women's health is centered in research on health disparities, while men's health issues are overlooked (e.g., Hankivsky, 2012; Richardson & Carroll, 2009; Smith & Robertson, 2008; Turshen, 2007; Wilkins & Savoye, 2009). Historically, however, this shift in focus to women's health was a significant step forward for activist scholars who critiqued biomedical research for excluding women from research and for falsely generalizing research findings on male samples to women (Khaw, 1993; Merton, 1993; Sechzer et al., 1994).

However, efforts to redress bias in health disparities research that simply account for gender differences do not go far enough. Hankivsky (2012) used intersectionality to critique the a priori primacy of gender in health disparities research. She argued that the focus on gender often is misguided and conceals true causes of health disparities, such as poverty and social policies. Other researchers questioned the common use of the phrase "women and minorities" in health disparities research (Bowleg, 2012; Weber & Fore, 2007). Bowleg (2012) illuminated the many ways this phrase is flawed, and in its clumsy attempt to be inclusive, actually excises women from minorities and minorities from women and simultaneously elides the possibility of identities at the intersections of gender and ethnicity.

Intersectional approaches are necessary tools for conceptualizing and investigating causes and solutions to health disparities. For example, Weber and Fore (2007) explained how intersectionality illuminates the role of macro structures in ethnic health disparities. Drawing on three areas of health disparities research (HIV/AIDs, infant mortality, smoking and pregnancy), Weber and Fore made the case that neither ethnicity nor gender alone explain health disparities and that an intersectional approach shifts the focus from individual deficits to power relations and social structures. Such a shift in focus can generate insights into more effective strategies to reduce health disparities and mobilize social justice efforts to improve marginalized social groups' health outcomes.

The intersectional move in health-related fields may advance social justice efforts to reduce health disparities. Drawing on Weber (2007), Rogers and Kelly (2011) proposed principles of feminist intersectionality to guide research into health disparities. For example, researchers should recognize that dimensions of difference are contextually dependent and fluid, that research questions and processes are socially constructed, that macro-level power relations shape micro-level experiences of health problems, and that social inequalities are mutually interdependent (Rogers & Kelly, 2011; Weber, 2007).

An interesting example of intersectionality in health disparities research illustrated how an intersectional framework illuminates the structural forces that put some groups at higher risk of contracting HIV than others (Collins, von Unger, & Armbrister, 2008). These researchers investigated the intersections of mental illness, gender, and ethnic identity in relation to both risk and resilience for Latina women living in New York City. Taking an intersectional approach allowed Collins et al. (2008) to identify how mental illness identity intersected with cultural norms to produce risky sexual behaviors. Findings indicated that mental illness stigma undermined these women's social standing as wives and mothers, as well as their self-confidence, making it difficult for them to successfully negotiate safe sex practices within the context of strongly gendered cultural norms (Collins et al., 2008).

This analysis of HIV risk offers educators an opportunity to illustrate intersectionality to students in a range of different disciplines, including medicine, nursing, public health, sociology, psychology, and social work. For example, educators in any of these disciplines could lead class discussions about this research and ask students to think about how their own intersecting identities act as protective or risk factors in their own lives, perhaps highlighting the role of privilege in protecting health and the role of disadvantage in harming health. Students could be encouraged to identify a comparison person with whom they share one social identity, but do not share another. They could, in turn, think through how that person's intersecting identities increase or decrease their health protection and risk. Discussions about the role of culture, subculture, and cultural norms could highlight the ways culture intersects with gender, mental illness identity, or social class to protect health or increase risk.

These kinds of classroom exercises could be used to implement best practice guidelines that recommend the use of intersectionality in health research, education, and practice (Rogers & Kelly, 2011; van Herk, Smith, & Andrew, 2011). For example, van Herk's et al. (2011) proposal is particularly interesting because of its focus on the importance of teaching nurses to examine connections between their own privileges and their research and practice. Van Herk and colleagues critiqued recent efforts to cultivate cultural sensitivity through curricula that focus singularly or additively on patients' subordinate identities and experiences of discrimination and oppression because they overlook the influence of privilege on nursing practice. Further, they argued that focusing on subordinated identities alone cannot interrupt the systems that contribute to disparities in nursing students' experiences and disparities in care delivered to different populations. Van Herk et al. proposed an alternate intersectional approach in which educators encourage nursing students to interrogate their own intersecting dominant and subordinate identities and reflect on the ways privileged identities impact nursing practice. Their suggestions for best practices in nursing education echo the pedagogical model proposed by Case (this volume) in which intersectional education for social justice incorporates personal reflection on both privileges and disadvantages to reveal how invisible intersections of power put some people at greater health risk and simultaneously buffer others.

Critiques of single-axis approaches in health-related research, practice, and education are also found in the social work literature. Social workers, like health researchers and educators, grow increasingly concerned with incorporating social justice into their research, practice, and education. Some of the intersectional critiques and solutions found in the social work literature are described in the next section.

Intersectionality in Social Work Research, Practice, and Education

In intersectional social work scholarship, a predominant theme is the importance of attending to macro-level forces such as time, history, and culture for understanding domination and subordination. By focusing attention on these macro-level forces, social work scholars highlight both the fluidity of social categories and the impermanence of power, domination, and subordination in a given individual's lived experiences (Gibson, 2015; Hulko, 2009; Mehrotra, 2010).

The power of context to dynamically shift privilege and disadvantage is illustrated by Hulko's (2009) story of a research participant born in Trinidad who immigrated to Canada. The immigrant woman described the ways her ethnicity is ascribed as Black in Canada, but White in Trinidad, as well as the corresponding shifts she experienced in belonging to dominant and subordinate groups depending on location. Bringing time, history, and context into social justice education is a powerful way to communicate to students not only the social construction of categories such as race, but also that no position of domination or subordination is ever fixed. For example, in a classroom exercise on patriarchy, students could discuss cross-cultural differences among women in agency and choice. Educators could challenge stereotypes of Muslim women as passive victims of Islamic patriarchy by highlighting the intersections of identity with location, such as the United Kingdom or United States compared to Afghanistan or Saudi Arabia. Equally, students could discuss the ways context shapes Muslim women's agency and choice to wear, or not to wear, hijab. These sorts of discussions could develop students' understanding of the ways that intersectional analyses can and should go beyond social category intersections and interrogate the roles of time, place, and history in experiences of power, dominance, and subordination. Kurtis and Adams (this volume) take these ideas even further in their chapter on decolonial intersectionality.

Anderson-Nathe et al. (2013) described the value of adding intersectionality to the graduate level social work curriculum. Anderson-Nathe and colleagues argued that intersectionality is an important tool for delivering the social justice elements of social work education. Echoing Case's (this volume) pedagogical model in which she encourages educators to reflect on how their own intersecting identities affect the learning environment, Anderson-Nathe et al. explained how they used their own intersecting identities as pedagogical tools to break down their students' binary thinking. For example, one of these authors, Anderson-Nathe, described how he deliberately shared his intersecting religious-queer-parent identities to compel his students to reflect on and question their own preconceived notions of these seemingly contradictory identities. In a classroom discussion, instructors could invite students to identify both the similar and the different challenges that might face instructors with seemingly contradictory or paradoxical intersecting identities. For example, students might be asked to discuss their expectations of and beliefs about an instructor who is a religious, heterosexual father, or an atheist Arab woman who has no children. Students could be asked to articulate how their different expectations illuminate both privilege and disadvantage.

Educators who take an intersectional approach to consciousness raising with their students should take care not to stop there, but go beyond mere formulaic and static "laundry lists" of hyphenated identities (Gibson, 2015; Shields, 2008). As Rivera (this volume), Knapp (2005), and Shields (2008) observed, nominally acknowledging hyphenated identities without deeply engaging with the ways these intersections sustain or interrupt power relations does nothing to advance our thinking about difference, and in fact, passes responsibility for that intellectual heavy lifting to others.

Similarly, Gibson (2015) noted that by merely listing hyphenated subjectivities, social work researchers risk losing sight of the social structures that shape individual experience. Like Hulko (2009), Gibson's intersectional approach emphasized macro-level forces, such as history, in shaping contemporary processes of dominance and subordination. For example, students can be asked to consider how the Supreme Court decision on same-sex marriage in the U.S. changed expectations about some queer parents but not others. Attending to the past can help researchers, educators, and students remember that present-day categories are not static and that ways of defining difference are always relational and impermanent. Looking at difference, as well as systems of domination and subordination, as situated in time, place, and history, and therefore dynamic and fluid, affords researchers, educators, and practitioners opportunities to adhere to some core principles of intersectionality: avoid reification of social categories; maintain focus on macro-level systems; and retain understanding of social relations as fluid, contingent, emergent, and constitutive.

Vervliet, de Mol, Broekaert, and Derluyn (2014) offered an example of an intersectional relational approach in social work in their research with young, unaccompanied refugee mothers in Belgium. Vervliet and colleagues analyzed interview data to identify the ways their participants constructed their identities as young refugee mothers and how these identity constructions were shaped by their experiences of the European asylum system. Illustrated in this analysis are the complex ways that daily living conditions disempowered these young mothers, while the identity "mother" afforded opportunities to find meaning and purpose in life. Importantly, these scholars maintained a parallel focus on macro-level forces, such as Belgian migration policies and how these policies construct definitions of social categories such as "refugee" and "unaccompanied minor" in ways that misrepresent young women's priorities and limit their access to material resources necessary for empowered parenting. Using an intersectional framework enabled Vervliet et al. to identify the challenges posed to effective social work with refugees in the context of policies that do not recognize the ways parenting needs shape the immigrant experience and exacerbate the difficult living conditions of refugee residence centers.

Research by Vervliet et al. (2014) could form the basis of a powerful teaching exercise in social worker education. These scholars illustrated how context shapes identity, power, domination, and subordination for women on the social and economic margins. They also highlighted the challenges social workers encounter when social policies clash with social work principles and ethics of care. Including this kind of scholarship in the social work curriculum helps prepare future social workers for the challenges they might face when social policies clash with their own values and their clients' needs.

Social policies that appear neutral or universal sometimes reflect the particular interests and characteristics of some groups and not others. Educators can create class exercises or assignments that ask students to analyze local, state, or national policy to reveal hidden intersections and identify the ways social policies reflect the needs and experiences of some group members and not others, how they create barriers or hurdles to access for some and not others, and how they fail to meet the particular needs of some groups and not others. For example, students could read Crenshaw's (1991) analysis of structural inequality that vividly illustrated the ways intersections of race, class, gender, and immigrant status create barriers to safety and access to social services for some battered women and not others. Crenshaw described how laws that limit access for citizens and legal residents create barriers to safety for undocumented women who must choose between battering and the risk of deportation. Educators could ask students to identify another social policy or law, analyze it to reveal the hidden intersections, biases, and barriers, and identify how the policy poses ethical and practical challenges for social workers.

Intersectionality in Psychological Theory, Research, and Pedagogy

As is the case with other disciplines including health and social work, feminist psychologists advocated for intersectionality as a solution to the problems inherent in single-axis approaches (Bowleg, 2008; Cole, 2009; Greenwood, 2012; Parent, DeBlaere, & Moradi, 2013; Shields, 2008). Beginning, as all writers do, from Collins's (1990) and Crenshaw's (1989) observations that social identities are mutually constitutive, these authors illustrated the ways the experience or expression of one social category, such as gender, is always given meaning through its intersections with other social categories such as race, class, or sexual orientation (Bowleg, 2008; Cole, 2009; Greenwood, 2012; Parent et al., 2013; Shields, 2008).

Psychologists described the different approaches that researchers in different disciplines take to intersectionality: as a framework, a theory, and an approach to social activism (Parent et al., 2013; Warner & Shields, 2013). As a framework, intersectionality offers psychologists a powerful tool for conceptualizing the experience or expression of a given social identity, such as gender, as always shaped by the individual's membership in other social categories, such as ethnicity, age, or sexual orientation. As theory, intersectionality is used to develop testable hypotheses about a set of core factors and as an approach to social activism when a researcher aims to articulate the processes through which intersecting identities shape social change-related phenomena ranging from mobilization to voting patterns to social protest (Cole, 2008; Swank & Fahs, 2013).

Psychologists have written extensively about the methodological challenges posed by intersectionality, probably because the discipline tends to privilege experimental methods above qualitative methods, which are generally viewed as most amenable to an intersectional approach (e.g., Bowleg, 2008; Cole, 2009; Shields, 2008; Warner, 2008). Both Warner (2008) and Cole (2009) published best practices and guidelines for intersectional psychological research. Both encouraged researchers to interrogate and articulate the reasoning behind the social categories/identities they select for inclusion in their research designs and analyses. For example, the researchers' explanation of sampling choices should include reflection on the decisions about whether to include both dominant and subordinate social categories, a question posed to intersectionality researchers in all disciplines.

One corrective to bias and exclusion is to center the experiences of minority group members in research. If, however, as Warner (2008) argues, researchers continue to focus solely on subordinated groups in intersectional research, then the roles of power, domination, and privilege in creating and sustaining injustice and inequality will remain under-examined, a warning that is echoed in Case's (this volume) pedagogical model. Warner argued that to do good intersectional research, researchers must be able to explain why they choose particular inter-sections and must be accountable for these decisions (see also Hankivsky, 2012, reflections on these concerns within the domain of health disparities research). One way intersectionality could easily be added to the curriculum within psychology and beyond is to incorporate intersectional questions into research methods classes that cover sampling theory, challenges, and decisions. These questions could require students to explain why they included certain groups and not others and how their decisions centered the experiences of some groups and also rendered invisible the experiences of others.

According to Cole (2009), researchers should center issues of inequality in their research in order to reveal the ways multiple category memberships influence one another. By deliberately interrogating issues of inequality, psychologists are better equipped to avoid what Shinn and Toohey (2003) call *context minimization error*, so that rather than homing in on individual deficit or pathology, attention is drawn further "upstream" to social structures (e.g., laws, policies, institutions) that perpetuate patterns of domination and subordination and maintain social inequality and injustice.

Deliberately asking where similarities lie across different intersectional positions also interrupts tendencies to see social identities as static and individuals as deficient or deviant. By looking across very different social category locations and identifying similarities in experience, Cole (2009) argued researchers can refocus attention on macro-level sources of inequality. Identification of such points of affinity and connection may facilitate coalitions of different groups in pursuit of common goals. Points of affinity sometimes reveal unexpected potential coalitions, such as when conservative Christians and some feminists find common ground in opposition to pornography. In classrooms, educators could lead discussions where students identify topics on which unlikely allies align in their social justice concerns.

Too often, efforts to mobilize participation in positive social change have relied on single-axis identification. A good example is the women's movement's focus on supposed "universal sisterhood" that relied on identification with a single social category and homogenized within-group differences. Educators can help students look upstream to identify how different groups experience discrimination manifested in distinct ways. Doing so may encourage coalitional and ally behavior, while simultaneously avoiding the trap of group homogeneity. Recent intersectional psychological research on intersectional political consciousness and intersectional awareness examined this potential (e.g., Curtin, Stewart, & Cole, 2015; Greenwood, 2008). Exercises in classrooms that raise students' consciousness about their own privileges, such as discussions about ordinary privileges that highlight heterosexual privilege, white privilege, or male privilege, can help students identify points of connection and realize how some of the experiences of ordinary unconscious privilege are shared by different dominant social categories, while others are distinctive.

These privileges, whether shared or unshared, may manifest differently in shifting contexts, but in combination operate to sustain systems of inequality, dominance, and subordination. In the classroom, privilege has many sources: white privilege, male privilege, heterosexual privilege, class privilege, and others. Each comes with its own set of invisible, unearned advantages (McIntosh, 1988) that facilitate comfort and performance in educational contexts, and confer attributions of intellectual competence to some but not others. Although these privileges arise from different sources, all operate to create, sustain, and legitimate inequalities in the classroom. Raising intersectional awareness about the ways these intersections operate in the classroom is not easy because privileged students may be defensive and resistant, but it is a vital component of social justice curriculum in any discipline. Examples and guidance for doing so are found throughout the current volume (e.g., Case & Rios, this volume; Dessel & Corvidae, this volume; Hall, this volume; Rios, Bowling, & Harris, this volume).

Most intersectional research in psychology falls into one of two types (Parent et al., 2013). The first type conceptualizes social categories/identities as predictor variables and examines both their additive and multiplicative effects on key outcomes such as attitudes toward outgroups (e.g., Norton & Herek, 2013). The second identifies a particular identity intersection and explores group members' subjective experiences of life at that intersection. For example, Nick Hopkins and I (Hopkins & Greenwood, 2013) took this approach in our examination of young Scottish Muslim women's decisions to adopt hijab and its importance to their identities.

A third, less common type of intersectional research examines the ways group members understand social justice issues. In my efforts to understand factors that predict solidarity amongst women from different groups (Greenwood, 2008), I examined the extent to which feminist consciousness reflected awareness of the ways that social hierarchies intersect and therefore produce qualitatively different experiences of gender discrimination for women differently positioned in the matrix of domination and subordination (Collins, 1990). I found that women expressed greater solidarity with diverse women's organizations when they also expressed greater intersectional feminist consciousness. In subsequent research, I found that women's intersectional political consciousness could be experimentally manipulated and that White women's intersectional consciousness predicted more positive and accepting attitudes toward Muslim women who wear hijab (Greenwood & Christian, 2008).

These findings were advanced and broadened by researchers who introduced the concept of intersectional awareness (IA; Curtin et al., 2015). IA is conceptualized as a way of thinking about social inequality and power hierarchies that influences individuals' processes of social information, attitudes, and behaviors. Curtin et al. (2015) investigated the extent to which IA was reflected in both men's and women's thinking about the experiences of different social groups as multiply determined by race, gender, and sexual orientation, and whether the tendency for one's thinking to reflect IA was associated with social activism. Findings demonstrated that IA correlated with actual involvement in social justice issues, a general orientation to social action, and pro-social attitudes toward outgroups, which are all important factors that support social change.

As Curtin and colleagues (2015) pointed out, anyone, whether a member of a dominant or subordinate group, may learn to think intersectionally. IA may hold promise for efforts to pursue positive social change on social justice issues, and educators and community organizers may incorporate efforts to raise intersectional awareness in their activities. More specifically, social justice educators should explicitly incorporate exercises into their curriculum that develop the student's intersectional awareness, ability to analyze social issues intersectionally, and skills for applying such awareness to research and practice. Examples of these kinds of exercises are distributed across the chapters in this book (e.g., Case & Lewis, this volume).

The utility of intersectional awareness for social justice education is illustrated in Case and Lewis's (this volume) reflections on teaching intersectional LGBT psychology. This trailblazing incorporation of intersectionality into the LGBT psychology curriculum simultaneously delivers psychological theory and research, develops students' critical thinking, stimulates intersectional awareness, and mobilizes actions that contribute to positive social change.

This curricular innovation transforms conventional approaches to teaching psychology which tend to focus on one social category at a time (gender or race or sexual orientation).

Case and Lewis (this volume) argue that educators can raise students' consciousness about domination and oppression and also increase students' participation in social change activities through effective use of intersectional pedagogical tools. Describing effects of the curriculum on students, both instructors note that at least some of their students began to adopt an ally identity and exhibit intersectional awareness through their group activities and written assignments. However, the students' progress toward development of intersectional awareness and ally identities was not linear, nor was it the same for all students. Case and Lewis report that one or more students dropped the class, and each witnessed some resistance to some portions of the curricular content. These findings suggest that any given individual has the potential to travel the road to intersectional awareness, regardless of her or his own positioning in the matrix of domination and subordination. The road may prove more challenging for some than others, and a few might ultimately choose other routes. Nevertheless, this excursion into intersectional pedagogy in the teaching of psychology demonstrates that the horizon is wide and holds great promise for advancing students' understanding of the complexity of social identities and for advancing social justice education.

While intersectionality has been embraced in many corners of the academy, the translation of intersectional theory and research into real-world social action for social justice concerns has not yet been fully realized. In order to fully realize the power of intersectionality to affect social change outside the academy, researchers and educators must extend their reach to practice, action, and policy. The next section describes one way academics, activists, and policy makers have taken intersectionality to the streets.

On the Ground: The Translational Promise of Intersectionality

According to their website, the African American Policy Forum (AAPF; www.aapf.org) is a think-tank that aims to change public policy and challenge structural inequality. AAPF takes an explicitly intersectional approach in its work. Kimberlé Crenshaw holds key founding roles in this organization, so this example also serves as an illustration of the ways academics can translate their scholarship into social actions that contribute to on-the-ground efforts to achieve social justice and make material changes in people's lives.

Two AAPF documents explicitly target use by organizers to raise consciousness about intersectionality: a primer on intersectionality (AAPF, n.d.) and a learning circle toolkit (AAPF, 2011). The Intersectional Primer is used in racial justice training with White allies to create and enhance intersectional awareness of those involved in racial justice activities. The Learning Circle Toolkit supports efforts to mobilize localized collective responses to over-incarceration of girls and women of color. These documents could easily be incorporated into social justice curricula as tools to raise students' intersectional awareness and provide examples of how to use intersectionality in social justice efforts. Educators could also develop coursework assignments in which students use these documents as templates for developing their own toolkits or primers for racial justice work tailored to their own locations, or for social justice work in domains that intersect with or complement racial justice efforts.

The AAPF broadly focuses on gendered racism and a range of social justice concerns related to policing, police brutality, and incarceration. The forum explicitly addresses these issues through the lens of intersectionality and examines the ways gendered racism affects the lives of people of color in the United States. The most recent document, "Say Her Name: Resisting Police Brutality against Black Women" (AAPF, 2015), highlighted the relatively invisible experiences of police brutality amongst Black women. The report included stories of gendered violence against Black women by police officers, rendered visible the often overlooked cases of police violence against women, and made recommendations for how activists can engage with communities on the topics of gendered police brutality and state violence. The report was accompanied by a media guide that advised activists how to leverage social media and contained a compilation of tweets (#SayHerName) and images used in social action aimed to resist police brutality against Black women. Again, these documents could be brought into the classroom to illustrate how intersectionality operates in people's lives, raise intersectional awareness, and inspire students to use intersectionality in their own social justice work on issues relevant to their own lives and communities.

Hazards in the Intersections: Challenges to the Intersectionality Construct

Perhaps inevitably, given its far-reaching influence, intersectionality has received its own share of criticism on a number of grounds. For critiques and challenges to intersectionality, see Lutz, Vivar, and Supik (2011) and the special issue of the *Du Bois Review* (for the issue's introductory article, see Carbado et al., 2013). Within this special issue, Cho (2013) wrote about the race-sexuality critique of intersectionality in legal studies. Ocen (2013) argued that legal scholars' use of single-axis analysis of Black men's mass incarceration has "shackled" intersectionality and limited its utility. Bilge (2013) stated that feminist debates about intersectionality have functioned to depoliticize the theory and undermine its power. Goff and Kahn (2013) criticized social psychological approaches to social identities such as race, class, and gender, labeling them inherently racist. They argued traditional methods used in psychological research impeded intersectional thinking and limited opportunities for intersectionality to take hold in and transform psychology. A cogent acknowledgement and response to Goff and Kahn's critique appears in Grzanka (this volume). Robertson (2013) responded to criticisms of intersectionality, explaining that the intersectional approach continues to hold its place as one of the most important tools that any researcher, practitioner, or educator may wield to understand social, cultural, and economic systems of domination, recognize the complexities of social identities, and advocate for positive social change. In response to Cho (2013), a recent examination of multiple discriminations in the European Union demonstrated how the European Union and its constituent countries have begun to grapple with issues of discrimination arising from multiple intersecting identities (Burri & Schiek, 2009). The African American Policy Forum (AAPF) illustrates how intersectionality can be used outside the academy to tackle social justice issues. Similarly, the growing literature on the intersection of social identities in social psychological research compellingly demonstrates how social psychologists effectively engage intersectionality in their theory and research to advance an activist science (Shields, 2008; Weisstein, 1968). Accounts such as that by Case and Lewis (this volume) provide concrete paths for incorporating intersectionality in the curriculum to pursue justice-oriented educational goals for and with students. Taken together, this body of evidence supports and validates McCall's (2005) claim that intersectionality is the single most important contribution made thus far by any feminist scholars.

Note

1 I would like to thank Abigail Stewart, Kim Case, and an anonymous reviewer for their comments and suggestions on earlier versions of this chapter.

References

African American Policy Forum (AAPF). (n.d.). *A primer on intersectionality*. Retrieved from www.aapf.org
AAPF. (2011). *Intersectionality learning circles practitioner's toolkit*. Retrieved from www.aapf.org
AAPF. (2015). *Say her name: Resisting police brutality against Black women* [report]. Retrieved from www.aapf.org
Alexander-Floyd, N. G. (2012). Disappearing acts: Reclaiming intersectionality in the social sciences in a post-black feminist era. *Feminist Formations, 24*, 1–25. doi:10.1353/ff.2012.0003
Anderson-Nathe, B., Gringeri, C., & Wahab, S. (2013). Nurturing "critical hope" in teaching feminist social work research. *Journal of Social Work Education, 49*, 277–291. doi:10.1080/10437797.2013.768477
Bates, L. M., Hankivsky, O., & Springer, K. W. (2009). Gender and health inequities: a comment on the final report of the WHO commission on the social determinants of health. *Social Science & Medicine, 69*, 1002–1004. doi:10.1016/j.socscimed.2009.07.0 22

Bilge, S. (2013). Intersectionality undone. *Du Bois Review: Social Science Research on Race*, *10*, 405–424. doi:10.10170S1742058X13000283

Bowleg, L. (2008). When Black + lesbian + woman ≠ Black lesbian woman: The methodological challenges of qualitative and quantitative intersectionality research. *Sex Roles*, *59*, 312–325. doi:10.1007/s11199-008-9400-z

Bowleg, L. (2012). The problem with the phrase women and minorities: Intersectionality-an important theoretical framework for public health. *American Journal of Public Health*, *102*, 1267–1273. doi:10.2105/AJPH.2012.300750

Burri, S., & Schiek, D. (2009). *Multiple discrimination in EU law: Opportunities for legal responses to intersectional gender discrimination?* European Commission Directorate-General for Employment, Social Affairs and Equal Opportunities.

Carbado, D. W., Crenshaw, K. W., Mays, V. M. & Tomlinson, B. (2013). Intersectionality. *Du Bois Review: Social Science Research on Race*, *10*, 303–312. doi:10.1017/S17420 58X13000349

Case, K. (2013). *Deconstructing privilege: Teaching and learning as allies in the classroom*. New York, NY: Routledge.

Case, K. A. (this volume). Toward an intersectional pedagogy model: Engaged learning for social justice. In K. A. Case (Ed.), *Intersectional pedagogy: Complicating identity and social justice* (pp. 1–24). New York, NY: Routledge.

Case, K. A., & Lewis, M. K. (this volume). Teaching intersectional psychology in racially diverse settings. In K. A. Case (Ed.), *Intersectional pedagogy: Complicating identity and social justice* (pp. 129–149). New York, NY: Routledge.

Case, K., & Rios, D. (this volume). Infusing intersectionality: Complicating the psychology of women course. In K. A. Case (Ed.), *Intersectional pedagogy: Complicating identity and social justice* (pp. 82–109). New York, NY: Routledge.

Cho, S. (2013). Post-intersectionality. *Du Bois Review: Social Science Research on Race*, *10*, 385–404. doi:10.1017/S1742058X13000362

Cole, E. R. (2008). Coalitions as a model for intersectionality: From practice to theory. *Sex Roles*, *59*, 443–453. doi:10.1007/s11199-008-9419-1

Cole, E. R. (2009). Intersectionality and research in psychology. *American Psychologist*, *64*, 170–180. doi:10.1037/a0014564

Collins, P. H. (1990). *Black feminist thought: Knowledge, consciousness, and the politics of empowerment*. New York, NY: Routledge.

Collins, P. Y., von Unger, H., & Armbrister, A. (2008). Church ladies, good girls, and locas: Stigma and the intersection of gender, ethnicity, mental illness, and sexuality in relation to HIV risk. *Social Science & Medicine*, *67*, 389–397. doi:10.1016/j.socscime d.2008.03.013

Crenshaw, K. (1989). Demarginalizing the intersection of race and sex: A Black feminist critique of antidiscrimination doctrine, feminist theory, and antiracist politics. *University of Chicago Legal Forum*, *1989*, 139–167.

Crenshaw, K. (1991). Mapping the margins: Intersectionality, identity politics, and violence against women of color. *Stanford Law Review*, *43*, 1241–1299.

Curtin, N., Stewart, A. J., & Cole, E. R. (2015). Challenging the status quo: The role of intersectional awareness in activism for social change and pro-social intergroup attitudes. *Psychology of Women Quarterly*, *39*, 512–529. doi:10.1177/0361684315580439

Dessel, A., & Corvidae, T. (this volume). Experiential activities for engaging intersectionality in social justice pedagogy. In K. A. Case (Ed.), *Intersectional pedagogy: Complicating identity and social justice* (pp. 214–231). New York, NY: Routledge.

Gibson, M. F. (2015). Intersecting deviance: Social work, difference and the legacy of eugenics. *British Journal of Social Work, 45*, 313–330. doi:10.1093/bjsw/bct131

Goff, P. A., & Kahn, K. B. (2013). How psychological science impedes intersectional thinking. *Du Bois Review: Social Science Research on Race, 10*, 365–384. doi:10.101 7/S1742058X13000313

Greenwood, R. M. (2008). Intersectional political consciousness: Appreciation for intra-group differences and solidarity in diverse groups. *Psychology of Women Quarterly, 32*, 36–47. doi:10.1111/j.1471-6402.2007.00405.x

Greenwood, R. M. (2012). Standing at the crossroads of identity: An intersectional approach to women's social identities and gender consciousness. In S. Wiley, G. Philogène, & T. A. Revenson (Eds.), *Social categories in everyday experience* (pp. 113–129). Washington, DC: American Psychological Association.

Greenwood, R. M., & Christian, A. (2008). What happens when we unpack the invisible knapsack? Intersectional political consciousness and inter-group appraisals. *Sex Roles, 59*, 404–417. doi:10.1007/s11199-008-9439-x

Grzanka, P. R. (this volume). Undoing the Psychology of Gender: Intersectional feminism and social science pedagogy. In K. A. Case (Ed.), *Intersectional pedagogy: Complicating identity and social justice* (pp. 63–81). New York, NY: Routledge.

Hall, N. (this volume). Quotes, blogs, diagrams, and counter-storytelling: Teaching intersectionality at a minority-serving institution. In K. A. Case (Ed.), *Intersectional pedagogy: Complicating identity and social justice* (pp. 150–170). New York, NY: Routledge.

Hankivsky, O. (2012). Women's health, men's health, and gender and health: Implications of intersectionality. *Social Science & Medicine, 74*, 1712–1720. doi:10.1016/j.socscimed.2011.11.029

Hopkins, N., & Greenwood, R. M. (2013). Hijab, visibility, and the performance of identity. *European Journal of Social Psychology, 43*, 438–447. doi:10.1002/ejsp.1955

Hulko, W. (2009). The time- and context-contingent nature of intersectionality and interlocking oppressions. *Affilia, 24*, 44–55. doi:10.1177/0886109908326814

Khaw, K. T. (1993). Where are the women in studies of coronary heart disease? *British Medical Journal, 306*, 1145–1146.

Knapp, G. A. (2005). Race, class, gender reclaiming baggage in fast travelling theories. *European Journal of Women's Studies, 12*, 249–265. doi:10.1177/1350506805054267

Kurtis, T., & Adams, G. (this volume). Decolonial intersectionality: Implications for theory, research, and pedagogy. In K. A. Case (Ed.), *Intersectional pedagogy: Complicating identity and social justice* (pp. 46–59). New York, NY: Routledge.

Lutz, H., Vivar, M. T. H., & Supik, L. (Eds.). (2011). *Framing intersectionality: Debates on a multi-faceted concept in gender studies*. London: Ashgate Publishing, Ltd.

McCall, L. (2005). The complexity of intersectionality. *Signs: Journal of Women in Culture and Society, 30*, 1771–800

McIntosh, P. (1988). *White privilege and male privilege: A personal account of coming to see correspondences through work in women's studies*. Working Paper No. 189. Wellesley, MA: Wellesley Centers for Women.

Mehrotra, G. (2010). Toward a continuum of intersectionality theorizing for feminist social work scholarship. *Affilia, 25*, 417–430. doi:10.1177/0886109910384190

Merton, V. (1993). The exclusion of pregnant, pregnable, and once-pregnable people (aka women) from biomedical research. *American Journal of Law and Medicine, 19*, 369–451.

Mullings, L., & Schulz, A. J. (2006). Intersectionality and health: An introduction. In A. Schultz & L. Mullings (Eds.), *Gender, race, class, & health: Intersectional approaches* (pp. 3–17). San Francisco, CA: Jossey-Bass.

Norton, A. T., & Herek, G. M. (2013). Heterosexuals' attitudes toward transgender people: Findings from a national probability sample of U.S. adults. *Sex Roles, 68,* 738–753. doi:10.1007/s11199-011-0110-6

Ocen, P. A. (2013). Unshackling intersectionality. *Du Bois Review: Social Science Research on Race, 10,* 471–483. doi:10.1017/S1742058X13000295

Parent, M. C., DeBlaere, C., & Moradi, B. (2013). Approaches to research on intersectionality: Perspectives on gender, LGBT, and racial/ethnic identities. *Sex Roles, 68,* 639–645. doi:10.1007/s11199-013-0283-2

Purdie-Vaughns, V., & Eibach, R. P. (2008). Intersectional invisibility: The distinctive advantages and disadvantages of multiple subordinate-group identities. *Sex Roles, 59,* 377–391. doi:10.1007/s11199-008-9424-4

Richardson, N., & Carroll, P. C. (2009). Getting men's health onto a policy agenda–charting the development of a National Men's Health Policy in Ireland. *Journal of Men's Health, 6,* 105–113. doi:10.1016/j.jomh.2009.03.004

Rios, D., Bowling, M., & Harris, J. (this volume). Decentering student "uniqueness" in lessons about intersectionality. In K. A. Case (Ed.), *Intersectional pedagogy: Complicating identity and social justice* (pp. 194–213). New York, NY: Routledge.

Rivera, D. P. (this volume). Revealing hidden intersections of gender identity, sexual orientation, race, and ethnicity: Teaching about multiple oppressed identities. In K. A. Case (Ed.), *Intersectional pedagogy: Complicating identity and social justice* (pp. 173–193). New York, NY: Routledge.

Robertson, E. (2013, December 23). In defense of intersectionality – one of feminism's most important tools. *The Guardian.* Retrieved from www.theguardian.com

Rogers, J., & Kelly, U. A. (2011). Feminist intersectionality: Bringing social justice to health disparities research. *Nursing Ethics, 18,* 397–407. doi:10.1177/0969733011398094

Sechzer, J. A., Rabinowitz, V. C., Denmark, F. L., McGinn, M. F., Weeks, B. M., & Wilkens, C. L. (1994). Sex and gender bias in animal research and in clinical studies of cancer, cardiovascular disease, and depression. *Annals of the New York Academy of Sciences, 736,* 21–48. doi:10.1111/j.1749-6632.1994.tb12816.x

Shields, S. A. (2008). Gender: An intersectionality perspective. *Sex Roles, 59,* 301–311. doi:10.1007/s11199-008-9501-8

Shinn, M., & Toohey, S. M. (2003). Community contexts of human welfare. *Annual Review of Psychology, 54,* 427–459. doi:10.1146/annurev.psych.54.101601.145052

Smith, J. A., & Robertson, S. (2008). Men's health promotion: A new frontier in Australia and the UK? *Health Promotion International, 23,* 283–289. doi:10.1093/heapro/dan019

Springer, K.W., Hankivsky, O., & Bates, L. M. (2012). Gender and health: Relational, intersectional, and biological approaches. [Special issue]. *Social Science and Medicine, 74,* 1661–1666.

Swank, E., & Fahs, B. (2013). An intersectional analysis of gender and race for sexual minorities who engage in gay and lesbian rights activism. *Sex Roles, 68,* 660–674. doi:10.1007/s11199-012-0168-9

Turshen, M. (2007). Gender and health. *Journal of Public Health Policy, 28,* 319–321. doi:10.1057/palgrave.jphp.3200141

Van Herk, K. A., Smith, D., & Andrew, C. (2011). Examining our privileges and oppressions: Incorporating an intersectionality paradigm into nursing. *Nursing Inquiry, 18,* 29–39.

Vervliet, M., de Mol, J., Broekaert, E., & Derluyn, I. (2014). "That I live, that's because of her:" Intersectionality as framework for unaccompanied refugee mothers. *British Journal of Social Work, 44,* 2023–2041. doi:10.1111/j.1440-1800.2011.00539.x

Warner, L. R. (2008). A best practices guide to intersectional approaches in psychological research. *Sex Roles, 59*, 454–463. doi:10.1007/s11199-008-9504-5

Warner, L. R., & Shields, S. A. (2013). The intersections of sexuality, gender, and race: Identity research at the crossroads. *Sex Roles, 68*, 803–810. doi:10.1007/s11199-013-0281-4

Weber, L. (2007). Future directions of feminist research: New directions in social policy: The case of women's health. In S. Hesse-Biber (Ed.), *Handbook of feminist research: Theory and praxis* (pp. 669–679). Thousand Oaks, CA: Sage.

Weber, L., & Fore, M. E. (2007). Race, ethnicity, and health: An intersectional approach. In H. Vera & J. R. Feagin (Eds.), *Handbooks of the sociology of racial and ethnic relations* (pp. 191-218). New York, NY: Springer

Weber, L., & Parra-Medina, D. (2003). Intersectionality and women's health: Charting a path to eliminating health disparities. *Advances in Gender Research, 7*, 181–230.

Weisstein, N. (1968). *Psychology constructs the female.* Retrieved from www.uic.edu/orgs/cwluherstory/CWLUArchive/psych.html

Wilkins, D., & Savoye, E. (Eds.). (2009). *Men's health around the world: A review of policy and progress across 11 countries* [report]. Brussels, Belgium: European Men's Health Forum.

3

DECOLONIAL INTERSECTIONALITY

Implications for Theory, Research, and Pedagogy

Tuğçe Kurtiş and Glenn Adams

Intersectionality refers to the idea that subjectivity is constituted by multiple, interrelated dimensions of experience (Collins, 2008; Crenshaw, 1989; hooks, 1984). Intersectionality is a key paradigm for analyzing identity, oppression, and privilege within feminist scholarship. The status of the theory as a gold standard within contemporary feminist scholarship is evident not only in the increasing number of anthologies, special issues, and conferences dedicated to intersectionality, but also in the inclusion of intersectionality as a central topic of study in university textbooks and curricula (Case & Rios, this volume; Cho, Crenshaw, & McCall, 2013). In light of its status, one might conclude that intersectionality is "the most important theoretical contribution that women's studies has made so far" (McCall, 2005, p. 1771).

Although the concept of intersectionality is feminism's success story (Davis, 2008), scholars suggested that the paradigm of intersectionality, perhaps especially as it manifests in psychological science, falls short of its transformative potential (Goff & Kahn, 2013; Patil, 2013). Prevailing approaches to intersectionality draw to a disproportionate extent on experience in the Global North, thereby reflecting and reproducing the racialized power and colonial violence of Euro-American domination (Lugones, 2007; Mignolo, 2007; Patil, 2013). This narrow scope of application contradicts a foundational premise of intersectionality, namely, attention to the voices of the marginalized (see Case, this volume), in that it silences or pathologizes experiences of people across diverse *Majority-World* (Kağıtçıbaşı, 1995) settings. Majority-World refers to people associated with the so-called developing world who constitute the numerical majority of humankind.

While embracing intersectionality as a tool for critical intervention, transnational feminist approaches reveal how conventional appropriations within hegemonic varieties of feminism carry traces of domination that limit their liberatory potential (Lugones & Spelman, 1983; Mohanty, 1991). In particular, these approaches reveal how conventional appropriations of intersectionality reflect what decolonial theorists refer to as the coloniality of power, knowledge, and being (Grosfoguel, 2002; Maldonado-Torres, 2007; Mignolo, 2007, 2011; Quijano, 2000). Standard narratives in intellectual and everyday social discourse represent everyday realities of the modern global order as the benign product of a steady march of human cultural progress. In stark contrast, decolonial theorists use the term *coloniality* to emphasize the extent to which everyday realities of the modern global order are the harmful legacy of the racialized colonial violence that enabled Euro-American global domination. To address concerns about coloniality in mainstream appropriations of intersectionality, perspectives of transnational feminism require what Salem (2014) refers to as *decolonial intersectionality*. Rather than contributing to the ongoing domination of the marginalized many for the benefit of a privileged few, a decolonial intersectionality draws upon silenced perspectives of people in Majority-World spaces to propose sustainable ways of being consistent with global social justice (Kurtiş & Adams, 2015).

We begin our discussion with a brief overview of the important contributions and critiques of intersectionality. We then discuss the concept of decolonial intersectionality and present two strategies of a cultural psychology analysis (Adams, Kurtiş, Salter, & Anderson, 2012) to apply the concept in intellectual work and teaching. The first decolonizing strategy is to normalize patterns of experience in diverse Majority-World settings that hegemonic discourses portray as abnormal or suboptimal. Although mainstream perspectives of feminism often portray women in Majority-World settings as oppressed junior sisters in need of education or rescue, the normalizing strategy of a cultural psychology analysis valorizes the experiences of women in Majority-World settings as a privileged source of insight about gender oppression. The second decolonizing strategy is to denaturalize patterns that hegemonic discourse considers as standards of optimal functioning. Rather than portray Western feminist understandings as the vanguard of gender liberation, the denaturalizing strategy of a cultural psychology analysis draws upon the epistemological perspectives of women in Majority-World settings to illuminate manifestations of privilege (e.g., based on race, social class, sexuality) that undermine their liberatory potential (Adams et al., 2012).

Theoretical Contributions of Intersectionality

The concept of intersectionality emerged within perspectives of Black feminism and critical race theory (especially Crenshaw, 1989, 1991) as an analytical and political tool that problematizes monolithic accounts of experience. In contrast to unidimensional conceptions of identity and identity-based oppression, intersectional analyses situate experience within a complex web of power relations including dimensions of gender, race, ethnicity, class, ability, and sexual orientation (Anthias & Yuval-Davis, 1983; Crenshaw, 1989; Collins, 2008; Hurtado, 1996). With particular reference to feminist scholarship, intersectional analyses illuminate and counteract essentialist and monolithic conceptions of gender and gender-based oppression (Chowdhury, 2009).

A primary contribution of intersectional analyses is to center the experiences of people in marginalized identity positions to rethink prevailing understandings of oppression and to illuminate problematic exclusions within both feminist and antiracist theory and practice. For example, Crenshaw (1989) focused on the experiences of Black American women to challenge prevailing understandings of both race and gender based oppression. Her analysis revealed that the experience of Black women is not simply a double jeopardy addition of gender and racial oppression. Instead, the standpoint of Black American women highlights how the experience of gender depends on the experience of race and vice versa.

Perhaps a more important contribution of intersectional analyses is to reveal how conventional understandings of women's liberation bear traces of racial privilege (Crenshaw, 1989, 1991). As an example, feminists of color within the U.S. highlighted how hegemonic forms of feminist discourse tend to emphasize individual rights, particularly within domains of sexuality and reproduction, that prioritize the concerns of White, Western, heteronormative, and middle-class women (Butler, 1995; Carby, 1997; hooks, 1981). From the marginalized standpoints of feminists of color, hegemonic feminist agendas do violence by ignoring concerns about security and everyday existence that are primary sites of gendered violence among women of color, poor women, and queer folk (e.g., Collins, 2008; Hurtado, 2001; Smith, 2005). In this way, intersectional analyses reveal how otherwise liberatory knowledge formations (feminism, anti-racism) can nevertheless reproduce forms of domination by constructing liberation from one dimension of oppression in ways that served the interests of privilege on another dimension of oppression.

Intersectionality is not only an academic project, but also provides a key site for critical intervention into social struggles. Scholars and activists go beyond mere analysis of intersectional dynamics and instead apply these analyses in attempts at social transformation. Examples of intersectional praxis include legal and policy advocacy that confronts gender and racial discrimination (e.g., Carbado, 2013; Crenshaw, Ocen, & Nanda, 2015; Verloo, 2013), movements demanding greater economic justice for women of color with low income (e.g., Carastathis, 2013; Chun, Lipsitz, & Shin, 2013), and movements targeting immigration restrictions that disproportionately harm communities of color (e.g., Spade, 2013).

In summary, intersectionality is an influential theory that has traveled to many disciplines and informed social justice efforts. It offers a key lens for examining experiences of marginalized people in the context of multilayered structures of

power and domination, illuminates obscured sites of privilege, and provides a
tool for practical intervention into vast inequalities.

Critiques of Intersectionality

Despite these contributions, intersectionality generated scholarly controversy
and contestation (Greenwood, this volume). One common critique concerns a
theoretical over-reliance on Black women as prototypical intersectional subjects
(Nash, 2008). Scholars argued that this tendency can both obscure other dimensions of power (e.g., class, nationality, and sexuality) that impact Black women's
experience and reproduce silence about other racialized positions.

A counter-critique concerns mainstream feminist appropriations of intersectionality. Although intersectionality has a genesis in Black feminist theory
and the particularities of Black women's experience, scholars across disciplines
employ intersectionality to examine multiple axes of difference including class,
sexual orientation, disability, immigration status, and religion. Critics suggest that these various articulations sanitize intersectionality and neutralize its
revolutionary potential. For instance, Bilge (2013) warned against the "whiten-
ing of intersectionality" (p. 405), particularly within European feminist work.
By treating intersectionality as the brainchild of hegemonic feminism, these
approaches fail to acknowledge not only the origins of intersectionality in Black
feminist thought, but also its primary agenda of confronting racism within white
feminism (Bilge, 2013; Tomlinson, 2013). Along parallel lines, Carbado (2013)
noted that mainstream appropriations refuse to acknowledge the operation
of whiteness in intersectionality, resulting in what he refers to as colorblind
intersectionality.

Transnational Feminist Perspectives

Our understanding of intersectionality reflects engagement with theoretical perspectives of transnational feminism (e.g., Alexander & Mohanty, 1997, Grewal &
Kaplan, 2005). Although they have different origins and often proceed in isolation, transnational feminisms and intersectionality make similar critiques of
hegemonic feminisms. Resonating with the framework of intersectionality,
transnational feminisms reject universalized notions of "women" and "global
sisterhood" that prevail in hegemonic feminist accounts and emphasize the diversity of women's experience and the multidimensional character of their subject
positions. Consistent with the emphasis of intersectionality accounts on attuning
to (multiply) marginalized voices, transnational feminisms draw on experience
within Majority-World spaces to decenter dominant discourses and reveal alternative, subjugated knowledges.

Despite these similarities, there are various tensions between intersectionality and transnational feminist perspectives. Again, a major criticism from

transnational feminist perspectives concerns the prevailing emphasis on what Patil (2013) refers to as domestic intersectionality or a narrow focus on experience in North American settings that leaves unexamined global dynamics of racial power. In contrast, the transnational feminist call for a decolonial intersectionality (Grabe & Else-Quest, 2012; Salem, 2014) challenges scholars to attend to experience in numerous Majority-World settings in order to reveal global dimensions of colonial history and racial power. One contribution of decolonial approaches is to illuminate how racism and its intersections within U.S. settings are local manifestations of such transnational processes as coloniality, Eurocentric modernity, and neoliberal globalization.

Another contribution of decolonial approaches is to reveal and disrupt tendencies of colorblind racial privilege in intersectional productions of knowledge (Lugones, 2007). Western feminist discourses often portray Majority-World women in a homogenizing and pathologizing fashion as ignorant cultural Others who are victims of their timeless, oppressive traditions (Mohanty, 1991; Narayan, 1997). These neocolonial and Orientalist discourses position the West as culturally superior (Fanon, 1963; Said, 1978) and embellish self-representations of Western women as relatively liberated (Mohanty, 1991). In contrast, decolonial approaches draw upon experience of people in Majority-World settings as a productive intellectual standpoint from which to observe typically obscured forms of everyday gender oppression that operate in Western settings (Grabe, 2013).

Toward a Decolonial Intersectionality: A Transnational Feminist Vision

We find it fitting to discuss perspectives of transnational feminism and decolonial intersectionality in the context of a book on pedagogy because our own introduction to these ideas arose from the activity of teaching. As instructors of cultural psychology courses, one of our overarching pedagogical goals is to prompt students to critically interrogate their beliefs of what is natural and good. Rather than pathologizing Other cultural practices as backward or ignorant, we encourage students not only to understand the worlds within which those practices might make sense, but also and perhaps more importantly to rethink the necessity or value of practices that students consider natural or normal. Yet, in our discussions of cultural diversity we invariably encounter practices (e.g., honor killing, genital cutting, polygyny, arranged marriage, and restrictions on women's education, dress, movement, and especially sexuality) that arouse the paternalistic indignation of our students and require our attention as feminist-oriented scholars concerned about issues of patriarchal oppression and ongoing gender-based inequality. Whereas prevailing accounts tend to obscure the operation of gendered power in ways that are antithetical to feminist political goals (Burman, 2005), prevailing perspectives of hegemonic feminisms tend to seize on these practices as backward, traditional expressions of a monolithic, universal patriarchy. How does one navigate these conflicting concerns of gender inequality and cultural imperialism?

Against this background, we aim to provide critical consciousness regarding gender oppression across diverse contexts while emphasizing the diversity of women's experience and avoiding universalized notions of women and global sisterhood. A decolonial intersectionality standpoint provides an especially effective framework for accomplishing these contradictory tasks. We illustrate this approach with an example from our own work on the experience of relationship at the intersection of gender and culture.

Conventional Accounts: Care as Silence and Sacrifice

Conventional accounts of psychological science that one might encounter in a typical psychology course valorize growth-oriented forms of relationality characterized by the pursuit of personal satisfaction and a construction of love as emotion-rich intimacy. This conception of relationship also informs a long strand of mainstream thought in feminist psychology (Belenky, Clinchy, Goldberger, & Tarule, 1986; Gilligan, 1982). Judged against this normative standard, hegemonic perspectives of mainstream psychology and feminist scholarship tend to look with suspicion at patterns in many Majority-World settings where women appear to sacrifice personal growth and intimacy in order to maintain relational harmony and satisfy obligations of care within broader networks of support. From these hegemonic perspectives, women's experiences of care and silence within Majority-World communities appear to constitute primary or prototypical examples of rampant patriarchy and gender-based oppression that force women to repress their desires, opinions, and other forms of self-expression in service to male power. In turn, this construction of care and silence as a manifestation of patriarchal oppression elicits paternalistic responses. Concerned intellectuals in Western, Educated, Industrialized, Rich, Democratic (i.e., WEIRD; Henrich, Heine, & Norenzayan, 2010) settings experience a sort of righteous indignation about the oppressive treatment of their Majority-World sisters that motivates them to intervene on their behalf.

In extreme cases, this motivation leads scholars and practitioners with otherwise anticolonial politics to call for neocolonial military violence to "save brown women from brown men" (Spivak, 1999, p. 93; see also Stabile & Kumar, 2005). In less extreme cases, this motivation to intervene on behalf of oppressed, Majority-World sisters leads researchers, practitioners, and educators to perform a sort of epistemic violence. Epistemic violence occurs when scholars, practitioners, and educators in WEIRD settings understand their particular ways of knowing and being as the pinnacle of human development and present these ways of knowing and being as universal standards for all humanity. The imposition of these standards on colonized Other societies subjugates Other ways of knowing and being in the process.

A Decolonial Intersectionality Analysis

Our own engagement with decolonial intersectionality arose in the context of research by Tuğçe (first author of this chapter) among women in Turkish settings. The initial inspiration for this work was silencing the self theory (Jack, 1991). Briefly, this theory proposes that women experience an oppressive loss of self (Jack, 1991) when they enact patriarchal norms that require burdens of care, inhibition of self-expression, and sacrifice of their aspirations or desires in service to others. From this perspective, an emphasis on silence in service of relationship harmony or obligations of care is a gendered phenomenon that disproportionately threatens women's well-being.

Engagement with perspectives of transnational feminism provided Tuğçe with a decolonial intersectional standpoint that led her to re-think silencing the self theory and conventional understandings of care and silence among women in Majority-World settings. Training in decolonial perspectives of cultural psychology provided a set of analytic strategies to articulate this standpoint.

Normalizing Silence. Resonating with the first decolonizing strategy of a cultural psychology analysis, one contribution of a decolonial intersectionality is to normalize patterns of marginalized Other experience that mainstream discourse portrays as abnormal. Without denying that particular relationship practices in various Majority-World spaces may have oppressive consequences, this strategy invites scholars to re-think the ways these patterns of relationship may be beneficial. Rather than a deficit in relationality or a sign of universal gender oppression (e.g., self-sacrifice), our research suggests an appreciation for care and silence as practices of maintenance-oriented relationality that are productive of broader well-being within cultural worlds of embedded interdependence that promote a sense of rootedness in context (Adams et al., 2012; Kurtiş, 2010; Salter & Adams, 2012). From this perspective, silence, care, and other manifestations of maintenance-oriented relationality are not antithetical to authentic personal desires and do not necessarily constitute a threat to women's well-being. In fact, they may even be expressive of authentic personal desires and promote well-being.

Denaturalizing Expression-Oriented Relationality. Resonating with the second decolonizing strategy of a cultural psychology analysis, another contribution of a decolonial intersectionality is to denaturalize the dominant patterns that hegemonic discourse portrays as natural standards. This strategy invites scholars to consider how the expression-focused patterns of growth-oriented relationality that constitute the dominant standard in hegemonic accounts are not naturally superior or inherently liberatory. Instead, they reflect engagement with neoliberal individualism associated with cultural worlds of abstracted independence, in other words, conceptual and material realities that afford an experience of bounded separation or insulation from physical or social context (Adams et al., 2012). These growth-oriented tendencies may produce narrow individual well-being within ecologies of abstracted independence associated

with WEIRD settings, where lack of affordances for social connection compel people to create intimacy and emotional connection through processes of
mutual disclosure (Oliker, 1998). However, these tendencies may produce harm
when elevated to the status of normative standard and imposed more broadly
as a universal prescription beyond the WEIRD settings that disproportionately
inform mainstream scientific imagination.

A clue to this harm lies in the idea that patterns of growth-oriented relationality require and reproduce a neoliberal individualist sense of abstraction from
context and freedom from constraint. As both decolonial and feminist scholars
note, this sense of ontological separation resonates with androcentric (Bem, 1993)
and Eurocentric (Markus & Kitayama, 1991) standpoints antithetical to feminist
and anti-racist concerns about social justice. Moreover, as decolonial and feminist
scholars also emphasize, this neoliberal individualist sense of ontological separation
is itself a product of privilege built upon colonial and patriarchal appropriation of
others' productive activity. As such, this experience of being is a manifestation of
domination and injustice not only because the associated sense of freedom from
constraint is unavailable to people in less privileged positions (i.e., the vast majority of humanity), but also because the exercise of abstracted independence reflects
and reproduces the marginalization of people in less privileged positions (Shaw,
2000). From this perspective, conceptions of gender justice that prescribe equal
enjoyment of growth-oriented relationality for women, at least those with enough
power to take advantage of resulting opportunities, may result in the reproduction
of racial, ethnic, and class domination in the name of gender equality.

To summarize, a decolonial intersectional standpoint invites scholars to
reconsider the apparently "optimal" patterns of growth-oriented relationality
that constitute normative standards in hegemonic forms of psychological and
feminist praxis. In the absence of such an analysis, one might organize feminist
efforts at social justice around rights of self-expression or equal opportunity for
women to enjoy the same pursuit of happiness and personal growth available
to men. Drawing on the insights of people in marginalized communities of the
Majority World, a decolonial analysis can alert scholars and students to the potential violence of this hegemonic approach. The point is not only that the focus on
growth-oriented relationality and rights of self-expression directs attention away
from concerns about sustainable security and freedom from violence that are
pressing concerns of people in the Majority World, but also that the androcentric
and racialized basis of this focus may make it counterproductive as a basis for
gender justice even in the WEIRD settings from which this focus arises.

Conclusion: Pedagogical Implications of Decolonial Intersectionality

Our work constitutes a preliminary attempt to articulate a decolonial intersectionality (Salem, 2014). In this concluding section, we consider possible

applications of a decolonial intersectionality, with particular attention to its implications for feminist pedagogy.

As Grewal and Kaplan (2005) pointed out in their discussion of a transnational feminist pedagogy, a decolonial intersectionality cannot be a mere add-on to "things as usual," constitute a bounded unit on an otherwise Eurocentric syllabus, or serve as a "special topic" within feminism. A decolonial intersectionality framework requires devising what De Lissovoy (2010) referred to as a curriculum against domination that decenters hegemonic discourses and challenges prevailing tendencies of Eurocentrism underlying the politics of knowledge in education. Rather than something limited to topics of prejudice and discrimination or discussions of cultural others, a decolonial intersectionality calls for rethinking the world and questioning hegemonic forms of knowledge at large.

Although we illustrated a decolonial intersectionality analysis in the context of a concrete example from our research on relationship, we frequently apply the same decolonizing strategies to a wide range of phenomena as a classroom exercise. Following the normalizing strategy of a decolonial intersectionality analysis, in the classroom we emphasize perspectives of marginalized Others and encourage learning about the worlds that they inhabit so that our students can better appreciate the larger systems in which seemingly pathological ways of being might make sense. Equally important, we model attitudes of epistemic humility to encourage students to resist responses of paternalistic superiority that are otherwise prevalent in society at large. Following the denaturalizing strategy of a decolonial intersectionality analysis, we draw upon the perspective of people in marginalized settings as an epistemological standpoint for students to gain critical consciousness (Freire, 1970/1993) about the cultural and historical foundations of their own experience. In particular, because the majority of our students are White Americans, the epistemological standpoint of oppressed Others provides an invaluable pedagogical tool to illuminate how the lifestyle of privilege that our students experience as just natural is the ongoing product of racialized colonial violence.

Both strategies of a decolonial intersectionality analysis emphasize the inclusion of marginalized voices from Majority-World perspectives in discussions of identity, oppression, power, and privilege. Decolonial intersectionality provides students with a means for "thinking through others" (Shweder, 1991, p. 101) not merely in the sense of pondering until one comes to an accurate account or proper appreciation of diverse others (a worthy endeavor, to be sure), but more profoundly in the sense of appreciating phenomena from the epistemic position of others. From this perspective, everyday experiences of people in Majority-World communities provide a privileged standpoint from which students can observe broader truth about humanity in general (Adams & Estrada-Villalta, 2015; Comaroff & Comaroff, 2012; Martín-Baró, 1994). In the example from our own work, the epistemological perspective of women in Majority-World spaces provides a standpoint to reveal elements of ethnocentrism and androcentrism lurking in otherwise progressive antiracist or feminist work, particularly in the commitment to a neoliberal individual model of the person. Alternatively stated, the act of listening to rather than silencing Majority-World women and their accounts of care and silence is not merely a matter of equal representation or an exercise of global multiculturalism. Instead, it provides an important learning opportunity to take an Other perspective on one's own experience.

Related to this point and consistent with intersectional approaches in general, another pedagogical contribution of a decolonial intersectionality analysis is its focus on the unique epistemological position of marginalized communities in order to articulate a more human(e) vision of equality and justice. Rather than pathologizing Majority-World settings as sites of ignorance that need rescuing via neocolonialist intervention and education, a decolonial intersectionality analysis proposes that students who are interested in social justice can fruitfully learn from the experiences of people inhabiting such spaces. For instance, everyday experience in various Majority-World spaces can provide students with insights about sustainable ways of being that derive from the foundation of embeddedness (Kurtiş & Adams, 2013). In turn, this reorientation can serve as an antidote to the neoliberal individualistic ontology that underpins much of psychological science, feminism, and current efforts at social justice (Tomlinson & Lipsitz, 2013).

Finally, as we hinted above, the most important pedagogical contribution of decolonial intersectionality is perhaps as a tool for teaching about privilege (see intersectional pedagogy model in Case, this volume). Students who are beneficiaries of racial and colonial privilege typically fail to recognize it, refuse to hold themselves accountable for it, and frequently act in ways that perpetuate it (Bilge, 2013). A decolonial intersectionality attempts to make invisible intersections visible (see Case, this volume) by illuminating privilege among people who otherwise claim a mark of oppression (e.g., hegemonic feminist claims of "global sisterhood") but fail to see how they are participants in systems of oppression and domination. A decolonial intersectionality provides a tool for people who are genuinely committed to struggles for social justice to confront their possessive investments in the products of racialized violence (Lipsitz, 1998), to disinvest in these stolen privileges for the benefit of broader humanity, and thereby to preserve their self-respect and redeem their own humanity (Freire, 1970/1993).

In conclusion, we propose that a decolonial intersectionality shifts the emphasis from an inward-looking celebration of multicultural diversity to a recognition of the modern global order and associated ways of being as the product of racial and colonial violence. As such, a decolonial intersectionality can more effectively confront the epistemic privilege of WEIRD spaces and more adequately serve the interests of the majority of humanity. Rather than liberating a privileged few to better participate in the ongoing racialized domination of the marginalized many, a decolonial intersectionality not only illuminates lurking forms of racial and colonial privilege in mainstream feminist or antiracist scholarship, but also provides students with models of personhood and social relations that are more consistent with the broader liberation of humanity.

References

Adams, G., & Estrada-Villalta, S. (2015). La psicología de la liberación: Un caso paradigmático de «Teoría desde el Sur» [Liberation psychology: A paradigmatic case of "theory from the South"]. *Teoría y Crítica de la Psicología, 6,* 196–216.

Adams, G., Kurtiş, T., Salter, P. S., & Anderson, S. L. (2012). A cultural psychology of relationship: Decolonizing science and practice. In O. Gillath, G. Adams, & A. D. Kunkel (Eds.), *Relationship science: Integrating across evolutionary, neuroscience, and sociocultural approaches* (pp. 49–70). Washington, DC: American Psychological Association.

Alexander, M. J., & Mohanty, C. T. (1997). *Feminist genealogies, colonial legacies, democratic futures.* New York, NY: Routledge.

Anthias, F., & Yuval-Davis, N. (1983). Contextualizing feminism: Gender, ethnic, and class divisions. *Feminist Review, 15,* 62–75. doi:10.1057/fr.1983.33

Belenky, M. F., Clinchy, B. M., Goldberger, N. R., & Tarule, J. M. (1986). *Women's ways of knowing: The development of self, voice, and mind.* New York, NY: Basic Books.

Bem, S. L. (1993). *Lenses of gender.* New Haven, CT: Yale University Press.

Bilge, S. (2013). Intersectionality undone: Saving intersectionality from feminist intersectionality studies. *Du Bois Review: Social Science Research on Race, 10,* 405–424. doi:10.1017/S1 742058X13000283

Burman, E. (2005). Engendering culture in psychology. *Theory & Psychology, 15,* 527–548. doi: 10.1177/0959354305054750.

Butler, J. (1995). Contingent foundations: Feminism and the question of "postmodernism." In S. Benhabib, J. Butler, D. Cornell, & N. Fraser (Eds.), *Feminist contentions: A philosophical exchange* (pp. 35–57). London, UK: Routledge.

Carastathis, A. (2013). Identity categories as potential coalitions. *Signs, 38,* 941–965. doi:10.108 6/669573

Carbado, D. W. (2013). Colorblind intersectionality. *Signs, 38,* 811–845. doi:10.1086/669666

Carby, H. (1997). White woman listen! Black feminism and the boundaries of sisterhood. In R. Hennessy & C. Ingraham (Eds.), *Materialist feminism: A reader in class, difference, and women's lives* (pp. 110–128). New York, NY: Routledge.

Case, K. A. (this volume). Toward an intersectional pedagogy model: Engaged learning for social justice. In K. A. Case (Ed.), *Intersectional pedagogy: Complicating identity and social justice* (pp. 1–24). New York, NY: Routledge.

Case, K. A., & Rios, D. (this volume). Infusing intersectionality: Complicating the psychology of women course. In K. A. Case (Ed.), *Intersectional pedagogy: Complicating identity and social justice* (pp. 82–109). New York, NY: Routledge.

Cho, S., Crenshaw, K. W., & McCall, L. (2013). Toward a field of intersectionality studies: Theory, applications, and praxis. *Signs, 38,* 785–810. doi:10.1086/669608

Chowdhury, E. H. (2009). Locating global feminisms elsewhere: Braiding U.S. women of color and transnational feminisms. *Cultural Dynamics, 21,* 51–78. doi: 10.1177/092137400810 0407

Chun, J. J., Lipsitz, G., & Shin, Y. (2013). Intersectionality as a social movement strategy: Asian immigrant women advocates. *Signs, 38,* 917–940. doi:10.1086/669575

Collins, P. H. (2008). *Black feminist thought: Knowledge, consciousness, and the politics of empowerment* (2nd ed). New York, NY: Routledge.

Comaroff, J., & Comaroff, J. L. (2012). Theory from the South: Or, how Euro-America is evolving toward Africa. *Anthropological Forum: A Journal of Social Anthropology and Comparative Sociology, 22,* 113–131. doi:10.1080/00664677.2012.694169

Crenshaw, K. (1989). Demarginalizing the intersection of race and sex: A Black feminist critique of antidiscrimination doctrine. *University of Chicago Legal Forum, 1989,* 139–168.

Crenshaw, K. (1991). Mapping the margins: Intersectionality, identity politics, and violence against women of color. *Stanford Law Review, 43,* 1241–1299.

Crenshaw, K. W., Ocen, P., & Nanda, J. (2015). Black girls matter: Pushed out, overpoliced, and underprotected. *African American Policy Forum.* New York, NY: Center for Intersectionality and Social Policy Studies.

Davis, K. (2008). Intersectionality as buzzword: A sociology of science perspective on what makes a feminist theory successful. *Feminist Theory, 9,* 67–85. doi:10.1177/1464700108086364

De Lissovoy, N. (2010). Decolonial pedagogy and the ethics of the global. *Discourse Studies in the Cultural Politics of Education, 31,* 279–293. doi:10.1080/01596301003786886

Fanon, F. (1963). *The wretched of the earth.* New York, NY: Présence Africaine.

Freire, P. (1970/1993). *Pedagogy of the oppressed.* New York, NY: Continuum.

Gilligan, C. (1982). *In a different voice.* Cambridge, MA: Harvard University Press.

Goff, P. A., & Kahn, K. B. (2013). How psychological science impedes intersectional thinking. *Du Bois Review: Social Science Research on Race, 10,* 365–384. doi:10.1017/S1742058X13000313

Grabe, S. (2013). Psychological cliterodectomy: Body objectification as a human rights violation. In M. Ryan & N. Branscombe (Eds.), *The SAGE handbook of gender and psychology* (pp. 412–428). London, UK: Sage.

Grabe, S., & Else-Quest, N. M. (2012). The role of transnational feminism in psychology: Complimentary visions. *Psychology of Women Quarterly, 36,* 158–161. doi:10.1177/0361684312442164

Greenwood, R. (this volume). Intersectionality foundations and disciplinary adaptations: Highways and byways. In K. A. Case (Ed.), *Intersectional pedagogy: Complicating identity and social justice* (pp. 27–45). New York, NY: Routledge.

Grewal, I., & Kaplan, C. (2005). *An introduction to women's studies: Gender in a transnational world.* New York, NY: McGraw-Hill.

Grosfoguel, R. (2002). Colonial difference, geopolitics of knowledge, and global coloniality in the modern/colonial capitalist world-system. *Review, 25,* 203–334.

Henrich, J., Heine, S. J., & Norenzayan, A. (2010). The weirdest people in the world? *Behavioral and Brain Sciences, 33,* 61–83. doi:10.1017/S0140525X0999152X

hooks, b. (1981). *Ain't I a woman.* Boston, MA: South End Press.

hooks, b. (1984). *Feminist theory: From margin to center.* Boston, MA: South End Press.

Hurtado, A. (1996). *The color of privilege: Three blasphemies on race and feminism.* Ann Arbor, MI: University of Michigan Press.

Hurtado, A. (2001). Sitios y lenguas: Chicanas theorize feminisms. *Hypatia, 13,* 134–161. doi:10. 1111/j.1527–2001.1998.tb01230.x

Jack, D. C. (1991). *Silencing the self: Women and depression.* Cambridge, MA: Harvard University Press.

Kaşıtçıbaşı, Ç. (1995). Is psychology relevant to global human development issues? *American Psychologist, 50,* 293–300. doi:10.1037/0003-066X.50.4.293

Kurtiş, T. (2010). *Silencing the self and depression among Turkish women* (Unpublished master's thesis). University of Kansas, Lawrence, KS.

Kurtiş, T., & Adams, G. (2013). A cultural psychology of relationship: Toward a transnational feminist psychology. In M. Ryan & N. Branscombe (Eds.), *The SAGE handbook of gender and psychology* (pp. 251–269). London, UK: Sage.

Kurtiş, T., & Adams, G. (2015). Decolonizing liberation: Toward a transnational feminist psychology. *Journal of Social and Political Psychology, 3*, 388–413. doi:10.5964/jspp. v3i1.326

Lipsitz, G. (1998). *The possessive investment in whiteness: How White people profit from identity politics.* Philadelphia, PA: Temple University Press

Lugones, M. (2007). Heterosexualism and the colonial/modern gender system. *Hypatia, 221*, 186–209. doi:10.2979/HYP.2007.22.1.186

Lugones, M., & Spelman, E. (1983). Have we got a theory for you! Feminist theory, cultural imperialism and the demand for "the woman's voice." *Women's Studies International Forum, 6*, 573–581. doi:10.1016/0277

Maldonado-Torres, N. (2007). On the coloniality of being: Contributions to the development of a concept. *Cultural Studies, 21*, 240–270. doi:10.1080/09502380601162548

Markus, H. R., & Kitayama, S. (1991). Culture and self: Implications for cognition, emotion, and motivation. *Psychological Review, 98*, 224–253. doi:10.1037/0033-295X.98.2.224

Martín-Baró, I. (1994). *Writings for a liberation psychology.* (A. Aron & S. Corne, Trans.). Cambridge, MA: Harvard University Press.

McCall, L. (2005). The complexity of intersectionality. *Signs, 30*, 1771–1800. doi:10. 1086/426800

Mignolo, W. D. (2007). Delinking: The rhetoric of modernity, the logic of coloniality and the grammar of de-coloniality. *Cultural Studies, 21*, 449–514. doi:10.1080/ 095023806011626 47

Mignolo, W. D. (2011). *The dark side of Western modernity: Global futures, decolonial options.* Durham, NC: Duke University Press.

Mohanty, C. T. (1991). Under Western eyes: Feminist scholarship and colonial discourses. In C. Mohanty, A. Russo, & L. Torres (Eds.), *Third world women and the politics of feminism* (pp. 333–358). Bloomington, IN: Indiana University Press.

Narayan, U. (1997). *Dislocating cultures: Identities, traditions, and third-world feminism.* New York, NY: Routledge.

Nash, J. C. (2008). Re-thinking intersectionality. *Feminist Review, 89*, 1–15. doi:10.1057/ fr.200 8.4

Oliker, S. J. (1998). The modernization of friendship: Individualism, intimacy, and gender in the nineteenth century. In R. G. Adams & G. Allan (Eds.), *Placing friendship in context: Structural analysis in the social sciences* (pp. 18–42). New York, NY: Cambridge University Press.

Patil, V. (2013). From patriarchy to intersectionality: A transnational feminist assessment of how far we've really come. *Signs, 38*, 847–867. doi:10.1086/669560

Quijano, A. (2000). Coloniality of power, Eurocentrism, and Latin America. *International Sociology, 15*, 215–232. doi:10.1177/0268580900015002005

Said, E. W. (1978). *Orientalism.* New York, NY: Vintage.

Salem, S. (2014, April 17). Decolonial intersectionality and a transnational feminist movement [Web log post]. Retrieved from thefeministwire.com

Salter, P. S., & Adams, G. (2012). Mother or wife? An African dilemma tale and the psychological dynamics of sociocultural change. *Social Psychology, 43*, 232–242.

Shaw, R. (2000). "Tok af, lef af": A political economy of Temne techniques of secrecy and self. In I. Karp & D. A. Masolo (Eds.), *African philosophy as cultural inquiry* (pp. 25–49). Bloomington, IN: Indiana University Press.

Shweder, R. A. (1991). *Thinking through cultures: Expeditions in cultural psychology.* Cambridge, MA: Harvard University Press.

Smith, A. (2005). Native American feminism, sovereignty, and social change. *Feminist Studies, 31,* 116–132. doi:10.2307/20459010

Spade, D. (2013). Intersectional resistance and law reform. *Signs, 38,* 1031–55. doi:10.1086/669 574

Spivak, G. C. (1999). *A critique of postcolonial reason: Toward a history of the vanishing present.* Cambridge, MA: Harvard University Press.

Stabile, C. A., & Kumar, D. (2005). Unveiling imperialism: Media, gender, and the war on Afghanistan. *Media, Culture, & Society, 27,* 765–782. doi:10.1177/0163443705055734

Tomlinson, B. (2013). Colonizing intersectionality: Replicating racial hierarchy in feminist academic arguments. *Social Identities: Journal for the Study of Race, Nation, and Culture, 19,* 254–272. doi:10.1080/13504630.2013.789613

Tomlinson, B., & Lipsitz, G. (2013). Insubordinate spaces for intemperate times: Countering the pedagogies of neoliberalism. *Review of Education, Pedagogy, and Cultural Studies, 35,* 3–26. doi:10.1080/10714413.2013.753758

Verloo, M. (2013). Intersectional and cross-movement politics and policies: Reflections on current practices and debates. *Signs, 38,* 893–915. doi:10.1086/669572

PART II

Intersectionality and Classroom Applications

4

UNDOING THE PSYCHOLOGY OF GENDER

Intersectional Feminism and Social Science Pedagogy

Patrick R. Grzanka

When I was first offered the opportunity to teach the psychology of gender as a new assistant professor at The University of Tennessee's flagship campus in Knoxville, I thought of this as a chance at pedagogical nirvana, an ideal unification of my interdisciplinary training in psychology and gender studies. I was especially excited for the challenge of teaching this course in the Bible Belt, where old-fashioned sexism and hyper-traditional, (hetero)sexist gender norms remain pervasive. This presented a genuine opportunity to use my skills as a feminist social scientist in a cultural context in which feminism is typically elided or lampooned. This was precisely what I was trained to do. I was not only going to design and implement a course on the psychology of gender, but would teach it through the lens of intersectionality so that my students would leave with competency in the key themes, methods, and concerns of feminist psychology, as well as robust understanding of how gender, as a system of domination, never works in isolation. As an experienced instructor, I knew these were somewhat ambitious goals, but I have taken seriously the calls from feminist psychologists to stop making excuses for one-dimensional, single-axis approaches to inequality that privilege gender at the expense of race, sexuality, class, and other dimensions of difference (Dill, Nettles, & Weber, 2001; Shields, 2008). To borrow a quote from the now well-known axiom coined by blogger Flavia Dzodan (2011), I decided my psychology of gender course "will be intersectional or it will be bullshit!"

An intersectional psychology of gender course was relatively straightforward as a proposition alone. But from the moment I began designing my syllabus, I was confronted with the unavoidable reality that teaching this course would present myriad conceptual and practical pitfalls. This chapter will explore those challenges and the steps I took to address them, including the limits of my own training and the normative orientation of the social sciences to the study of identity, difference, and inequality. This essay is based on ongoing, critical self-reflection on designing and teaching a psychology of gender course for the first time, as well as analyses of multidisciplinary scholarship that asks whether "gender" as a construct may fundamentally resist an intersectional perspective (e.g., May, 2015; Wiegman, 2012). I foreground two apparent paradoxes I have encountered in my attempts and failures to work through this course with an intersectional approach. Indeed, intersectionality presents serious challenges to the constitutive elements of psychology of gender insomuch as theories of inter-sectionality generally (a) reject a psychological framing of the social world and (b) question the primacy of gender in feminist discourse. I explore these issues, explain how I attended to them in terms of my course content and assignments, and reflect on the strengths and weaknesses of my pedagogical strategies, particu-larly in light of Case's (this volume) proposed model of intersectional pedagogy. Ultimately, I arrive at a certain degree of ambivalence toward the psychology of gender as a course and consider the capacities of social science courses on gen-der to expand and inhibit intersectionality-informed discourse. And though my discussion focuses on a cross-listed course in psychology and women's studies, my interdisciplinary training and study of intersectionality's uptake across the disciplines leads me to believe that these issues are relevant beyond the walls of a psychology department or women's studies program.

What Is the Psychology of Gender?

In designing and implementing this course for the first time, I inherited learning outcomes that were partially predetermined but could also be tailored to my interests and expertise. The University of Tennessee, Knoxville's (UTK) course catalog description of *Psychology of Gender*, a 400-level class that is cross-listed in the university's interdisciplinary Women's Studies Program, reads as follows: "Biological, psychological, and social factors in gender. Importance of gender roles and stereotypes for behavior and experience" (UTK, 2015). Traditionally, courses like this function as upper-division undergraduate or graduate-level electives for psychology degree-seekers and sometimes count as diversity cred-its. Though non-psychologists might assume that this course offers an inherently critical perspective on gender, sexism, and social inequality, psychologists typi-cally study gender from a post-positivist and essentialist perspective. This means that gender is approached as a knowable entity that can be understood, meas-ured, and predicted through the mostly quantitative methods of psychological science (Eagly & Riger, 2014). Someone who adheres to this position may acknowledge that gender is influenced by social and cultural norms, but simulta-neously take the biology of sex differences for granted and believe that relatively universal bio-psychological mechanisms undergird the differences between men and women that can be empirically observed, such as differences in aggression, academic performance, and relational styles (Hyde, 2005). While feminist psychology has offered long-standing critiques of this perspective, and robust empirical work has debunked many of the most pervasive stereotypes about gender differences (Eagly, Eaton, Rose, Riger, & McHugh, 2012; Fine, 2010; Tavris, 1993), psychological research on gender tends to reify rather than undermine the discipline's dominant conceptualization of gender. So, if the goal of a course on the psychology of gender is solely or primarily to introduce students to the ways that psychologists study gender, the course may not actually reflect feminist or social justice-oriented principles. One might compare this to a course on gender and crime or women and politics. It would be a mistake to assume that any of these courses were necessarily feminist.

Accordingly, within the discipline of psychology, the "psychology of gender" is not equivalent to "feminist psychology" and indeed includes many perspectives that are actually hostile to the goals of 21st century multicultural feminist perspectives, including intersectionality (see also Case & Rios, this volume). On the other hand, I faced the very practical question of how to convey important contributions of feminist social science research on gender while simultaneously teaching texts that interrogate whether science has the potential to do anything but harm members of marginalized social groups (e.g., Fausto-Sterling, 2000). However, the cross-listed nature of my course meant that the class should theoretically introduce students to the standard psychology of gender and how feminism informs the psychological study of gender, because it is also a women's studies course. Presenting these multifarious and contradictory perspectives is a complicated pedagogical endeavor, particularly if one is willing to consider that students are generally poised to embrace evolutionary and biological determinist concepts and to reject what they see as subjective, unscientific accounts of power relationships that ask them to interrogate their own gender. I became perplexed when I reviewed potential textbooks that presented feminist perspectives as one among a buffet of approaches students should grasp during the 15-week course. This seemed patently absurd to me. What would I even say to my students? "In week one, evolutionary psychology will teach us how ovaries determine women's behavior. In week two, feminist science studies will show you that sex hormones were basically invented to make billions of dollars for pharmaceutical companies." Books about gender from outside of psychology seemed better equipped to introduce the students to feminism, but these texts failed to address relevant psychological concepts, such as stereotype threat, research design, mental health issues, etc. Furthermore, none of the psychology of gender textbooks that I reviewed addressed race, sexuality, or other dimensions of identity in more than a cursory way, and none attended to intersectionality. The perfect book may exist, but it eluded me. I realized that this would be an uphill climb and I could not rely on any single book to do the work I wanted it to do, including presenting multiple perspectives while addressing feminist psychology's political and radical critique of those disembodied positivist approaches that claim a neutral or apolitical relationship to gender (or any other element of social life, for that matter). In a widely cited article on intersectional approaches to the study of gender in psychology, Shields (2008) argued that failing to address how gender never operates in isolation is a particularly egregious failure in the 21st century after decades of academic critique by women of color feminists who highlighted the weaknesses of such single-axis approaches that imagine gender or race or class as parallel, discrete phenomena. The limitations of one's training/expertise, word counts, or the scope of a given research project are not valid excuses for avoiding intersectionality. Shields (2008) essentially demanded that psychologists embrace the multidimensional complexity of intersectionality, especially in feminist research that portends to do social justice work. Other psychologists (Bowleg, 2012; Cole, 2008, 2009; Syed, 2010) and scholars across the social sciences and humanities (Hancock, 2007; Kennedy, 2005; Valentine, 2007) made similar claims. Though these calls for an intersectional revolution, so to speak, tend to share a commitment to thinking about categories relationally, foregrounding the ways systems of power and domination are co-constitutive, and generating scholarship that makes a tangible contribution toward social transformation, they also tend not to offer prescriptive explanations of how to go about doing such work. Intersectionalizing research and teaching within the confines of disciplines that are expressly or implicitly anti-intersectional necessitates a sustained interrogation of the discipline's core assumptions, epistemology, and methodological precepts (Syed, 2010). In the context of an undergraduate course, how precisely can one accomplish this with students who are barely yet familiar with the discipline's normative assumptions? How can one do the work of explaining the complexity of intersectionality when students are lacking familiarity with how power, privilege, and inequality function in any single domain, such as gender?

I suggest that the single-axis paradigms indoctrinated into so many educators are fundamentally antithetical to the kind of intersectional pedagogy that Case (this volume) and others propose (e.g., Grzanka, 2010; Naples, this volume; Rivera, this volume). Educators often face questions about the impossibility of intersectional approaches or fixate on the complexity of intersectionality (McCall, 2005), because they begin from a place of anti-intersectionality (for an overview, see May, 2015). Rather than take an additive approach to intersectionality that would imagine teaching one content domain (e.g., race) first and then complicating it with other issues (e.g., gender), an intersectional pedagogy should begin from the place of intersectional complexity and work forward toward specific sites and issues through which this complexity can be rendered comprehensible to students at any developmental level. For me, I found that this was not about teaching gender first and then adding race and sexuality, for example, but instead teaching gender contextually and always with race, sexuality, class, and other axes of inequality in the foreground. I arrived at this strategy, however, after wrestling with two paradoxes that emerged as I planned my new course.

Intersectionality vs. Psychology

The first paradox is what might be characterized as intersectionality's immanent opposition to psychology. Though psychologists are quick to discuss intersectionality in ways that suggest it is primarily a theory of identity (or identities), intersectionality was developed by Black feminists as a structural critique of the ways systems of domination co-construct each other and collaborate in the production and maintenance of oppressions. Crenshaw's (1989, 1991) work in critical race theory articulated a robust critique of how Black women were positioned in the U.S. legal system in ways that fundamentally denied their experiences as simultaneously gendered and racialized subjects (see also Williams, 1992). In sociology, Collins (2000) theorized the matrix of domination as a framework for understanding and resisting the ideological, political, and economic configurations of oppression and privilege that produce intersectionality which she understood as the specific ways that dimensions of inequality are organized in particular times and spaces. Collins (1998) also argued that Black feminist thought is a counter-hegemonic epistemology (i.e., theory of knowledge) generated by Black women's "outsider-within" standpoint which positions them simultaneously inside yet excluded from mainstream feminist and antiracist discourse that centers White women's and Black men's experiences, respectively. This work was explicitly indebted to centuries of Black women's scholarly and creative work that had been systemically marginalized in formal academic institutions but which nonetheless flourished and developed into a critical social theory (Collins, 2000) that works to both describe and contest structures of intersectional oppression. For these scholars and the work of other Black feminists they draw upon, including Angela Davis, bell hooks, Audre Lorde, and Alice Walker, intersectionality represents a political agenda for social transformation as much as a descriptive theory of U.S. Black women's experiences and similarly oppressed groups throughout the world.

Though intersectionality's widespread travels throughout academic research are beyond the scope of this chapter (for overviews see Collins, 2015; Davis, 2008; Dhamoon, 2011; and Grzanka, 2014), one major concern of intersectionality theorists is the ways social scientists used or even co-opted intersectionality in the interest of a reductive explanation of how individuals possess multiple social identities. According to legal theorist Carbado (2013),

> Intersectionality reflects a commitment neither to subjects nor to identities per se but . . . to marking and mapping the production and contingency of both. Nor is the theory an effort to identify, in the abstract, an exhaustive list of intersectional social categories and to add them up to

determine—once and for all—the different intersectional configurations those categories can form. (p. 815)

Similarly, MacKinnon (2013) rejects an identity-based framing of intersectionality by positing stereotypes and social classifications as the "ossified outcomes of the dynamic intersections of multiple hierarchies" (p. 1023) rather than the causes of systemic inequality. When intersectionality is framed primarily as a way to talk about multiple social identities, which political psychologists recognized far outside the context of multicultural psychology or Black feminist thought (e.g., Crisp & Hewstone, 2006), intersectionality runs the risk of being reduced to a descriptive metaphor for capturing an apolitical maxim of human experience (i.e., that we all are multiple things at the same time). In other words, to say that Black feminism's principal contribution to social science is the recognition that individuals possess more than one social identity is a gross reduction of intersectionality's theoretical robustness, analytic capacities, and political aims.

Intersectionality's focus on structural, systemic social forces (Crenshaw, 2000/2014) is at odds with disciplinary psychology's epistemic anchoring in individuals' and small groups' behaviors, attitudes, emotion, and cognition (Bowleg, 2008; Orford, 2008). I do not mean to suggest that an intersectional psychology is impossible, however. While thinking about gender in the terms of multiculturalism and diversity is not inherently anti-psychological, actually taking an intersectional approach to the psychology of gender means doing more than providing examples of diverse individuals' experiences or showcasing people of color while teaching an otherwise gender-first, single-axis oriented form of psychology. For example, much of the content of intersectional scholarship that might be included in a psychology of gender course undermines psychology's authority in ways that are potentially empowering and confusing for students. Whereas traditional psychological training might provoke research questions that focus on the degree to which men and women are different on X variable, Cole (2009) suggested that intersectionality-sensitive research questions focus on:

- across-group similarities (as opposed to fixating on hypothesized differences);
- categorical exclusion (as opposed to tacit understandings of social categorizations such as race, gender, sexuality, and nationality); and
- power (the historical and cultural dynamics that produce a given form of inequality).

According to Cole's (2009) framework, a research question about potential gender differences might be transformed into something like, for example, "How is X variable shaped by social forces including but not limited to racism, sexism, and classism, and how might observed gender differences reflect the interplay of those social forces?" Therefore, taking a critical, multicultural, feminist approach to the psychology of gender means, in many ways, teaching against psychology.

Intersectionality vs. Gender

The second paradox that emerged as I prepared my syllabus encompasses the tension between intersectionality and gender itself. If the political motivation for the intersectionality framework is rooted in white, middle-class, Eurocentric feminism's inability to seriously theorize race or account for the experiences of people of color, then how might the psychology of gender implicitly reinforce a gender-first or single-axis framing of psychology that negates the significance of other oppressive social forces in shaping behavior, emotion, and cognition?

Scholarly debates about the political efficacy and limitations of concepts such as "women," "sisterhood," and "gender" heralded major changes in the ways academic feminists approached intersectionality in both teaching and research (Dill, 1979; Smith, 1980; Wiegman, 2012). Much of this work suggests that a feminist pedagogy that embraces intersectionality necessarily involves some decentering of gender itself so that the curriculum affords sufficient space to race, sexuality, nation, religion, social class, ability, and other interlocking systems of inequality. In an intersectional pedagogy, gender must not fall out completely but rather is theorized as always implicated within other intersecting dimensions of oppression. However, the discourse of psychology that generally treats gender as a subject variable or independent variable is largely resistant to such an intersectional rendering of social dynamics (Bowleg, 2008; Syed, 2010). In Helgeson's (2012) widely used textbook, theories that may explain gender differences, such as social identity theory, peer group socialization, social learning theory, and gender schema theory, are presented first as scientific, empirically grounded ways of studying observed gender differences in phenomena such as identity development, conflict style, and attachment. Then, typically toward the end of the chapter, Helgeson (2012) offers a summary of research data gathered among samples that include people of color or sexual minorities and may challenge the key precepts of supposedly race- and sexuality-neutral theories. This exemplifies a gender-first approach insomuch as this pedagogical style does not deny the consequences of race or sexuality but subordinates racial and sexual issues to gender, which has the effect of rendering gender white and heterosexual. In teaching such unfamiliar psychological concepts and theories to undergraduates, I faced the pedagogical hurdles of explaining important, widely cited theories that are not intersectional and then challenging these ideas with intersectional perspectives. My goal is for my students to hear something like, "These ideas are foundational to the study of gender in psychology, and here are some of their strengths and weakness in terms of their ability to account for diverse groups' experiences."

My concern, of course, is that students are actually thinking, "All of this is arbitrary," or, even worse, "I thought this was a course about gender, so why are we talking about race?" (Case, Miller, & Jackson, 2012).

Intersectionality theory's rejection of gender-first approaches includes consequences for the identity politics that inevitably manifest in classrooms. Sociologists Schilt and Westbrook (2009) define cisgender as "individuals who have a match between the gender they were assigned at birth, their bodies, and their personal identity" (p. 461). In other words, cisgender refers to non-transgender individuals with gender-identity privilege. As a White, queer man, I find myself personally and politically troubled by any efforts to displace gender that might inadvertently obscure my own cisgender privilege in the classroom and in society at large. For example, while displacement has been a powerful heuristic in critical whiteness studies and other domains influenced by poststructural and postmodern approaches (e.g., Frankenberg, 1997), Black feminist scholars such as Collins (1998) have taken postmodernism to task for its rubrics of decentering and deconstruction that often elide the material realities of systemic inequalities (see also Grzanka, 2014). In the context of the psychology of gender, then, how can one balance the imperative to attend to gender's co-constitutive relationships with other dimensions of identity and difference that are just as consequential as gender while also insisting on gender's preeminent place in historical and contemporary hegemonies? And how can this be pragmatically accomplished with students who may be developing a critical consciousness around gender for the first time (Gramsci, Hoare, & Smith, 1971)?

Doing Intersectional Pedagogy

With these paradoxes in mind, I developed a syllabus organized around two broad learning goals, the first of which was explicitly psychologically oriented and the second of which was driven by the reality that most of my students will not become professional psychologists.

- Students should gain an understanding of feminist psychology's key contributions to the discipline and how intersectional feminist perspectives can inform psychological research.
- Students should be able to apply intersectional feminist perspectives to their everyday lives and in seemingly non-psychological contexts, such as mass media, popular culture, and their own education.

To actualize these goals, I designed a series of assignments to be completed multiple times during the semester to facilitate an iterative process of consciousness-raising, critical introspection, and skills development, all of which are elements of the knowledge-skills-awareness rubric frequently deployed in psychological training around multicultural competencies (Vera & Speight, 2003).

Fieldwork Assignments

Embracing Bowleg (2008) and Syed's (2010) critical stance toward the (im)possibility of quantitative intersectionality and recognizing that my students will be inundated with examples of experimental research prior to taking my class, I designed three fieldwork assignments to foster skills in flexible, interpretive, critical qualitative reflection. After spending a week studying feminist approaches to empirical research, specifically qualitative interviewing and ethnography, students completed the first fieldwork assignment that asked them to "Go to a public space where a meal is occurring, observe gender, and synthesize your observations into a three-page fieldwork report that attempts an argument as opposed to stream of consciousness anecdotes." At this point in the semester (week five), students have been introduced to intersectionality but have not studied the concept in detail. The goal for the first assignment is development of basic skills in observing gendered dynamics that usually go unnoticed, such as who takes care of children at the dinner table, who dominates conversations, whom waiters address for payment, etc. Students are also instructed not to pretend to be mind-readers or to try to guess the intentions of the individuals and groups they observe. To the contrary, I encouraged them to interrogate their own assumptions about others' behavior and to reflect on what they were drawn to observe. In other words, I asked them, "What did you see, and what did you not see? Where did you look and why?" The argument they present in their write-up should not take the form of a thesis that disregards other feasible accounts but that attempts to offer a theoretically grounded, accurate, and insightful interpretation of their observation. Students received written feedback on all assignments, therefore this approach may not be feasible for sections with 50 or more students, but it afforded me the opportunity to help them develop skills in integrating theory and research and articulating their ideas precisely on paper.

The second and third fieldwork assignments required students to attend a public event, preferably one that they do not normally attend, such as a concert for a musical genre they do not know well or a religious service they have not previously encountered. Doing something unusual (for them) or interacting with cultural groups in settings with which they are unfamiliar can cultivate multicultural competencies and qualitative research skills. Indeed, embracing unfamiliar experiences helped to make visible interactions that may normally be invisible (Case, this volume). This newfound awareness of other peoples' experiences also encouraged students to reflect on their own everyday lives and to consider what about their social environments are shaped by unspoken or arbitrary social norms (Case, this volume). Specifically in terms of intersectionality, this assignment linked research to lived experience, and the qualitative scope of the project encourages students not to use predetermined variables to interpret others' behavior. Instead, the students take a more radically inductive approach, characteristic of intersectionality theories' emphasis on social categories as dynamic and emergent rather than static and uncontested (Grzanka, 2014). Because the course stressed intersectional thinking, students tackle the intersections of sexuality, race, and class early in the semester, and I encouraged them to interrogate how their lived experiences inform their assumptions about others' social group memberships. When students wrote up their fieldwork, I asked them to consider the following:

• What evidence led you to arrive at your conclusion about that person's social identity? In other words, if you think you observed a lesbian couple, a mixed-race individual, or a person whose social class status made them exceptional in this group, how do you know this?

These concerns transcend psychology and are relevant to critical thinking in any academic discipline or professional field.

The first time I taught this class, I asked the students to focus on gender and sexuality for the second fieldwork assignment and on gender and race for the third assignment. This approach was ineffective for multiple reasons. First, this approach reflected an implicitly additive model such that dimensions of identity were folded into the analysis with increasing complexity throughout the semester. Second, it suggested that sexuality and gender are closer together conceptually than gender and race, and it marginalized racial analysis to the end of the semester. Finally, I found that my students were the least capable of thinking complexly about sexuality before extensive study of sexuality-related issues. In the second iteration of the course, I moved the intersectionality unit of the course up and pushed the sexualities section to later in the semester. Students then attended to intersectionality in the second fieldwork assignment and focused specifically but not exclusively on sexuality in the final fieldwork assignment. I instructed them to keep in mind the following:

One of the key empirical and analytic strengths of participant observation and qualitative, ethnographic methods is that they enable us to make visible the otherwise invisible interactions that shape our everyday lives. It is not easy, of course, to notice what is designed to go unnoticed, but you will use theories and concepts from our class to inform and enrich your observations about gender, race, class, sexuality, and other dimensions of diversity. Finally, remember that intersectionality is not only pertinent to multiply marginalized groups; you can see intersectional dynamics at play within groups that might possess several markers of privilege, as well.

This approach enabled me to treat intersectionality not as a kind of analytic crescendo, but rather as the foundation for approaching all conversations about identity and inequality in the course. Anecdotally, I observed that interrogation of both race and sexuality improved and students were better able to make insightful observations about dynamics that would previously be unnoticeable, such as the intersections of heterosexism, femininity, whiteness, and social class. For example, one student wrote about an end-of-the-year celebration in which her sorority sisters' mothers presented graduating seniors with speeches and gifts that suggested the students were about to transition from college to marriage. She wrote that those around her did not seem to notice that the entire ceremony was extremely patriarchal, even in the presence of explicit claims to sisterhood. This school-to-marriage dynamic was ingrained in the culture of the sorority, which she began to view as co-produced by gender, race, and social class. Her field-work assignment explained that pervasive middle-class whiteness of the sorority was intersectionally co-constituted by patriarchal heterosexism. Other students reflected on the ways Black couples negotiate predominantly White dance clubs, Black women servers' experiences of discrimination relative to White staff, and perceptions of gender non-conforming individuals in cisgender and apparently heterosexual friend groups. And while most write about their observations of strangers, some students have written on their own social settings, including workplace friendship circles.

Research Critique

Whereas the fieldwork assignments reflected intersectionality theory's invest-ment in doing social research that takes the relationships among social categories seriously (Dill & Kohlman, 2012), I assigned two research critiques at the middle and end of the semester to encourage students to be more critical consumers of psychological science. Both assignments were take-home components of the midterm and final exams. For the midterm, I chose the articles they analyzed, but the final exam asked them to identify an article of their choice. Because so much of the course provided them with tools to constructively criticize positiv-ist and evolutionary approaches to social psychology, I directed them toward the kinds of gender differences-focused experimental research commonly published in leading social psychology journals. For example, on the midterm, I asked them to critique one of two experimental studies, both of which use terror management theory to explore women's objectification. The first suggests that mortality salience drives men's attraction to women (Morris & Goldenberg, 2015), and the second suggests women may self-objectify in ways that are not always harmful to them (Goldenberg, Cooper, Heflick, Routledge, & Arndt, 2011). Students were asked to critique multiple aspects of the article, including the literature review, research questions, hypotheses, methods, findings, limita-tions, and implications. I provided them peer reviewer guidelines directly from the feminist social science journal *Gender & Society* that they used to structure 3–4 page essays. Accordingly, they provided constructive feedback to the article authors as if peer reviewers of the manuscripts.

Though these published articles offered what I might call "low hanging fruit," the students struggled to integrate theories from the course into their critiques. Perhaps I should not have been surprised that many of the students only attempted to criticize the articles on the basis of the college student participant samples drawn from predominantly White institutions, as opposed to engaging with the theoretical and cultural assumptions undergirding the authors' empirical inquiry. While identifying the limitations of a convenience sample is important, one does not need the psychology of gender or intersectionality to make this point. Accordingly, based on trial and error, I ultimately directed students away from the authors' methods and toward the assumptions underlying the studies' research questions:

> Your critique may address multiple aspects of the article, including multiple components of the research process: review of literature, research questions, hypotheses, methods, findings, and limitations/implications. Nonetheless, you may choose to highlight one major area of concern in your paper. I strongly discourage you from focusing your critique exclusively or even primarily on methods; you will likely be much more successful in this assignment if you critique the theory and assumptions driving the study rather than the particular methods employed . . . I discourage you from making superficial arguments about the weaknesses of college student convenience samples on the basis of claims about "external validity" and "generalizability."

This strategy proved more useful because it allowed my students, many of whom were not psychology majors nor proficient in quantitative research, to interrogate the premises of concepts such as terror management theory, which like so much of evolutionary psychology can be read as an attempt to justify sexist or otherwise oppressive behaviors (Fine, 2010).

Though students also struggled to think about intersectionality in the midterm beyond relatively superficial feedback (e.g., "The authors should consider how race might affect these findings"), the final exam yielded more substantive results in both semesters. For example, a student critiqued an article about young African American men's so-called risky sexual behaviors for its failure to attend to intersectionality. Specifically, she highlighted the scholars' gesture toward intersectionality theory when they noted that discrimination does not affect all men equally but proceeded to treat their sample as a homogeneous group defined by race and gender. By allowing students to select their own articles, I found they searched for research that reflected their own interests, including gender and sport, women in STEM fields, and LGBT issues. They also moved away from studies that solely focused on gender, which helped them to showcase their emerging intersectional imaginations. Students offered critiques of quantitative studies that might have benefited from a qualitative approach, research on sexism that neglected to attend to racism and hetero-sexism, and gender studies that failed to attend to gender's situatedness in the matrix of domination (Collins, 2000). For example, another student critiqued a quantitative study of drug use among LGB clients in substance abuse treatment for its exclusion of transgender participants, reduction of race to White/non-White, reduction of ethnicity as Hispanic/non-Hispanic, elision of social class status, and insufficient attention to the problems immanent to studying sexual orientation without attending to its intersections. Nonetheless, several students inevitably struggled in developing their arguments and some even picked articles from feminist and multicultural journals which offered few entry points for cri-tique. Overall, however, I found this exercise beneficial for developing students' self-efficacy in navigating research databases, identifying appropriate studies, reading science critically, and offering substantive feedback in a respective and constructive scholarly exchange.

Gender Autobiography

Various articulations of intersectionality theory emphasize its radical capacity to undermine the imagined distance between subjects (i.e., researchers) and objects of study (i.e., participants). The concept of the standpoint, in particular, is about looking inward toward the identities, life histories, and individual dif-ferences that inform who one is and how one sees the world (Grzanka, 2014). Throughout the semester, I assigned deeply introspective readings from women of color scholars such as Anzaldúa (1987) and Williams (1992) that model ways to connect the personal to the political in intersectional ways. In both take-home portions of the midterm and final exam, students wrote what I refer to as a "gender autobiography." The midterm required a 4-5 page critical self-reflection on an important moment of gender socialization. The final asked for a reflection on how the course material influenced the student's conceptualization of their own identity. Both assignments required students to integrate course readings to inform their self-analyses:

> You will be graded not on your creativity, but on the way you can con-nect academic scholarship on the psychology of gender to everyday life experiences of gender socialization, gender identity development, and social inequalities (including privilege and oppression across multiple dimensions of difference, including but not limited to gender, sexuality, race, and class).

I am sympathetic to instructors' concerns that these kinds of exercises can devolve into narcissistic or self-indulgent musings that diverge from course con-tent and fail to evaluate students' learning. I am also cognizant that these kinds of exercises may showcase students' abilities to regurgitate what they think

I want to hear, rather than an honest reflection of their beliefs, feelings, and learning. But by requiring them to use structural theories of power and inequality to make sense of their own lives, they were challenged to think and write across individual and structural registers of their lives. For example, a woman of color wrote about her experiences of gendered racism while working at a local restaurant known for objectifying female servers (similar to Hooters). By connecting her job to our theories of enlightened sexism (Douglas, 2010), objectification, and sexualization (Gill, 2009), she unpacked her own conflicted feelings about being empowered to earn money for school in a place that profits off of women's exploitation and objectification. Accordingly, this assignment addressed intersectionality theory's emphasis on the connections between lived experiences and structures of oppression and gave students an opportunity to reflect on their life histories as manifestations of intersectional forms of privilege and marginalization.

For the final assignment, I was most surprised at how little prompting my students needed to focus on intersectionality. I will not pretend that each student earned an "A" on every assignment and demonstrated mastery of the course material, but many of their autobiographies focused on experiences of gendered racism, masculinity and sexuality, class privilege and sexism, religion and heteropatriarchy, and other collisions of power and privilege. That is not to say that the autobiographies were not about gender, because they certainly were, but they were about more than gender.

Conclusion: Toward a Pedagogy of Critical Ambivalence

At the 2015 National Multicultural Conference and Summit, Kim Case (2015) suggested that intersectional pedagogy presents social science educators with an important dilemma: Do we incorporate intersectionality into our existing curriculum or rebuild our degree programs from the ground up? Case did not answer this question nor do I believe that there is a simple solution to curriculum transformation that will realize a fully intersectional pedagogy. Instead, as many other authors in this volume illustrate (e.g., Dessel & Corvidae, this volume), there are a variety of practical strategies that push educators and students toward an intersectional perspective, all of which open new questions about the politics, methods, and epistemology of multicultural-focused curricula across the disciplines. At the core of Case's (2015) provocation, I assert, is a superordinate question about intersectionality's capacity to transform systems that were never designed to accommodate it.

Cultural theorist Wiegman (2012) referred to many of the diversity and social justice oriented educational programs developed in the last 50 years as "identity-knowledges," because most of them were organized around particular identity-based political agendas, such as women's studies, queer studies, whiteness studies, American studies, etc. One inherent limitation of these identity-based frameworks is that they have been artificially limited in scope by their objects of study, which privilege one dimension of identity that is sometimes narrowly construed (Wiegman, 2012). In women's studies, for example, there has been a push in recent decades to foreground "gender" instead of "women" as the field's primary object of study, because gender is thought to be more inclusive of transgender identities and to facilitate the critique of masculinities. However, Wiegman (2012) is somewhat suspicious of the term gender and the promise of its transcendental inclusiveness, particularly because the phrase "women of color" represents yet another salient critique of the implicit whiteness of gender-first approaches to women's and gender studies. Likewise, as intersectionality becomes mainstreamed (Dhamoon, 2011), advocates often position the theory as offering a utopian politics of inclusivity that can attend to all imaginable intersections of identities (Carbado, 2013). Yet what can intersectionality do in disciplinary contexts, such as multicultural psychology, whose architecture is characterized by identity-based silos, including LGBT psychology, African American psychology, Latina/o psychology, and the psychology of gender? What happens to intersectionality in English, history, political science, and other disciplines that historically bucket diversity into special topics courses? Will intersectional perspectives be effectively understood as critical of the compartmentalization of race, gender, sexuality, and ethnicities, or merely become a celebratory rubric of "diversity" while single-axis approaches continue to dominate multicultural inquiry throughout the disciplines?

To return to Case's (2015) question of whether or not intersectionality should be incorporated into existing frameworks or serve as the blueprint for an entirely new curriculum, I suggest that a pedagogy of ambivalence may function as a critical rubric for doing intersectional work within the confines of disciplinary settings in which single-axis approaches to the study of inequality and identity remain dominant. Insomuch as ambivalence represents the simultaneity of negative and positive feelings towards an object, a pedagogy of ambivalence in regards to identity categories may help scholar-teachers maintain a critical relationship with the very topics faculty are charged with teaching. In the context of the psychology of gender, for me this meant teaching gender at an oblique angle, constantly pivoting between normative psychological framings of gender, feminist psychological approaches to gender, and intersectional perspectives that refuse a one-dimensional understanding of sex, gender, or sexuality. Rather than bucket the course into various identity-based units (e.g., race week, sexual orientation week), I tried to underscore the relationality of identity categories and systems of inequality, particularly how gender and sexism never function in isolation. I tried to resist presenting gender as a kind of master category, instead highlighting the strengths and weaknesses of gender's potential to capture what is actually occurring in any given empirical situation ranging from the laboratory, the therapy session, the classroom, or the field. And while feminist psychology guided the design and implementation of the class, I tried to illuminate rather than obfuscate the limitations of mainstream feminist psychology's capacity to account for how racism, classism, xenophobia, and heterosexism co-construct experiences of oppression. I did not teach intersectional perspectives as universalizing or infallible, but as critical, imperfect perspectives that aim to promote more precise explanations of social problems and to catalyze the amelioration of those problems.

Ambivalence denotes neither an absence of feeling nor complacency. Scholar-teachers and activists continue to advocate for curriculum transformation within institutions and disciplines that are explicitly hostile to intersectional commitments. This activism often means negotiating curriculum committees, teaching evaluations, and other bureaucratic structures that fundamentally limit the extent to which one can implement an intersectional approach in teaching and scholarship. A critical ambivalence toward the structures we inherit and inhabit can help sustain the kinds of intersectionality-grounded conversations this volume encourages. Critical ambivalence helps me resist fetishizing feminist and multicultural approaches while considering where, how, and when intersectionality is missing, flourishing, or failing to work in my courses and in my various intellectual communities more broadly. As I continue to teach the psychology of gender, I am reminded of feminist philosopher Judith Butler's (2004) discussion of the multiple meanings of "becoming undone" when it comes to gender. To Butler (2004), on the one hand, normative gender politics (i.e., heterosexism and cisgenderism) restrict one's ability to persevere in a livable life. On the other hand, resisting or "undoing" these politics can open up new ways of being. Likewise, an intersectional approach to the psychology of gender can mean facing the limits of gender, and then undoing its restrictions to imagine new ways of teaching, learning, and living.

References

Anzaldúa, G. (1987). *Borderlands/La Frontera*. San Francisco, CA: Aunt Lute Books.

Bowleg, L. (2008). When Black + woman + lesbian ≠ Black lesbian woman: The methodological challenges of qualitative and quantitative intersectionality research. *Sex Roles, 59*, 312–325. doi:10.1007/s11199-008-9400-z

Bowleg, L. (2012). The problem with the phrase "women and minorities": Intersectionality – an important theoretical framework for public health. *American Journal of Public Health, 102*, 1267–1273. doi:10.2105/AJPH.2012.300750

Butler, J. (2004). *Undoing gender*. New York, NY: Routledge.

Carbado, D. W. (2013). Colorblind intersectionality. *Signs: The Journal of Women in Culture and Society, 38*, 811–845. doi:10.1086/669666

Case, K. A. (2015, January). *Infusing intersectionality: Setting goals for the psychology curriculum.* Paper presented at the National Multicultural Conference and Summit, Atlanta, GA.

Case, K. A. (this volume). Toward an intersectional pedagogy model: Engaged learning for social justice. In K. A. Case (Ed.), *Intersectional pedagogy: Complicating identity and social justice* (pp. 1–24). New York, NY: Routledge.

Case, K. A., Miller, A. R., & Jackson, S. B. (2012). "We talk about race too much in this class!" Complicating the essentialized woman through intersectional pedagogy. In S. M. Pliner & C. A. Banks (Eds.), *Teaching, learning, and intersecting identities in higher education* (pp. 32–48). New York, NY: Peter Lang Publishing.

Case, K. A., & Rios, D. (this volume). Infusing intersectionality: Complicating the psychology of women course. In K. A. Case (Ed.), *Intersectional pedagogy: Complicating identity and social justice* (pp. 82–109). New York, NY: Routledge.

Cole, E. R. (2008). Coalitions as a model for intersectionality: From practice to theory. *Sex Roles, 59,* 443–453. doi:10.1007/s11199-008-9419-1

Cole, E. R. (2009). Intersectionality and research in psychology. *American Psychologist, 64*(3), 170–180. doi:10.1037/a0014564

Collins, P. H. (1998). *Fighting words: Black women and the search for justice.* Minneapolis, MN: University of Minnesota Press.

Collins, P. H. (2000). *Black feminist thought: Knowledge, consciousness, and the politics of empowerment* (2nd ed.). New York, NY: Routledge.

Collins, P. H. (2015). Intersectionality's definitional dilemmas. *Annual Review of Sociology, 41,* 1–20. doi:10.1146/annurev-soc-073014-112142

Crenshaw, K. W. (1989). Demarginalizing the intersection of race and sex: A Black feminist critique of antidiscrimination doctrine, feminist theory and antiracist politics. *University of Chicago Legal Forum, 140,* 139–167.

Crenshaw, K. W. (1991). Mapping the margins: Intersectionality, identity politics, and violence against women of color. *Stanford Law Review, 46,* 1241–1299.

Crenshaw, K. W. (2000/2014). The structural and political dimensions of intersectional oppression. In P. R. Grzanka (Ed.), *Intersectionality: A foundations and frontiers reader* (pp. 16–22). Boulder, CO: Westview Press.

Crisp, R. J., & Hewstone, M. (2006). Multiple social categorization: Context, process, and social consequences. In R. J. Crisp & M. Hewstone (Eds.), *Multiple social categorization: Processes, models and applications* (pp. 3–22). New York, NY: Psychology Press.

Davis, K. (2008). Intersectionality as buzzword: A sociology of science perspective on what makes a feminist theory successful. *Feminist Theory, 9,* 67–85. doi:10.1177/14647001080 86364

Dessel, A., & Corvidae, T. (this volume). Experiential activities for engaging intersectionality in social justice pedagogy. In K. A. Case (Ed.), *Intersectional pedagogy: Complicating identity and social justice* (pp. 214–223). New York, NY: Routledge.

Dhamoon, R. K. (2011). Considerations on mainstreaming intersectionality. *Political Research Quarterly, 64,* 230–243. doi:10.1177/1065912910379227

Dill, B. T. (1979). The dialectics of Black womanhood. *Signs: The Journal of Women in Culture and Society, 4,* 543–555. doi:10.1086/493637

Dill, B. T., & Kohlman, M. H. (2012). Intersectionality: A transformative paradigm in feminist theory and social justice. In S. N. Hesse-Biber (Ed.), *The handbook of feminist research: Theory and praxis* (2nd ed., pp. 154–174). Thousand Oaks, CA: Sage.

Dill, B. T., Nettles, S. M., & Weber, L. (2001). Defining the work of the consortium: What do we mean by intersections? *Connections: Newsletter of the Consortium on Race, Gender, & Ethnicity at the University of Maryland.* Retrieved from www.crge.umd.edu

Douglas, S. J. (2010). *Enlightened sexism: The seductive message that feminism's work is done.* New York, NY: Times Books.

Dzodan, F. (2011, October 10). My feminism will be intersectional or it will be bullshit! [Blog post]. *Tiger Beatdown.* Retrieved from: tigerbeatdown.com

Eagly, A. H., Eaton, A., Rose, S., Riger, S., & Mchugh, M. (2012). Feminism and psychology: Analysis of a half-century of research. *American Psychologist, 67,* 211–230. doi:10.1037/ a0027260

Eagly, A. H., & Riger, S. (2014). Feminism and psychology: Critiques of methods and epistemology. *American Psychologist, 69,* 685–702. doi:10.1037/a0037372

Fausto-Sterling, A. (2000). *Sexing the body: Gender politics and the construction of sexuality.* New York, NY: Basic Books.

Fine, C. (2010). *Delusions of gender: How our minds, society, and neurosexism create difference.* New York, NY: W. W. Norton & Company.

Frankenberg, R. (Ed.). (1997). *Displacing whiteness: Essays in social and cultural criticism.* Durham, NC: Duke University Press.

Gill, R. (2009). Beyond the 'sexualization of culture' thesis: An intersectional analysis of 'sixpacks,' 'midriffs,' and 'hot lesbians' in advertising. *Sexualities, 12,* 137–160.

Goldenberg, J. L., Cooper, D. P., Heflick, N. A., Routledge, C., & Arndt, J. (2011). Is objectification always harmful? Reactions to objectifying images and feedback as a function of self-objectification and mortality salience. *Journal of Experimental Social Psychology, 47,* 443–448. doi:10.1016/j.jesp.2010.11.013

Gramsci, A., Hoare, Q., & Smith, G. N. (Eds.). (1971). *Selections from the prison notebooks of Antonio Gramsci (1929–1935).* New York, NY: International Publishers.

Grzanka, P. R. (2010). Buffy, the Black feminist? Intersectionality and pedagogy. In J. A. Kreider & M. K. Winchell (Eds.), *Buffy in the classroom: Essays on teaching with the vampire slayer* (pp. 186–201). Jefferson, NC: McFarland Press.

Grzanka, P. R. (2014). Intersectional objectivity. In P. R. Grzanka (Ed.), *Intersectionality: A foundations and frontiers reader* (pp. xi-xxvii). Boulder, CO: Westview Press.

Hancock, A.-M. (2007). When multiplication doesn't equal quick addition: Examining intersectionality as a research paradigm. *Perspectives on Politics, 5,* 63–79. doi:10.1017/S 1537592707070065

Helgeson, V. (2012). *The psychology of gender* (4th ed.). New York, NY: Pearson.

Hyde, J. S. (2005). The gender similarities hypothesis. *American Psychologist, 60,* 581–592. doi:10.1037/0003-066x.60.6.581

Kennedy, H. (2005). Subjective intersections in the face of the machine. *European Journal of Women's Studies, 12,* 471–487. doi:10.1177/1350506805057102

MacKinnon, C. A. (2013). Intersectionality as method: A note. *Signs: The Journal of Women in Culture and Society, 38,* 1019–1030. doi:10.1086/669570

May, V. (2015). *Pursuing intersectionality, unsettling dominant imaginaries.* New York, NY: Routledge.

McCall, L. (2005). The complexity of intersectionality. *Signs: The Journal of Women in Culture and Society, 30,* 1711–1800. doi:10.1086/426800

Morris, K. L., & Goldenberg, J. (2015). Objects become her: The role of mortality salience on men's attraction to literally objectified women. *Journal of Experimental Social Psychology, 56,* 69–72. doi:10.1016/j.jesp.2014.09.005

Naples, N. (this volume). Pedagogical practice and teaching intersectionality intersectionally. In K. A. Case (Ed.), *Intersectional pedagogy: Complicating identity and social justice* (pp. 110–128). New York, NY: Routledge.

Orford, J. (2008). Challenging psychology over its neglect of the social. In J. Orford (Ed.), *Community psychology: Challenges, controversies, and emerging consensus* (pp. 1–34). West Sussex, UK: John Wiley & Sons.

Rivera, D.P. (this volume). Revealing hidden intersections of gender identity, sexual orientation, race, and ethnicity: Teaching about multiple oppressed identities. In

K. A. Case (Ed.), *Intersectional pedagogy: Complicating identity and social justice* (pp 173–193). New York, NY: Routledge.

Schilt, K., & Westbrook, L. (2009). Doing gender, doing heteronormativity: "Gender normals," transgender people, and the social maintenance of heterosexuality. *Gender & Society, 23,* 440–464. doi:10.1177/0891243209340034

Shields, S. A. (2008). Gender: An intersectionality perspective. *Sex Roles, 59,* 301–311. doi:10.1 007/s11199-008-9501-8

Smith, B. (1980). Racism and women's studies. *Frontiers: A Journal of Women's Studies, 5,* 48–49. doi:10.2307/3346304

Syed, M. (2010). Disciplinarity and methodology in intersectionality theory and research. *American Psychologist, 65,* 61–62. doi:10.1037/a0017495

Tavris, C. (1993). *The mismeasure of woman.* New York, NY: Touchstone.

University of Tennessee, Knoxville. (2015). *2015–2016 Undergraduate Catalog.* Retrieved from catalog.utk.edu

Valentine, G. (2007). Theorizing and research intersectionality: A challenge for feminist geography. *The Professional Geographer, 59,* 10–21. doi:10.1111/j.1467-9272.2007.00587.x

Vera, E., & Speight, S. L. (2003). Multicultural competence, social justice, and counseling psychology: Expanding our roles. *The Counseling Psychologist, 31,* 253–272. doi:10.117 7/0011000002250634

Wiegman, R. (2012). *Object lessons.* Durham, NC: Duke University Press.

Williams, P. (1992). *The alchemy of race and rights: Diary of a law professor.* Cambridge, MA: Harvard University Press.

5

INFUSING INTERSECTIONALITY

Complicating the Psychology of Women Course

Kim A. Case and Desdamona Rios

Scholars have framed the utility of intersectionality as either useful for examining systems of power or divisive due to the misconception of intersectionality having an "alleged emphasis on categories of identity versus structures of inequality" (Cho, Crenshaw, & McCall, 2013, p. 797). Despite common challenges raised by both scholars who use intersectionality as an analytic tool and students learning about intersectionality, little attention has been paid to pedagogical strategies for teaching intersectionality theory, this book and its intersectional pedagogy model (Case, this volume) being an exception (see also Pliner & Banks, 2012). For example, students often conceptualize intersectionality as a defining feature of uniqueness (Rios, Bowling, & Harris, this volume), express frustration about the complexities of the matrix of infinite identities (Cho et al., 2013), or rely on additive jeopardy, all of which result in an individual rather than structural level of analysis. To address these challenges, we offer strategies for infusing intersectionality into a Psychology of Women class with the goal of shifting students to understand intersectionality as a frame for thinking about "the way things work rather than who people are" (Cho et al., 2013, p. 797). How do educators carve out spaces for making invisible aspects of intersectionality visible to students?

In the introductory chapter to this volume, I (Kim) described my early experiences teaching Psychology of Women from a categorical perspective that neglected intersectional concerns. Like many colleagues who seek to infuse intersectionality into their courses (Grzanka, this volume), as an early career, then tenured, and now full professor, my journey toward more intersectional pedagogy continues. However, the course presented here represents moving away from additive models in favor of more complicated infusion of interconnections of identity and systemic oppression and privilege. Below, we provide educators with a detailed map for infusing intersectional pedagogy that could apply to a wide range of courses within psychology as well as across social sciences, education, humanities, and interdisciplinary studies. Although the course described here occurred over five weeks as a summer online course, the pedagogical approaches lend themselves to both face-to-face and hybrid (partially online) models.

Setting the Syllabus Stage for Complicating Assumptions

In designing the syllabus, I (Kim) made a concerted effort to infuse intersectional theory throughout the document. When I began my career as a junior faculty member, syllabi for my undergraduate women's studies courses (e.g., Introduction to Women's Studies, Psychology of Women) typically included a learning goal alluding to, but not naming, intersectionality such as:

- to identify concepts of class, race, age, gender, and sexuality as constructions by societies and *interrelated* throughout women's lives; or
- to foster critical reading and thinking about women's lives and the ways *interlocking systems* of colonialism, racism, sexism, ethnocentrism, ageism, and heterosexism shape women's and men's lives.

A few years later, this developed into a learning goal bullet point that mentioned gender's intersections with race, class, and sexuality:

- to use the social constructivist paradigm as an approach to understanding the meaning and *intersections* of constructs such as gender, woman, man, race, class, sexual orientation.

Students reading these bulleted learning goals are highly unlikely to recognize all the tenets and complexities of intersectional theory within words like "interrelated" and "interlocking." Even though the literal mention of the word "intersections" may represent an improvement, that bullet was merely one among five total learning goals on the syllabus and therefore potentially lost as students shuffled to quickly identify requirements and due dates. Rather than limit intersectional cues to one sentence in the syllabus, I added sections on intersectional theory, critical race theory, and queer theory to the existing section on the academic feminist framework of the course. The intersectional theory section (paraphrased from Case, Miller, & Jackson, 2012) served to orient students to the major influence and infusion of intersectionality within this undergraduate Psychology of Women course:

In 1989, Crenshaw introduced the term "intersectionality" to explain that complex identities (based on race, gender, sexuality, class, age, etc.)

contrast with categorical generalizations about social groups. Patricia Hill Collins' (1990) "matrix of domination" also provides a conceptual structure to aid current understanding of the various social locations that result from complex identities in both privileged and oppressed groups. The intersectional approach provides instructors and students with a sophisticated critical framework for examining the complexity of identity. The lens of intersectionality provides a framework for:

- making connections across/within forms of oppression and privilege;
- identifying the complexity of social identity and the consequences of social location in the matrix of oppression;
- unveiling invisible systems of power that support and perpetuate oppression based on race, class, gender, sexuality, and more;
- challenging "traditional disciplinary boundaries and the compartmentalization and fixity of ideas" (Dill & Zambrana, 2009, p. 2) that currently dominate student learning environments;
- validating subjugated knowledge; and
- constructing a vision for change.

This newly included section in the course syllabus featured intersectional theory on the first day of class following the syllabus section describing academic feminist theory. Immediately after this explanation of the learning benefits of intersectional theory, students read sections on critical race theory and queer theory to further disrupt student assumptions of "women" as a gender-only topic of scholarly consideration and encourage thinking beyond privileged norms. The assignment descriptions in the syllabus also include an emphasis on intersectionality and are explained in more detail below.

Intersectional Infusion throughout Course Materials

Required Readings

The chosen textbook sends implicit messages to students about the values and goals of the course, what is worthy of study, and whose experiences form the foundation of the course. With the main goal of infusing intersectionality, *Women's Lives: A Psychological Exploration* (Etaugh & Bridges, 2013) served as the textbook for the course. As the main reading source, students gained direct access to intersectional theory from the very first chapter, which blatantly names intersectionality learning goals outlined by Etaugh and Bridges. Among the handful of textbooks available for a course on the psychology of women, the text authors made an obvious effort to infuse intersections of gender with social class, race, sexual orientation, ability, age, gender identity, and nationality in each and every chapter. In fact, these typically invisible intersections are not bracketed off into special "diversity" boxes, but rather included throughout each section and topic. This form of inclusion of women's varied social locations in the matrix of oppression avoids the marginalization of mentioning these intersections only in special boxes or only at the end of a chapter as an afterthought, as texts tend to do. As argued by Kurtis and Adams (this volume), this process of normalizing the experiences of marginalized groups of women and denaturalizing the mythical norms of White, middle-class, heterosexual, able-bodied, young, gender-identity privileged women creates a new inclusive narrative with diverse intersections of women's lives at the core of the text.

The course was structured as 10 topical learning modules. Therefore, some models included one textbook chapter and others covered two chapters. Each module also required students to read 2–3 peer-reviewed journal articles[1] for more in-depth access to research studies beyond the general summaries of decades of empirical findings provided by the text. To begin the course, module 1 asked students to read:

1. the introductory chapter of Etaugh and Bridges (2013) which focused on intersectionality as a core frame for the book;
2. the influential Cole (2009) *American Psychologist* article on the need for intersectional theory in psychological research; and
3. an article presenting data countering the stereotype of feminists as "man-haters" (Anderson, Kanner, & Elsayegh, 2009).

The journal article readings in each module provided students with direct exposure to empirical feminist research in the field, both qualitative and quantitative studies, and invisible intersections in women's and men's lives. Most of the selected articles contributed to learning goals for deeper understanding of intersectionality at the individual and structural levels. For example, the textbook chapters on gender self-concept and infant to adolescent development complemented articles on transgender identity development (Levitt & Ippolito, 2014) and training for educators and counselors to support gender-diverse youth (Case & Meier, 2014). Via reading articles that highlighted intersectionality, students in the course explored interconnections among sex, gender, and gender identity beyond the textbook coverage that some students might gloss over. Across the course, students read journal articles covering intersectional topics such as portrayals of women of color in magazine advertisements, Latina and White girls' experiences with academic sexism, abuse of women with disabilities, lesbian identity development, partner violence in tribal communities, and more. Table 5.1 provides the full list of modules and assigned readings. These readings served to support the intersectional pedagogy model's tenet of uncovering invisible intersections (Case, this volume).

TABLE 5.1 Assigned Peer-Reviewed Journal Articles by Course Module

Module	Topic(s)	Article	Author(s) & Year
1	Introduction to the Psychology of Women: History and Research	*Are Feminists Man Haters? Feminists' and Nonfeminists' Attitudes Toward Men*	Anderson, Kanner, & Elsayegh (2009)
		Intersectionality and Research in Psychology	Cole (2009)
2	Cultural Representations of Gender	*Reading Representations of Black, East Asian, and White Women for Adolescent Girls*	Sengupta (2006)
		Killing Us Softly? Investigating Portrayals of Women and Men in Contemporary Magazine Advertisements	Conley & Ramsey (2011)
3	Gender Self-Concept and Gender Attitudes Infancy, Childhood, and Adolescence	*Being Transgender: The Experience of Transgender Identity Development*	Levitt & Ippolito (2014)
		Developing Allies to Transgender and Gender-Nonconforming Youth: Training for Counselors and Educators	Case & Meier (2014)
		Mixed Drinks and Mixed Messages: Adolescent Girls' Perspectives on Alcohol and Sexuality	Livingston, Bay-Cheng, Hequembourg, Testa, & Downs (2012)
4	Gender Comparisons: Social Behavior, Personality, Communication, and Cognition	*The Swimsuit Becomes Us All: Ethnicity, Gender, and Vulnerability to Self-objectification*	Hebl, King, & Lin (2004)
		Carrying the World with the Grace of a Lady and the Grit of a Warrior: Deepening Our Understanding of the "Strong Black Woman" Schema	Abrams, Maxwell, Pope, & Belgrave (2014)
5	Sexuality	*An Empirical Analysis of Factors Affecting Adolescent Attachment in Adoptive Families with Homosexual and Straight Parents*	Erich, Kanenberg, Case, Allen, & Bogdanos (2009)

		Conceptualizing Lesbian Sexual Identity Development: Narrative Accounts of Socializing Structures and Individual Decisions and Actions	Shapiro, Rios, & Stewart (2010)
	Reproductive System and Childbearing	Identity and Agency: The Meaning and Value of Pregnancy for Young Black Lesbians	Reed, Miller, & Timm (2011)
6	Education and Achievement	Latina and European American Girls' Experiences with Academic Sexism and their Self-concepts in Mathematics and Science During Adolescence	Brown & Leaper (2010)
	Employment	Dimensions of Disrespect: Mapping and Measuring Gender Harassment in Organizations	Leskinen & Cortina (2014)
		When Professionals Become Mothers, Warmth Doesn't Cut the Ice	Cuddy, Fiske, & Glick (2004)
7	Balancing Family and Work	Speaking on Behalf of Others: A Qualitative Study of the Perceptions and Feelings of Adolescent Latina Language Brokers	Villanueva & Buriel (2010)
		"Live to Work" or "Work to Live"? A Qualitative Study of Gender and Work-life Balance Among Men and Women in Mid-life	Emslie & Hunt (2009)
	Relationships	Is Traditional Gender Ideology Associated with Sex-typed Mate Preferences? A Test in Nine Nations	Eastwick et al. (2006)
8	Violence against Girls and Women	Abuse of Women with Disabilities: Toward an Empowerment Perspective	Foster & Sandel (2010)
		"A Disease of the Outside People": Native American Men's Perceptions of Intimate Partner Violence	Matamonasa-Bennett (2015)

(continued)

TABLE 5.1 *(continued)*

Module	Topic(s)	Article	Author(s) & Year
		Don't Rock the Boat: Women's Benevolent Sexism Predicts Fears of Marital Violence	Expósito, Herrera, Moya, & Glick (2010)
9	Physical Health	*Understanding the Link Between Multiple Oppressions and Depression Among African American Women: The Role of Internalization*	Carr, Szymanski, Taha, West, & Kaslow (2014)
		Cultural Body Shape Ideals and Eating Disorder Symptoms Among White, Latina, and Black College Women	Gordon, Castro, Sitnikov, & Holm-Denoma (2010)
	Mental Health	*Older Women of Color: A Feminist Exploration of the Intersections of Personal, Familial, and Community Life*	Conway-Turner (1999)
10	A Feminist Future	*Transgender Inclusion in University Nondiscrimination Statements: Challenging Gender-Conforming Privilege through Student Activism*	Case, Kanenberg, Erich, & Tittsworth (2012)
		Discovering the Privilege of Whiteness: White Women's Reflections on Anti-racist Identity and Ally Behavior	Case (2012)
		Positive Portrayals of Feminist Men Increase Men's Solidarity with Feminists and Collective Action Intentions	Wiley, Srinivasan, Finke, Firnhaber, & Shilinsky (2012)
		Seeing the Unseen: Attention to Daily Encounters with Sexism as a Way to Reduce Sexist Beliefs	Becker & Swim (2011)

Global Feminism Project Interviews

In addition to required readings, students viewed at least one interview video from the Global Feminisms Project (GFP) online resource maintained by the Institute for Research on Women and Gender at the University of Michigan (Cole & Luna, 2010; McGuire, Stewart, & Curtin, 2010; Stewart, Lal, & McGuire, 2011; Zheng & Zhang, 2010). The GFP offers students and instructors "comparative case studies of women's activism and scholarship" (umich.edu/~glblfem). This archive houses over 50 in-depth interviews with feminist activists from China, India, Nicaragua, Poland, and the U.S., as well as pedagogical resources such as syllabi, assignments, and PowerPoints. Rios and Stewart (2013) provided a more thorough review of the GFP as well as innovative uses of the interviews for student assignments aimed at invisible intersections of privilege.

For the Psychology of Women course, each module directed students to at least one GFP interview with these instructions:

> This website was created by researchers to provide you with access to women social justice activists from all over the world. This set of interviews is an amazing resource full of women's diverse experiences with working to improve the lives of girls and women globally. Your task is to watch the video and consider the various ways that oppression, privilege, and intersectional theory inform your understanding of the activist. What overall themes does the woman being interviewed present to us?

These videos with feminist activists and scholars from a variety of international sites served to disrupt student assumptions of the U.S. as the central location of feminist work and of Western feminism as the ideal model for non-Western women to adopt in their local contexts (Kurtis & Adams, this volume). Quite the contrary, students learned about women who developed the first women's hotline, provided domestic violence training to police, judges, and doctors, and organized for migrant rights in China, fought for minority rights and against dowry-related violence and death in India, campaigned against homophobia and trafficking women in Poland, and raised awareness of racial and gender discrimination using radio programs in Nicaragua. In addition, the GFP interviews with U.S. feminist activists helped students question and dismantle assumptions of feminist movements as exclusively White, heterosexual, middle-class, able-bodied women working on sexism as an isolated form of oppression. As illustrations of the often invisible intersectional social justice work within U.S. feminism, these interviews presented students with women providing food, shelter, and clothing to the poor, organizing for reproductive rights with women with disabilities and women of color, countering violence against women of color, and opposing racist hate groups. In sum, the GFP archive highlights shared social justice issues (e.g., violence against women or poverty; Greenwood, this volume) for groups of women who differentially experience these same issues based on systems of domination (e.g., sexism, racism, heterosexism, classism/caste system, and religion) in their national contexts.

Although students in the course read one assigned journal article that used GFP as the data source, this approach was under-utilized. Given their direct access to the raw data interviews, students could be assigned viewing key videos before reading a GFP-based publication (publications are all listed on the website). For example, they could view 2–3 interviews with Chinese feminist activists and then read the Zheng and Zhang (2010) article on Chinese feminisms. Through this process, they could explore the process of translating women's voices in the form of qualitative data into an empirical research article. In face-to-face courses, these videos could also be viewed in class to promote small group discussions with guided questions for recognizing intersectionality at individual (identity) levels, but especially structural levels for analysis of power and systemic privilege and oppression (Case, this volume). Table 5.2 provides the full list of assigned GFP interviews.

TABLE 5.2 Assigned Global Feminisms Project Interview Videos by Course Module

Module	Interviewee	Country/Site	Length (mins)	Interviewer(s) & Year
1	Wang Xingjuan	China	90	Jian (2004)
2	Sista II Sista	US	65	Naber (2004)
3	Yamileth Mejía	Nicaragua	63	Grabe (Interviewer) & Baumgartner (Interpreter) (2011b)
4	Maureen Taylor & Marian Kramer	US	93	Lyle (2004)
5	Loretta Ross	US	81	Luna (2006)
	Adrienne Asch	US	57	Kirkland (2006)
6	Wang Cuiyu	China	106	Xueyu (2003)
7	Anna Gruszczyńska	Poland	75	Piela & Wydrych (2004)
8	Flavia Agnes	India	90	Datta (2003)
	Matilde Lindo	Nicaragua	68	Grabe (Interviewer) & Baumgartner (Interpreter) (2011a)
9	Ge Youli	China	131	Jian & Tong (2002)
10	Barbara Limanowska	Poland	54	Walczewska & Iwasiow (2005)

Current Events Curriculum

Pedagogical literature on increasing student engagement suggests the use of current events, popular culture, and news stories to help students recognize the immediate relevance of course content in their lives (Platt, 2013) and "deconstruct dominant narratives" (Morrell, 2002, p. 72). Platt (2013) argued that this approach also aids in bringing privileged students into difficult conversations about oppression and privilege while minimizing student resistance. Along with these benefits, my primary pedagogical goal for the current events curriculum was enhancing the intersectionality presence in the course (see Table 5.3 for assigned readings and videos). For each Psychology of Women course module, students viewed videos and read news stories or essays intended to connect text and journal article readings with current real-world events. Students received this description of the relevance of the current events curriculum for their learning:

> The current events area within each module will address some news story, event, movement, etc. that is making major headlines nationally or internationally or it may focus on some little-known story that did not make the mainstream media coverage. Some current events will be happenings from last week while others may be from a few years ago. The main point here is to connect our readings and other course materials to real world issues. The Psychology of Women does not happen within the academy or within a textbook. This course applies to all aspects of our lives far and wide. Therefore, we want to be sure and consider how what we learn in each module helps us be more informed citizens, social action leaders, voters, critical thinkers, family members, and responsible members of the global society.

Early on, the current events section worked toward expanding student conceptualizations of "woman" and challenging cultural assumptions of the mythical norm (Lorde, 1984). For example, the very first two modules included a magazine article, "My Feminism Is Black, Intersectional, and Womanist: And I Refuse to Be Left Out of the Movement" (McCrayer, 2015) plus a short video, "Things Black Men are Tired of Hearing" (BuzzFeed, 2015), addressing stereotypical cultural misrepresentations. Students also viewed Kerry Washington's 2015 GLAAD Award speech on the intersectionality, complexity, and diversity of LGBT identities and experiences. The current events curriculum infused student access to topics such as intersex communities, acceptance of transgender students into Wellesley, forced sterilization of Native, Latina, and Black women, police violence and racism, as well as intersectional analyses of campus rape, same-sex partner violence, climate justice, and the Hobby Lobby employee birth control access court decision. Of particular relevance to students attending a university in Houston, the current events modules also covered

TABLE 5.3 Assigned Current Event Items by Course Module

Module	Current Events	Type	Author & Year
1	Gloria Steinem on the Colbert Report	Video (6:04)	The Colbert Report (2011)
	My feminism is Black, intersectional, and womanist	Online article	McCrayer (2015)
	TED Talk - Chimamanda Ngozi Adichie	Video (30:15)	TEDx Talks (2013a)
2	Media representations of ethnic and racial minorities	Online article	Halusic (2015)
	Cultural representations of Black men	Video (1:50)	Edewi (2015)
	Killing Us Softly - Introduction by Jean Kilbourne	Video (4:56)	ChallengingMedia (2010)
	Miss Representation - movie trailer	Video (8:52)	Anthony M (2011)
3	What it's like to be intersex	Video (3:25)	Warner & Ruggirello (2015)
	8-year-old calls out Clarks for its lack of dinosaur-themed shoes for girls	Online article	Clements (2015)
	Wellesley College accepts transgender women	Online article	Kellaway (2015)
4	Kerry Washington's 2015 GLAAD Awards Speech	Video (7:15)	GLAAD (2015)
5	"No Más Bebés" documentary on sterilization abuse	Online article & video (2:50)	Pérez (2015)
	Elaine Riddick's forced sterilization testimony	Video (3:45)	Ptah (2011)
	History of forced sterilization & current U.S. abuses	Online article	Krase (2014)
6	Store charges women less than men	Online article	Wang (2015)
	Study shows challenges for Latina and Black women scientists	Online article	Desmond-Harris (2015)
	Why "girl" scientists cause trouble in the lab	Blog post	Dusenbery (2015)
	Oscar acceptance speech by Patricia Arquette	Video (3:15)	Oscars (2015)
	Intersectional analysis of Patricia Arquette's Oscar acceptance speech	Online article	Grimes (2015)

7	Women's groups in D.C. address rights of women in forced marriages	Online article	Constable (2015)
	TED Talk by Sehba Sarwar	Video (16:16)	TEDx Talks (2013b)
8	Intimate partner violence in queer communities	Blog post	Gattuso (2015b)
	McKinney pool party & the history of policing Black women's bodies	Blog post	Niles (2015)
	Human trafficking in Houston	Video (7:41)	Donor Houston (2014)
	Intersectional analysis of national discussion of campus rape	Blog post	Rodriguez (2015)
	The women of #Blacklivesmatter	Ms. magazine article	Cooper (2015)
9	Deterioration found in DNA of urban poor	Online article	Pitney (2015)
	Hobby Lobby Supreme Court ruling about denying employees access to certain healthcare rights	Online article	Sementelli & Edelman (2014)
	What the Hobby Lobby ruling means for LGBT employees: Applying intersectional theory	Blog post	Johnson (2014)
	Response to the court from American Association of University Women (AAUW)	Blog post	Maatz (2014)
10	Radical Brownies: Teaching girls the value of social justice & activism	Blog post	Bobadilla (2015)
	Climate justice: Intersectional feminism in action	Blog post	Gattuso (2015a)
	Ms. Magazine highlights the work of anti-rape activists	Blog post	Heldman & Dirks (2015)

Note: Video length is provided in parentheses in minutes and seconds.

Houston's local-global connections for sex trafficking women and girls. With this direct exposure to marginalized voices and intersectional analyses of both mainstream news and subjugated knowledge, students explored the practical applications of intersectional theory in timely real-world scenarios happening to actual people. This aspect of the course facilitated students' understanding of the Psychology of Women beyond, but in connection to, textbook and research-based readings.

Intersectional Infusion throughout Assessment and Assignments

Reflective Discussion Posts

As a component for each module, and as preparation for in-class discussions when the course meets in person, students completed reflective discussion posts that established connections between the text, journal articles, GFP, and current events which addressed intersectional social locations within each module:

> For each course module, you will complete the posted readings (textbook chapters and research articles). You will also view a Global Feminisms Project video and review the current event materials provided (e.g., news story, video). Please write your post about at least two of the following in connection to the textbook readings:
>
> • Peer-reviewed journal articles
> • Global Feminisms Project video
> • Current event materials.
>
> An appropriate post might address questions that arose while you read, new ideas or implications that result from the readings, connections between course topics, etc. Make sure you are clearly connecting the textbook concepts AND other aspects of the module (journal articles, GFP video, current events).

The instructions also asked students to address the following two questions in their posts:

• How does intersectional theory help you understand more perspectives on this issue?
• How might privilege affect your ability to fully comprehend various perspectives on this topic?

These brief reflective papers challenged students to individually grapple with recognizing intersectionality within and across course materials in preparation for broader class discussions.

Chapter Quizzes

With the goal of encouraging students' attentiveness to intersectional theory, each chapter quiz included strategically chosen questions addressing intersectional content. For example, quiz questions tested student comprehension of intersectional theory as distinct from an additive model, womanist critiques of the U.S. feminist movement, the impact of race on gender attitudes, and transgender identity. In addition, women of color's experiences with wage inequality, academic racism and sexism, and stereotypes and media portrayals were infused throughout. Quizzes assessed understanding of stereotypes as well as sexuality and dating for women with disabilities and older women. The feminization of poverty was addressed within questions on older low-income women, single mothers, and women in developing countries. Additional global women's concerns were covered in items about female infanticide, dowry assaults and killings, and human trafficking. Other questions concerned issues for lesbian and bisexual women such as workplace discrimination, stressors on same-sex couples, access to healthcare, and positive outcomes for children in lesbian families. This summary serves as only a sampler of intersectional quiz items rather than an exhaustive list.

Paper Options

For the course paper, each student chose either the *privilege paper* (Case, 2015) with an intersectional component or the *photovoice project* with a central focus on intersectionality (Case, 2015; Case & Lewis, this volume; Case et al., 2012). Although the privilege paper contributed to student intersectional awareness in the sense that students reflected on understandings of privileged social identities and structural power through privilege, the assignment does not truly infuse an intersectional analysis. Students must write about their own personal privilege (Case, this volume) as described in these truncated privilege paper instructions:

> The essential goal of your paper is to think about how a form of privilege affects your life as a dominant group member. People have a much easier time recognizing prejudice and individual and institutional discrimination when we are part of the targeted group. However, we tend to have more difficulty when we experience the advantages and benefits of dominant group memberships as they tend to be invisible. This paper will be your space for exercising your privilege-recognition muscles. Your paper should reflect your ability to think critically about prejudice and privilege and successfully apply the concepts to real life and the course readings and materials.

Detailed questions to be answered within the paper prompted students to critically analyze their daily privilege, institutional privilege, the psychological and behavioral impact of privilege, and ways to take action within their own spheres of influence. In addition, all students choosing to complete this assignment answered the following intersectional question within the final paper:

- How does this form of privilege connect to intersectional theory? How does intersectionality relate to the ways that privilege affects your lived experiences, psychology, and interactions with others?

Given that only one of eight questions required intersectional analysis, this paper did not reflect a complete infusion of intersectional theory.

In contrast, the photovoice project and reflective paper clearly focused on intersectional theory and application to students' own lives. After some background information on photovoice as a research methodology, students received instructions:

Your photovoice project and paper must include intersectionality as a central focus. Your charge will be to take pictures that capture your voice with regard to aspects of your own intersectionality and social location (both marginalized and privileged). Thinking about two main sections of the photovoice PPT (or other creative choice such as a website), you will include both of the following along with text explanations or voiceover:

- *Personal:* Photos that represent the intersections of your own various identities, including those that are associated with privilege and oppressed positionalities.
- *Conceptual:* Photos that illustrate intersectionality as a concept. You might take pictures of items, locations, and abstract images that would help others understand intersectional theory and the matrix of oppression and privilege.

The rubric informed students that grading depended on the relevance of the photos, explanation of the photos, connections to intersectionality, connections to course readings, concepts, theories, GFP, and current event materials, as well as organization and clarity. Given the required and explicit centrality of intersectional analysis, this project and paper represented enhanced pedagogical infusion of intersectionality compared with the privilege paper.

Intersectionality Project

Although other sources described versions of this project in graduate psychology courses (Case, 2015; Case & Lewis, this volume; Case et al., 2012; Rios et al., this volume), this Psychology of Women course was the first attempt to convert this project for use with undergraduates, most of whom had zero exposure to women's and gender studies. All students completed the intersectionality assignment as their final project in the course. For the undergraduates, students received learning goals and step-by-step project details. At each stage, the undergraduates needed more scaffolding and support such as approving their topics and providing consistent, clear, and rapid feedback in the final weeks before the project deadline.

Intersectionality Project Learning Goals:

- to create a product that helps raise awareness of intersectionality and can be used to teach about intersectionality;
- to promote understanding of multiple social identities, intersectionality theory and the complexity of group membership and identities, and the matrix of oppression;
- to provide experiential learning opportunities for direct and applied social action with regard to intersecting identities;
- to develop prosocial behavior and strengthen their public education skills for building community awareness of social inequalities.

Step 1: Identify a Topic – In order for you to effectively educate others, you first need to understand intersectional theory and its application to real world social identities. Once you understand the intricacies of the theory, you will choose an intersectionality topic as the focus of the project. The main goal is to create something that helps raise awareness of intersectionality and can be used to teach about it.

Step 2: Select Target Audience – With a topic chosen, you will investigate options with regard to appropriate target audiences. Will the project be for a completely general audience, college students in the classroom, adults, children, K-12 teachers, etc.?

Step 3: Create the Education Project – You will design and create your project for educating others about intersectional theory and its applications. For example, you might create videos, documentaries, games, cartoons, class activities, interactive exercises, new intersectional privilege list, teaching modules, websites, handouts, etc. Possible avenues and inspirations for creating your project:

- Intersectional privilege list such as the Black male privilege checklist. You will need to choose an intersection that does not yet have a privilege list.
- Create a video such as this video (4 min) explaining intersectionality with pizza (by Smoothiefreak, 2015): www.youtube.com/watch?v=FgK3NFvGp58
- Create a cartoon such as "Intersectionality: A Fun Guide" (Dobson, 2013). See Case (this volume) for the full cartoon.
- See my website for links to previous graduate student projects: www.drkimcase.com/resources

> **Step 4: Refection Paper** – Your reflection paper (5–7 pages) will connect the project to course readings, theory, concepts, videos, essays (anything within the course modules). The reflection will include sections addressing: choosing your topic and the target audience, the rationale and logic for the design of your project, an explanation of how your project could be used to raise awareness of intersectionality, and what you learned.

Unlike the graduate student requirements, undergraduates did not present their final projects to the target audiences. They were simply required to create the product, but not present it to the public or specific targeted group. Although that extra step could be incorporated with undergraduates, it would likely work best in a full 15-week course with seniors, students with previous exposure to women's and gender studies, and perhaps graduate teaching assistant support for guiding the final public education component.

Student Outcomes: Intersectional Awareness

Reflective Discussion Posts

Students' discussion posts provided insight into their development of intersectional awareness. For example, posts illustrated newfound considerations of their own intersectional identity connections with oppression:

> Personally I cannot think of a specific time that stands out in my mind that I feel that I was treated unequally because I am a woman or because I am a Hispanic woman. Perhaps it has happened to me and I just did not pick up on it.

Although new to the concept, students expressed awareness of the need for intersectionality in feminism after reading "My Feminism Is Black, Intersectional, and Womanist" (McCrayer, 2015):

> As a White female, I have never thought about the fact that minority women may have different struggles than I have. When we talk about feminism and sticking up for women's rights, you would like to think that we are referring to all women, not just White women. Often times though, like McCrayer says, the feminist movement leaves out females who are not White and able-bodied. This is why she says that her two identities of being black and being a woman cannot be separated. This is a good example of how the intersectional theory works.

After reading stories and viewing videos about forced sterilization of women of color, poor women, and immigrant women, one student commented on the lack of intersectional awareness in the reproductive rights movement: "Privileged (White and/or educated) women may not fully comprehend various perspectives on this topic because it does not concern them . . . reproduction and abortion are rarely looked at from the points of view of the poor, minority, or immigrant women." Students also wrote about the importance of considering intersectionality in terms of access to quality healthcare approaches:

> Look at intersectionality; this is not just as simple as a woman problem, it affects women of all ages, colors and even the LBGT community. Because say an older woman of color who also happens to be a lesbian would then not only need a doctor that understood women's problems, but who also understood health issues faced by women of color, older women and a doctor that a lesbian would also be comfortable with.

After reading about the Radical Brownies' (now called Radical Monarchs) approach to social justice, one mother posted about her plan of action to "use any opportunity to be an example of feminism that breaks stereotypes . . . I am active in their Cub/Boy Scout activities and wonder how I can integrate some lessons on intersectionality that are age appropriate and effective." Not only did this student express her understanding of intersectionality's potential influence on feminism, she also planned to apply intersectional theory to her work with boys.

Final Papers and Projects

The privilege paper, photovoice reflections, and final project papers demonstrated student learning with regard to intersectionality's complexity and relationship to feminism and privilege. Unlike when they entered the course, students articulated intersectional theory's argument against separating "all of the distinguishing features that are interwoven because each characteristic works with the others to make up who they are as a whole." To visually display simultaneous interaction, one student created an interactive class exercise on race, gender, and sexual orientation for her intersectionality project. The activity involved students choosing colorful ribbons to represent each identity then braiding bracelets that represent interwoven, mutually influential privileges and oppressions. She explained the "bracelets will be used to introduce the intersectional theory, along with opening discussion of the simultaneous effects of privilege and oppression that can occur when we see various intersections of race, gender, and sexual orientation." Another student mentioned the course readings helped her "expand on the basic categories of my identity" and see that "intersectionality theory shows that I am much more than my 'race-class-gender.'" A White woman discussed her discovery that "intersectional theory brings different levels or aspects to the table. White privilege is only one slice of the pie. If I were a White male,

I would experience privileges in a different way." This student began to dismantle interactions of male and White privilege in relation to her own social location as a racially privileged, marginalized woman.

A few of the students specifically critiqued feminists and feminisms that lack intersectional analysis. For example, one student labeled non-intersectional feminist identity as problematic:

> A feminist that is not intersectional is incomplete and ineffective . . . Intersectionality is also about understanding that we all exist in a variety of different systems, and sometimes one system is acting on us more strongly than another . . . Intersectionality has shown me that it is the missing piece of the puzzle, someone is not simply oppressed or privileged; rather they are simultaneously privileged and oppressed by different aspects of our identities.

Similarly, a student created an extensive Pinterest board focusing on intersectionality, feminism, and white privilege for her final intersectionality project and claimed a new self-determined identity label of *intersectionalist*:

> At the start of this class, I couldn't define feminist much less intersectionality, or the matrix of domination. I was able to walk away defining myself as a feminist. I didn't realize until I had grasped the idea of intersectionality that I [identify] more as an intersectionalist. Feminism without intersectionality is unfinished work.

These students recognized and named the simultaneity of identity and oppression along with the problematic nature of non-intersectional feminists and feminisms, arguably essential elements of intersectional theory.

Several students also reflected on how intersectional theory helped them become more aware of their own privileges despite their marginalized group memberships. While acknowledging her new awareness of the impact of the white beauty standard on her as an Asian woman and what she termed "a racialization of femininity," she also noted "though I may be marginalized as an Asian woman, I am also privileged that I have not had to experience oppression based on my family's social or economic status." As a result of her final intersectionality project creating a new privilege list specific to able-bodied women, one student shared her insights related to several of her own forms of privilege:

> Being an African American woman, I have easily been able to identify with the struggles and inequality that these identities face in our society. After this course and after the intersectionality project I realize that I am also a part of groups that are privileged. I am a heterosexual and I am an able-bodied adult. In these identities our society allows me advantages and

rights that people with disabilities, gay men, lesbian women, and bisexuals do not have.

One student wrote about her realization that not all members of her own groups will have the same experiences as her:

> I may identify with another person's gender, but I don't identify with somebody else's race or sexual orientation. I may identify with someone else's race, but I don't experience the same issues on disabilities and ageism . . . I realized that there are a lot more issues that need to be addressed in the hopes of spreading feminist attitudes and changing society's attitudes.

By recognizing that many experiences may not actually be shared with her ingroup members, she expressed awareness of more complex diversity within groups assumed to be homogenous.

Student Responses: What I Learned

Students' final discussion posts during the last few days of the course again highlighted their lack of previous exposure to intersectional theory:

> I had never heard the term intersectionality before this course, nor had I ever stopped to think about how people who face discrimination may possibly be affected in more than one way. In addition to this, when we think about certain groups who are privileged, the intersectional theory also made me realize that although they may appear to be privileged from the outside, many of these people who we considered privileged may be facing other types of discrimination as well.

This student's response revealed her new awareness of more complicated notions of simultaneous identity taking not only marginalized identities, but also privileged status into account. Although students sometimes used wording potentially additive in nature, they expressed awareness of the value of intersectionality for understanding the whole person:

> When you look through the eyes of intersectionality, you see people in their true light. You see the oppression that is occurring to people not just because of their gender, but because of gender and race, or race and orientation and gender. You must acknowledge these oppressions in order to obtain a better understanding into inequality.

Indications of understanding of co-constitutive influence among social identities and systems of oppression arose such as in another student's post about the impact of "sexual orientation, ethnicity, social class, age, ableness, marital status, and nationality, and that these factors create a varied mixture of privilege and discrimination all at the same time." Students also recognized the difficulty in conversation about intersectionality due to denial of privilege. One student posted that she learned "people identify strongly with their own areas of oppression, they are defensive about privilege, thus a discussion about intersectionality often turns into a competition for who has worked the hardest through tougher circumstances." Her experiences with discussing these topics with friends and family highlighted the challenges of these conversations that maintain barriers to intersectional analyses.

Many students commented on the textbook focus on intersectionality in women's lives as "informative and helpful" as well as within the journal articles and assignments:

> The writing assignment and the intersectionality project helped me to grasp this concept even better . . . it made me more aware of how people are affected multiple ways by discrimination.

However, student feedback overwhelmingly tuned in to the GFP interview videos and current events videos, stories, and essays within modules. One student explained the impact of the videos and interviews as due to her exposure to "true life stories in which you got to hear about personal encounters with discrimination and how it affected these people." This sentiment was expressed by several students:

> I enjoy hearing people's stories. It makes the content seem more real and authentic. It no longer just sounds like concepts but real life, because that's exactly what it is. Real people with real stories going through real issues and it really made an impact on me.

> Chimamanda Ngozi Adichie's TedTalk was a major turning point and eye opener for me, personally. I would share that with anyone that subscribed to the stereotypical ideas of feminism.

The second student's mention of the stereotypical ideas of feminism revealed her new awareness of critiques of mainstream U.S. feminisms by women of color activists and scholars.

Conclusions

Our main advice to educators is to identify and implement concrete ways to infuse intersectionality at every single decision point within the pedagogical design for a particular course. This specific course occurred online over five weeks in the summer. One student shared her understandable concerns about the condensed summer session:

I was challenged by this class and enjoyed it very much. I do wish I had taken it in a regular semester session because I felt it was a lot to process and might have been able to absorb and sort out my thoughts more clearly if I had more time to do so.

The tight timeline gave students little time to process and absorb the tenets of intersectional theory, therefore a regular full session course might be more effective. In addition, face-to-face classes allow for more community building and group discussions of complex issues that often work better in person. For these students, a variety and plethora of quality examples to illustrate intersectionality advanced student learning and especially aided in their final project development. Intersectional theory and application represented a foreign concept to most students, and they tended to gravitate back to old frames embedded in the culture. Students are often drawn back like boomerangs to thinking only about individual uniqueness while neglecting structural analyses (Rios et al., this volume) as illustrated by one student's declaration that "every person is a unique combination of identities." Students often revert to a lack of power analysis and the additive model without consideration of how each form of oppression and privilege alters the others as a matrix of infinite interactions.

The pedagogical strategies described here could apply to a broad range of social sciences, education, humanities, fine arts, counselor and therapist practitioner training (Case, 2015), and interdisciplinary courses even when the course title implies a single-axis focus (e.g., Women in Literature, Sociology of Race and Ethnicity, Gender in Higher Education). In fact, we argue that consistent and persistent infusion of intersectionality is perhaps most important within courses previously developed to address only one social group identity category.

As mentioned above, these undergraduate final projects did not include social action in the form of educating the public or target group. However, this project works well for graduate students with the added requirement of implementing the final project as a true public education tool. See Case and Lewis (this volume) for examples of graduate student projects such as designing and facilitating workshops on masculinity and homophobia with juvenile detention officers. Graduate-level courses might also assign a research study proposal that uses intersectional theory and answers questions posed by Cole (2009) to bring intersectionality into research design.

Educators teaching Psychology of Women, gender studies, ethnic studies, LGBT studies, and other diversity courses across psychology, other social sciences, humanities, and beyond commonly claim to value intersectionality in the curriculum, but less often purposefully incorporate this theory into courses. Our anecdotal observation of this pattern led us to conclude that instructors want to infuse intersectionality, but lack the pedagogical tools and resources, and therefore confidence, to enact their values. Using some of the ideas presented here, instructors will offer students a learning experience that embraces complexity, highlights structural intersections, examines privilege, and challenges them to recognize typically invisible locations of identity and oppression (for additional ideas for teaching on gender see Grzanka, this volume). Almost 30 years since Crenshaw's (1989) introduction of the term intersectionality, now is the time for action to transform the curriculum for in-depth intersectional infusion throughout. This may require some bravery and the willingness to keep moving forward even when one feels inept, unqualified, or unsure of the path. As allies in the classroom, educators must overcome the tendency to teach the comfortable, avoid risks, and play it safe. As Doctor Who once said, "Do what I do. Hold tight and pretend it's a plan!" (Moffat & Blackburn, 2011).

Note

1 In designing the course described here, my gratitude goes out to both Desdamona Rios and Amanda Johnston for sharing the journal article reading lists. Many of the readings I assigned came from their lists.

References

Abrams, J. A., Maxwell, M., Pope, M., & Belgrave, F. Z. (2014). Carrying the world with the grace of a lady and the grit of a warrior: Deepening our understanding of the "Strong Black Woman" schema. *Psychology of Women Quarterly, 38*(4), 503–518. doi:10.1177/03 61684314541418

Anderson, K. J., Kanner, M., & Elsayegh, N. (2009). Are feminists man haters? Feminists' and nonfeminists' attitudes toward men. *Psychology of Women Quarterly, 33*(2), 216–224. doi:10.1111/j.1471-6402.2009.01491.x

Anthony M. (2011, October 13). *Miss Representation extended trailer* [Video file]. Retrieved from www.youtube.com/watch?v=S5pM1fW6hNs

Becker, J. C., & Swim, J. K. (2011). Seeing the unseen: Attention to daily encounters with sexism as a way to reduce sexist beliefs. *Psychology of Women Quarterly, 35*(2), 227–242. doi:10.1177/0361684310397509

Bobadilla, S. (2015, April). The feministing five: Anayvette Martinez [Web log post]. Retrieved from feministing.com

Brown, C. S., & Leaper, C. (2010). Latina and European American girls' experiences with academic sexism and their self-concepts in mathematics and science during adolescence. *Sex Roles, 63*, 860–870. doi:10.1007/s11199-010-9856-5

Carr, E. R., Szymanski, D. M., Taha, F., West, L. M., & Kaslow, N. J. (2014). Understanding the link between multiple oppressions and depression among African American women: The role of internalization. *Psychology of Women Quarterly, 38*(2), 233–245. doi:10.1177/036 1684313499900

Case, K. A. (2012). Discovering the privilege of whiteness: White women's reflections on anti-racist identity and ally behavior. *Journal of Social Issues, 68*(1), 78–96. doi:10.1111/j.154 0-4560.2011.01737.x

Case, K. A. (2015). White practitioners in therapeutic ally-ance: An intersectional privilege awareness training model. *Women & Therapy, 38*(3–4), 263–278. doi:10.1080/02703149.2 015.1059209

Case, K. A. (this volume). Toward an intersectional pedagogy model: Engaged learning for social justice. In K. A. Case (Ed.), *Intersectional pedagogy: Complicating identity and social justice* (pp. 1–24). New York, NY: Routledge.

Case, K. A., Kanenberg, H., Erich, S. A., & Tittsworth, J. (2012). Transgender inclusion in university nondiscrimination statements: Challenging gender-conforming privilege through student activism. *Journal of Social Issues, 68*(1), 145–161. doi:10.1111/j.1540-4560.2011.01741.x

Case, K., & Lewis, M. (this volume). Teaching intersectional psychology in racially diverse settings. In K. A. Case (Ed.), *Intersectional pedagogy: Complicating identity and social justice* (pp. 129–149). New York, NY: Routledge.

Case, K. A., & Meier, S. C. (2014). Developing allies to transgender and gender-non-conforming youth: Training for counselors and educators. *Journal of LGBT Youth, 11*, 62–82. doi:10. 1080/19361653.2014.840764

Case, K., Miller, A., & Jackson, S. B. (2012). "We talk about race too much in this class!" Complicating the essentialized woman through intersectional pedagogy. In C. Banks & S. Pliner (Eds.), *Teaching, learning, and intersecting identities in higher education* (pp. 32–48). New York, NY: Peter Lang.

ChallengingMedia. (2010, March 12). *Killing us softly 4: Advertising's image of women* [Video file]. Retrieved from www.youtube.com/watch?v=PTlmho_RovY

Cho, S., Crenshaw, K. W., & McCall, L. (2013). Toward a field of intersectionality studies: Theory, applications, and praxis. *Signs, 38*(4), 785–810. doi:10.1086/669608

Clements, E. (2015, March 19). 8-year-old calls out Clarks for its lack of dinosaur-themed shoes for girls. Retrieved from www.today.com

Cole, E. R. (2009). Intersectionality and research in psychology. *American Psychologist, 64*(3), 170–180. doi:10.1037/a0014564

Cole, E. R., & Luna, Z. T. (2010). Making coalitions work: Solidarity across difference within U.S. feminism. *Signs, 36*(1), 71–98.

Collins, P. H. (1990). *Black feminist thought: Knowledge, consciousness, and the politics of empowerment.* New York, NY: Routledge.

Conley, T. D., & Ramsey, L. R. (2011). Killing us softly? Investigating portrayals of women and men in contemporary magazine advertisements. *Psychology of Women Quarterly, 35*(3), 469–478. doi:10.1177/0361684311413383

Constable, P. (2015, March 21). Women's groups campaign in D.C. to help victims of forced marriages. *Washington Post.* Retrieved from www.washingtonpost.com

Conway-Turner, K. (1999). Older women of color: A feminist exploration of the inter-sections of personal, familial and community life. *Journal of Women & Aging, 11*(2), 115–130. doi:10.1300/J074v11n02_09

Cooper, B. (2015). The women of #Blacklivesmatter [online magazine article]. *Ms. Magazine, Winter.* Retrieved from www.msmagazine.com/Winter2015/

Crenshaw, K. (1989). Demarginalizing the intersection of race and sex: A Black femi-nist critique of antidiscrimination doctrine, feminist theory, and antiracist politics. *University of Chicago Legal Forum, 1989,* 139–167.

Cuddy, A. J. C., Fiske, S. T., & Glick, P. (2004). When professionals become mothers, warmth doesn't cut the ice. *Journal of Social Issues, 60*(4), 701–718. doi:10.1111/j.0022-4537.20 04.00381.x

Datta, M. (Interviewer). (2003). *Interview with Flavia Agnes* [Video file]. Retrieved from umich.edu/~glblfem/en/index.html

Desmond-Harris, J. (2015, June 4). Study: Half of Black and Latina women scientists have been mistaken for admin or custodial staff. *Vox*. Retrieved from www.vox. com

Dill, B. T., & Zambrana, R. E. (Eds.). (2009). Critical thinking about inequality: An emerging lens. In B. T. Dill & R. E. Zambrana (Eds.), *Emerging intersections: Race, class, and gender in theory, policy, and practice* (pp. 1–21). New Brunswick, NJ: Rutgers.

Dobson, M. (2013, April 24). Intersectionality: A fun guide [Web log post]. Retrieved from beyondthesemountains.wordpress.com/

Donor Houston. (2014, February 25). *Hiding in plain sight: Human trafficking in Houston and pathways for greater impact* [Video file]. Retrieved from www.youtube.com/watc h?v=qTM7UpkNsec

Dusenbery, M. (2015, June). Quote of the day: Why "girl" scientists cause trouble in the lab [Web log post]. Retrieved from feministing.com

Eastwick, P. W., Eagly, A. H., Glick, P., Johannesen-Schmidt, M. C., Fiske, S. T., Blum, A. M. B., . . . Volpato, C. (2006). Is traditional gender ideology associated with sex-typed mate preferences? A test in nine nations. *Sex Roles, 54*, 603–614. doi:10.1007/s11199-006-902 7-x

Edewi, D. (2015, March 1). *Things Black men are tired of hearing* [Video file]. Retrieved from www.buzzfeed.com/dayshavedewi/that-is-not-who-i-am#.yrrn7Kyo5

Emslie, C., & Hunt, K. (2009). 'Live to work' or 'work to live'? A qualitative study of gender and work-life balance among men and women in mid-life. *Gender, Work and Organization, 16*(1), 151–172. doi:10.1111/j.1468-0432.2008.00434.x

Erich, S., Kanenberg, H., Case, K., Allen, T., & Bogdanos, T. (2009). An empirical analysis of factors affecting adolescent attachment in adoptive families with homosexual and straight parents. *Children and Youth Services Review, 31*, 398–404. doi:10.1016/ j.childyouth.2008 .09.004

Etaugh, C. A., & Bridges, J. S. (2013). *Women's lives: A psychological exploration* (3rd ed.). Boston, MA: Pearson Education.

Expósito, F., Herrera, M. C., Moya, M., & Glick, P. (2010). Don't rock the boat: Women's benevolent sexism predicts fears of marital violence. *Psychology of Women Quarterly, 34*, 36–42. doi:10.1111/j.1471-6402.2009.01539.x

Foster, K., & Sandel, M. (2010). Abuse of women with disabilities: Toward an empowerment perspective. *Sexuality and Disability, 28*, 177–186. doi:10.1007/s11195-010-9156-6

Gattuso, R. (2015a, May). Climate justice is intersectional feminism in action [Web log post]. Retrieved from feministing.com

Gattuso, R. (2015b, June). Intersectional justice: On intimate partner violence in queer communities [Web log post]. Retrieved from feministing.com

GLAAD. (2015, March 21). *Kerry Washington accepts the Vanguard Award at the #glaadawards* [Video file]. Retrieved from www.youtube.com/watch?v=ruv8As-_CMg

Global feminisms: Comparative case studies of women's activism and scholarship. (n.d.). Retrieved from umich.edu/~glblfem/en/index.html

Gordon, K. H., Castro, Y., Sitnikov, L., & Holm-Denoma, J. M. (2010). Cultural body shape ideals and eating disorder symptoms among White, Latina, and Black college women. *Cultural Diversity and Ethnic Minority Psychology, 16*(2), 135–143. doi:10.1037/a00186 71

Grabe, S. (Interviewer) & Baumgartner, J. (Interpreter). (2011a). *Interview with Matilde Lindo* [Video file]. Retrieved from umich.edu/~glblfem/en/ind ex.html

Grabe, S. (Interviewer) & Baumgartner, J. (Interpreter). (2011b). *Interview with Yamileth Mejía* [Video file]. Retrieved from umich.edu/~glblfem/en/ind ex.html

Greenwood, R. (this volume). Intersectionality foundations and disciplinary adaptations: Highways and byways. In K. A. Case (Ed.), *Intersectional pedagogy: Complicating identity and social justice* (pp. 27–45). New York, NY: Routledge.

Grimes, A. (2015, February 23). Patricia Arquette's spectacular intersectionality fail. *RH Reality Check.* Retrieved from rhrealitycheck.org

Grzanka, P. (this volume). Undoing the psychology of gender: Intersectional feminism and social science. In K. A. Case (Ed.), *Intersectional pedagogy: Complicating identity and social justice* (pp. 63–81). New York, NY: Routledge.

Halusic, M. (2015, May). The Black criminal, the sexy Latin, and the invisible Native: Media representations of ethnic and racial minorities remain problematic. *Psychology Today.* Retrieved from www.psychologytoday.com

Hebl, M. R., King, E. B., & Lin, J. (2004). The swimsuit becomes us all: Ethnicity, gender, and vulnerability to self-objectification. *Personality and Social Psychology Bulletin, 30*(10), 1322–1331. doi:10.1177/0146167204264052

Heldman, C., & Dirks, D. (2015, March 22). Blowing the whistle on campus rape [Web log post]. Retrieved from msmagazine.com

Jian, Z. (Interviewer). (2004). *Interview with Wang Xingjuan* [Video file]. Retrieved from umich.edu/~glblfem/en/index.html

Jian, Z. & Tong, S. (Interviewers). (2002). *Interview with Ge Youli* [Video file]. Retrieved from umich.edu/~glblfem/en/index.html

Johnson, A. (2014, May 25). What Hobby Lobby can mean for the LGBT community [Web log post]. Retrieved from www.huffingtonpost.com

Kellaway, M. (2015, March 6). Wellesley College opens its doors to transgender women. *Advocate.* Retrieved from www.advocate.com

Kirkland, Anna. (Interviewer). (2006). *Interview with Adrienne Asch* [Video file]. Retrieved from umich.edu/~glblfem/en/index.html

Krase, K. (2014, October 1). History of forced sterilization and current U.S. abuses. *Our Bodies Ourselves.* Retrieved from www.ourbodiesourselves.org

Kurtis, T., & Adams, G. (this volume). Deolonial intersectionality: Implications for theory, research, and pedagogy. In K. A. Case (Ed.), *Toward an intersectional pedagogy model: Engaged learning for social justice* (pp. 46–59). New York, NY: Routledge.

Leskinen, E. A., & Cortina, L. M. (2014). Dimensions of disrespect: Mapping and measuring gender harassment in organizations. *Psychology of Women Quarterly, 38*(1), 107–123. doi:10.1177/0361684313496549

Levitt, H. M., & Ippolito, M. R. (2014). Being transgender: The experience of transgender identity development. *Journal of Homosexuality, 61,* 1727–1758. doi:10.1080/00918369. 2014.951262

Livingston, J. A., Bay-Cheng, L. Y., Hequembourg, A. L., Testa, M., & Downs, J. S. (2012). Mixed drinks and mixed messages: Adolescent girls' perspectives on alcohol and sexuality. *Psychology of Women Quarterly, 37*(1), 38–50. doi:10.1177/036168431246420 2

Lorde, A. (1984). *Sister outsider: Essays and speeches.* Freedom, CA: Crossing Press.

Luna, Z. (Interviewer). (2006). *Interview with Loretta Ross* [Video file]. Retrieved from umich.edu/~glblfem/en/index.html

Lyle, J. (Interviewer). (2004). *Interview with Maureen Taylor & Marian Kramer* [Video file]. Retrieved from umich.edu/~glblfem/en/index.html

Maatz, L. (2014, July 3). What does the Hobby Lobby decision mean? [Web log post]. Retrieved from www.aauw.org

Matamonasa-Bennett, A. (2015). "A disease of the outside people": Native American men's perceptions of intimate partner violence. *Psychology of Women Quarterly, 39*(1), 20–36. doi:10.1177/0361684314543783

McCrayer, J. (2015, May). My feminism is Black, intersectional, and womanist—and I refuse to be left out of the movement. *Everyday Feminism.* Retrieved from everyday-feminis m.com/2015/05/black-womanist-feminism

McGuire, K., Stewart, A. J., & Curtin, N. (2010). Becoming feminist activists: Comparing narratives. *Feminist Studies, 36*(1), 99–125.

Moffat, S. (Writer.), & F. Blackburn (Director.) (2011). The doctor, the widow, and the wardrobe [television series episode]. In S. Moffat & C. Skinner (Producers), *Doctor Who.* United Kingdom: BBC.

Morrell, E. (2002). Toward a critical pedagogy of popular culture: Literacy development among urban youth. *Journal of Adolescent and Adult Literacy, 46*, 72–77.

Naber, N. (Interviewer). (2004). *Interview with Sista II Sista* [Video file]. Retrieved from umich.edu/~glblfem/en/index.html

Niles, E. (2015, June 10). McKinney and the history of policing Black women's bodies [Web log post]. Retrieved from msmagazine.com/blog

Oscars. (2015, March 9). *Patricia Arquette winning Best Supporting Actress* [Video file]. Retrieved from www.youtube.com/watch?v=6wx-Qh4Vczc

Pérez, M. Z. (2015, June 1). "No Más Bebés" exposes sterilization abuse against Latinas in L.A. *Colorlines.* Retrieved from www.colorlines.com/articles

Piela, O., & Wydrych, J. (Interviewers). (2004). *Interview with Anna Gruszczyńska* [Video file]. Retrieved from umich.edu/~glblfem/en/index.html

Pitney, N. (2015, May 8). Scientists find alarming deterioration in DNA of the urban poor. *Huffington Post.* Retrieved from www.huffingtonpost.com

Platt, L. F. (2013). Blazing the trail: Teaching the privileged about privilege. In K. A. Case (Ed.), *Deconstructing privilege: Teaching and learning as allies in the classroom* (pp. 207–222). New York, NY: Routledge.

Pliner, S. M., & Banks, C. A. (Eds.). (2012). *Teaching, learning, and intersecting identities in higher education* (1st ed.). New York, NY: Peter Lang.

Ptah, A. (2011, April 4). *Elaine Riddick's forced sterilization testimony* [Video file]. Retrieved from www.youtube.com/watch?v=cFJNX5bHYVI

Reed, S. J., Miller, R. L., & Timm, T. (2011). Identity and agency: The meaning and value of pregnancy for young Black lesbians. *Psychology of Women Quarterly, 35*(4), 571–581. doi:10.1177/0361684311417401

Rios, D., Bowling, M., & Harris, J. (this volume). Decentering student "uniqueness" in lessons about intersectionality. In K. A. Case (Ed.), *Intersectional pedagogy: Complicating identity and social justice* (pp. 194–213). New York, NY: Routledge.

Rios, D., & Stewart, A. J. (2013). Recognizing privilege by reducing invisibility: The Global Feminisms Project as a pedagogical tool. In K. A. Case (Ed.), *Deconstructing privilege: Teaching and learning as allies in the classroom* (pp. 115–131). New York, NY: Routledge.

Rodriguez, P. H. (2015, February 12). How the myth of the "ideal" survivor hurts campus anti-violence movements [Web log post]. Retrieved from www.blackgirl-dangerous.org

Sementelli, S., & Edelman, G. (2014, June 30). Texas conservatives laud court ruling on birth control. *Texas Tribune.* Retrieved from www.texastribune.org

Sengupta, R. (2006). Reading representations of Black, East Asian, and White women in magazines for adolescent girls. *Sex Roles, 54,* 799–808. doi:10.1007/s11199-006-9047-6

Shapiro, D. N., Rios, D., & Stewart, A. J. (2010). Conceptualizing lesbian sexual identity development: Narrative accounts of socializing structures and individual decisions and actions. *Feminism & Psychology, 20*(4), 491–510. doi:10.1177/095935 3509358441

Smoothiefreak. (2015, April 8). *On intersectionality and pizza* [Video file]. Retrieved from www.youtube.com/watch?v=FgK3NFvGp58

Stewart, A. J., Lal, J., & McGuire, K. (2011). Expanding the archives of Global Feminisms: Narratives of feminism and activism. *Signs, 36*(4), 889–914. doi:10.1086/658683

TEDx Talks. (2013a, April 12). *We should all be feminists: Chimamanda Ngozi Adichie* [Video file]. Retrieved from www.youtube.com

TEDx Talks. (2013b, October 29). *What is home? Sehba Sarwar at TEDxHouston* [Video file]. Retrieved from www.youtube.com

The Colbert Report. (Producer). (2011, August 11). *Gloria Steinem* [Video file]. Retrieved from www.cc.com/video-clips

Villanueva, C. M., & Buriel, R. (2010). Speaking on behalf of others: A qualitative study of the perceptions and feelings of adolescent Latina language brokers. *Journal of Social Issues, 66*(1), 197–210. doi:10.1111/j.1540-4560.2009.01640.x

Walczewska, S. & Iwasiow, I. (Interviewers). (2005). *Interview with Barbara Limanowska* [Video file]. Retrieved from umich.edu/~glblfem/en/ind ex.html

Wang, C. (2015, November 6). Update: This store lets women pay 66 cents to every man's dollar. *Refinery29*. Retrieved from www.refinery29.com/wage-gap-store#slide

Warner, L., & Ruggirello, J. (2015, March 28). *What it's like to be intersex* [Video file]. Retrieved from www.buzzfeed.com/lizzwarner

Wiley, S., Srinivasan, R., Finke, S., Firnhaber, J., & Shilinsky, A. (2012). Positive portrayals of feminist men increase men's solidarity with feminists and collective action intentions. *Psychology of Women Quarterly, 37*(1), 61–71. doi:10.1177/0361684312464575

Xueyu, G. (Interviewer). (2003). *Interview with Wang Cuiyu* [Video file]. Retrieved from umich.edu/~glblfem/en/index.html

Zheng, W., & Zhang, Y. (2010). Global concepts, local practices: Chinese feminism since the fourth UN Conference on Women. *Feminist Studies, 36*(1), 40–70. doi:10.2307/40607999

6

PEDAGOGICAL PRACTICE AND TEACHING INTERSECTIONALITY INTERSECTIONALLY

Nancy A. Naples

When I began teaching women's studies courses in the mid-1980s, many feminist scholars and teachers had become disillusioned with the rigidity of the theoretical constructions of feminisms that frequently contoured pedagogical approaches in women's studies as well as social movement scholarship on the women's movement.[1] In fact, the first course I taught on the sociology of gender was informed by frameworks such as liberal, Marxist, socialist, and radical feminisms. The clarity of the distinctions between them made it easy to teach. Each framework had a very different origin story, strategies for social change, and goals for social transformation. At the core of much of these debates were the ways these frameworks either disappeared race or class, as in liberal feminism, or centered one form of oppression over others, such as Marxist feminism or radical feminism. As Kim Case (this volume) describes in her introduction, the intervention of women of color in the U.S. context revealed the limits of feminist approaches that could not account for the power of white supremacy and racism to structure the experiences of all social actors. Their challenges were grounded in praxis, insights generated in the context of struggle, and therefore deepened the complexity of theoretical practice.

   In an effort to go beyond an additive approach to theorizing multiple oppressions, a bridging paradigm emerged in the form of standpoint epistemology. Rather than adding oppressions together as in white supremacist capitalist patriarchy, standpoint epistemologies argued for a materialist understanding of how knowledge derives from different social experiences and therefore influences perceptions of the social and political context (Naples, 2003). Debates arose around whether and to what extent different women's experiences were more or less privileged in accurately assessing the complex matrix of domination (Collins, 2000) or relations of ruling (Smith, 1990) that contoured different social locations. Intersectional feminism can be understood as a further effort to go beyond the additive approach but one that is more self-consciously derived from anti-racist praxis than many standpoint epistemologies with the exception, of course, of Collins's (2000) analysis of Black feminist thought.

For contemporary feminist studies scholars and teachers, intersectionality is one of the primary theoretical lenses through which women's studies is envisioned and taught. Many programs now situate their mission statements and pedagogical practice through an intersectional lens. As Wiegman (2012) noted, intersectionality is "repeatedly posited as both a core pedagogical tenant and a field-defining analytic and institutional goal" (p. 240) in women's studies programs and national organizations. In fact, she concluded, "it is no longer exaggeration to say that intersectionality circulates today as the primary figure of political completion in U.S. identity knowledge domains" (p. 240).

The ubiquity of intersectionality in feminist teaching and scholarship led some commentators to see it as a buzzword (Davis, 2008) that has lost its meaning as a powerful analytic term. Some critics are concerned that as intersectionality traveled across academic sites and disciplinary investments, a "tendency to treat intersectionality as a feminist account of identity . . . [and confusing] personal kinds of identity and structural identities" developed (Cooper, 2015, p. 4). Quoting Nash (2008), Cooper (2015) pointed to another problem in contemporary intersectional theorizing and argued that "'vectors of race, gender, and class, and sexuality,' are conflated with a discussion of remedying 'racism, sexism, and classism'" (p. 5). Another concern relates to debates over the centrality of Black women's experience to intersectional analyses. Cooper (2015) noted that because "Crenshaw constructed the intersectional proposition on the ground of black women's erasure in civil rights law, intersectionality has come to stand in as a kind academic and/or theoretical pronoun, whose antecedent is, or has at different turns been, black women, the black woman, and the black female experience" (p. 9). She explained that for some "feminist scholars . . . black women anchor intersectionality to a kind of particularity that seems difficult to overcome" (p. 10). While I cannot resolve these challenges to the utility of intersectionality approaches, I outline below a way to orient students to the diverse approaches with special attention to intersectional feminist praxis.

How intersectionality achieved such a central place in women's studies curriculum and scholarship reflects, on the one hand, "its lack of definition and analytic specificity" (Wiegman, 2012, p. 242) and its perceived power to resolve the tensions within and between different feminisms. If this is the case in some settings, then I see several significant problems for feminist pedagogy. First, the lack of definition and specificity and the wide-ranging ways intersectionality is defined by different scholars makes it very difficult to teach (Grzanka, this volume). Students come away more confused than before the course started if intersectionality has an endless array of definitions and intersections that occur everywhere and with no specific analytic focus. As Wiegman (2012) explained, "By posing itself as a counter to single-axis analysis, intersectionality pursues not only complexity but particularity, specifically through the critical location attributed to both black women and black feminism *and* in such a way that no configuration of identity as a constructed social relation of power and subordination is thought to be beyond its analytic reach" (p. 240).

Second, the tensions with and between different feminisms produced diverse insights into how inequality is constructed and reproduced and effective ways to challenge it in different settings. Third, the loss of a historical perspective on feminist praxis may result in intersectional theories disappearing other modes of theoretical engagement, even as intersectionality relies upon the analytic work of earlier feminist, critical race, and materialist feminist theories. As a fourth concern, I also wonder to what extent intersectionality can capture the ever-changing insights of queer and trans theories, if in fact, these perspectives should be brought into the frame.

Below, I take up the challenge of teaching intersectionality intersectionally. This effort examines the intellectual and activist history of the conceptualization of the term and the ways different scholar-activists adopted and reformulated it to analyze specific social phenomena and activist goals. I also offer a way to conceptualize the different approaches to intersectionality and conclude with a reflexive approach that retains the power of intersectionality as a feminist praxis.

The Changing Context for Teaching Intersectionality

Even before I had a word for it, the intersection of race, class, and gender as it shaped different women's experiences captured my intellectual imagination and activist energies. My dissertation project, along with almost every other research study I initiated since then, was informed by my desire to capture the complexity of social relations, experiences, inequalities, and structural dynamics that contour the diversity of women's lives, situated knowledges, and resistance strategies.

Not surprisingly, every course I teach is organized around an intersectional frame. When I first began teaching in the 1980s, I struggled to go beyond the additive approach of race, class, and gender that was dominant at the time to produce a more nuanced course outline (see also Case, this volume). As the term became popularized following Crenshaw's (1989) influential article, I sought to identify any research study or analysis that claimed intersectionality as the organizing frame or methodological approach to inform my syllabi. Fortunately, the number of feminist analyses using an intersectional frame has grown exponentially since the 1980s. It is now possible to chronicle a wide array of approaches to intersectionality that differ significantly by discipline, epistemology, methodology, and conceptualization.

Many of the scholars who have adopted intersectionality as a central analytic approach generated studies incorporating data from women of different racial-ethnic and class backgrounds as a way to advance their intersectional projects (see Naples, 1998). These scholars argued that incorporating an intersectional perspective forces a reconceptualization of their understanding of different conceptual frames. For example, Glenn, Chang, and Forcey (1994) contested the traditional constructions of mothering based on white, middle-class, nuclear family models (see James & Busia, 1993). My development of the conceptualization of *activist mothering* (Naples, 1992) and Abramovitz's (1988) analysis of the *family ethic* also reflected the power of intersectional analysis for reconfiguring notions of politics and family. Starting from the lives of Black women, Springer (2002) used an intersectional approach to contest the wave approach to women's movement activism in the U.S. By 2013, the application of intersectionality had moved beyond what I call the *embodied approach* to encompass social movement strategies and decolonizing methodologies (Chun, Lipsitz, & Shin, 2013). Intersectionality as a feminist framework also foregrounded a number of challenging critiques that raise important intellectual and activist dilemmas that I address below.

Teaching Theories of Intersectionality: Mapping a Course

Many of my graduate students have engaged in the challenging and sometimes elusive goal of designing and implementing intersectional research studies. They struggled, along with many of the anonymous authors whose manuscripts I reviewed over the years, to conceptualize and operationalize intersectionality. In many instances, their efforts fall short of their goals. Many realized that it is not enough to assert that one's study is intersectional. To succeed, a researcher must clearly specify what makes the study intersectional, discuss why certain methodologies chosen for the study are the most productive for intersectional research, and reflect on which aspects of intersectionality are brought into the frame and which are left out or treated less centrally in the analysis (Naples, 2003). Given the diversity of conceptualizations and disciplinary approaches, it is often difficult for new researchers to identify the most effective intersectional perspectives and models for their own research.

To facilitate my students' understanding and application of intersectionality, I constructed an interdisciplinary course that would highlight the diversity of approaches to intersectionality and attempt to map the field of intersectional studies. My goal was to help provide students with a roadmap for their own efforts to produce intersectional research. The course, Theories of Intersectionality, was designed to focus on how different scholars theorize, research, and analyze intersectionality. I considered the following questions in designing the course:

- What are the limits and possibilities of different disciplinary and interdisciplinary approaches to intersectionality for understanding and analyzing difference?
- How have social scientists taken up the call to intersectionality in their research?
- What types of methodologies are most effective for an intersectional analysis?
- How does intersectionality inform feminist praxis?

My course readings drew from the fields of law, policy studies, science studies, comparative historical research, disability studies, sexuality studies, and cultural studies. I also reviewed work by feminist scholars in social, cultural, and political geography, anthropology, sociology, economics, and political science. The resulting overview incorporated postcolonial, postmodern, and queer theoretical approaches as well as other epistemological approaches including Marxist and symbolic interactionist inspired studies.

In constructing the course, I made my own approach to intersectionality explicit. I began with the following assumption to guide my course development: an intersectional framework should attend to historical, cultural, discursive, and structural dimensions that contour the intersections of race, class, gender, sexuality, national, and religious identity, among other identities. In my view, the most powerful approaches to intersectionality examine the ways these interactions produce contradictions and tensions across various levels of analysis and dimensions of difference with the goal of producing insights for feminist praxis (e.g., Maynard, 1994). I used this conceptualization to guide my organization of the outline and identify readings to illustrate the weekly topics.

The call for intersectional analyses were first heard from feminists of color who critiqued approaches that constructed women's concerns without attention to the ways race, class, and sexuality inform the experiences of women. Early challenges to reductive feminist analyses are found in the analyses of: Johnnie Tillmon who organized ANC Mothers Anonymous, the welfare rights group in Los Angeles; the Combahee River Collective (1977/1997); and Angela Davis's (1983) now classic book *Women, Race, and Class*. I decided to open the course with the Combahee River Collective's (1977/1997) "A Black Feminist Statement" and other early articles, such as Anthias and Yuval-Davis's (1983) essay on "Contextualizing Feminism: Gender, Ethnic and Class Divisions," to demonstrate some of the origins of the concept in different geographic regions (see also Anthias & Yuval-Davis, 1992). I also assigned a more recent article by Brah and Phoenix (2004) to set the stage for discussion of an historical overview of the changing definitions and approaches to intersectionality.

The next class focused on defining intersectionality. Here, I wanted to include both early and more recent conceptualizations, keeping in mind regional differences as well as postcolonial interventions and philosophical debates. I used the following readings: Collins' (1998) "It's All in the Family: Intersections of Gender, Race, and Nation" and Crenshaw's (1991) "Mapping the Margins: Intersectionality, Identity Politics, and Violence against Women of Color." I also added Stephan's (1986/1996) "Race and Gender: The Role of Analogy in Science" and a more recent article by Yuval-Davis (2006) on "Intersectionality and Feminist Politics." Drawing on these readings, students considered:

- whether and in what ways the notion of intersectionality functioned as an analogy or metaphor;
- what intersectionality offered as a way of capturing the complexity of positionality and structural differences; and
- what other metaphors might prove more effective or more useful for different analytic purposes.

The class also contrasted the American and British approaches to intersectionality. For example, Prins (2006) argued that, in contrast to the U.S. model, the "British approach to intersectionality has adopted this more relational and dynamic view of power . . . [and] elaborated a constructionist interpretation of intersectionality" (p. 280).

After mapping the field, I recognized several major differences in emphases that differentiate approaches to intersectionality. Early work offered what I call an embodied or individual approach, emphasizing the ways women's social locations at the intersections of race, class, gender, and sexuality contour their lived experiences. Writings in this vein included analyses that theorized difference by race, class, and gender as they affect individual experiences, worldviews, and oppression. Subsequent work tended toward a relational approach and offered a more historical and regional variation on the earlier themes of difference. I found Glenn's (2004) *Unequal Freedom: How Race and Gender Shaped American Citizenship and Labor* most useful in illustrating these variations. While Glenn's study offered a powerful historical and regionally diverse lens through which to view intersectionality, I also introduced students to the more focused social constructionist methodology offered by Fenstermaker and West (2002) and the rich ethnographic case study by Bettie (2002) as examples of the significance of social interaction and context for shaping identity construction and intersections of race, class, and gender.

A third approach adopts a social structural stance toward intersectionality and typically draws on quantitative data. McCall (2001) used the construct *configurations of inequality* in her analysis of how "race, gender, and class intersect in a variety of ways depending on underlying economic conditions in local economies" (p. 6). She emphasized the importance of regional variation, an emphasis also featured in Glenn's (1992) historical analysis of gender, race, and class in three different regions of the U.S. While Glenn focused on the relationships between White women and women of color within interdependent labor contexts, McCall used quantitative data to examine the structure of inequality in the labor markets as they vary across different regions. McCall (2005) differentiated between anti-categorical and intra-categorical approaches to intersectionality. Finding both inadequate for her purposes, she offered a third strategy that she called *intercategorical*, which she applied to the new inequality within the American labor market. In her weekly memo, class member Jayme Schwartzman described the approach as follows:

> Following the directives of the intercategorical approach introduced by McCall, the analysis brought out in Complex Inequality (2001) empha-sizes the relationships of inequality that exist between social categories such as race, gender, and class and uses them as "anchor points" (McCall 2005: 1784–5) to further substantiate how they should be used as the focus of the analysis itself.

One class member, Jamie Gusrang, found McCall's approach one of the most valuable for her own research. As she explained, "inequality is an economic condition directly affected by a combination of race, class, and gender, [but] given the gaps in much of the (new) inequality literature, [McCall] pays par-ticular attention to gender in her work." Gusrang appreciated the effort to apply intersectional analysis to quantitative data. McCall's comparative method also revealed the importance of examining the intersection of race, class, and gender in a regional context.

Prins (2006) drew a distinction between systemic and constructionist approaches to intersectionality, both of which "adhere to an anti-essentialist view of identity" (p. 6). On the one hand, Prins (2006) argued that the systemic approach "upholds that the meanings of social identities are determined by racism, classism, sexism, etc., which are taken to be static and rigid systems of domination," thus ignoring "the agency of individual subjects by interpreting identity constructions as not only made and as such contingent, but as made by the powers-that-be and as such false" (p. 6). On the other hand, for constructionist approaches, "constructions of identity are not ideological distortions of a suppressed and authentic experience, but the (symbolic-material) effects of performative actions" (Butler, 1990, p. 6). However, a more effective approach to intersectionality requires a nuanced conceptualization of the relationship between systemic and constructionist processes.

Many scholars who adopted an intersectional perspective emphasized the interactional construction of power and oppression. For example, as former University of Connecticut graduate student Maura Kelly explained in her gender field exam:

> This tradition understands systems of oppression as grounded in relational power differentials. Men's domination is thus related to (and dependent upon) women's subordination and the status of poor women of color is

related to (and dependent upon) the status of affluent White women. Using a multi-lens approach or a race/gender/class approach allows researchers to understand consequential power differentials among women as well as those between women and men. Hence, this framework can help explain why women's common structural location as women is not sufficient for mobilization against gender inequalities.

Feminist work on intersectionality is often linked to standpoint epistemological frameworks with overlapping concerns with the construction of experience, politics, and epistemology. My own intersectional approach is especially indebted to Smith's (1987, 1990) institutional ethnographic methodology that avoids viewing women's embodied experiences as the endpoint of analysis and also resists reifying systems of oppressions, arguing instead for a contextualized and historicized angle of vision. Smith's (1987) formulation of the *relations of ruling* captures "the intersection of the institutions organizing and regulating society . . . [and] grasps power, organization, direction, and regulation as more pervasively structured than can be expressed in traditional concepts provided by the discourses of power" (p. 3).

In exploring the epistemological grounds for different intersectional perspectives, I conceptualized a fourth framework that, in my view, offers more analytic power than the other approaches in that it brings into view the multiple dimensions of intersectionality. This epistemological approach to intersectional analysis is rooted in insights from the different theoretical perspectives designed to analyze gender, race, and class inequalities as well as sexuality and culture. For example, within my intersectional research on social policy, citizenship, and community activism, I drew on materialist feminism, critical race theory, political economic theory, and queer theory (Naples, 1998). An epistemological view is also evident in the work of both Collins (2000) and Smith (1987, 1990). Collins's (2000) intersectional approach, which centered the construct of the matrix of domination, identified four dimensions of power woven together to contour Black women's social, political, and economic lives:

- a structural dimension (i.e., "how social institutions are organized to reproduce Black women's subordination over time" (Collins, 2000, p. 277);
- a disciplinary dimension, which highlights the role of the State and other institutions that rely on bureaucracy and surveillance to regulate inequalities;
- a hegemonic dimension, which deals with ideology, culture, and consciousness; and
- an interpersonal dimension, the "level of everyday social interaction" (Collins, 2000, p. 277).

Collins (2000) argued that by "manipulating ideology and culture, the hegemonic domain acts as a link between social institutions (structural domain), their organizational practices (disciplinary domain), and the level of everyday social interaction (interpersonal domain)" (p. 284).

Smith's (1987) approach to intersectionality incorporates historical, cultural, textual, discursive, institutional, and other structural dimensions that contour the intersections of race, class, gender, sexuality, national, and religious identity, among other social phenomena. She used the term *relations of ruling* to capture the ways these different dimensions shape everyday life. Her institutional ethnographic approach is especially powerful for revealing how interactions within and across these different dimensions of social life produce contradictions and tensions that can create the grounds for resistance and politicization.

In order to broaden the factors to be incorporated into an intersectional frame, I foregrounded disability and sexuality studies in my course. We read Smith and Hutchison's (2004) book, *Gendering Disability,* and Beckett's (2004) "Crossing the Border: Locating Heterosexuality as a Boundary for Lesbian and Disabled Women." Class member Michael Hardej found the focus on disability useful for his interest in issues of the body. As he explained in his weekly memo:

> By taking the disability framework and incorporating it into feminist critiques and more importantly using intersectionality the ability/disability binary can be problematized to further understand the body. Not just one monolithic body, but variations of the body that take into consideration issues of gender, sexuality, race and class. Bodies with disabilities show how genders can be rethought of and understood. When . . . a body . . . no longer works in [traditional ways in] a given capacity alternatives are formed. It is with these alternatives that gender is reinvented.

Furthermore, I wanted to make sure that our discussion of intersectionality included sensitivity to contemporary globalization as it influences conceptualizations of difference, feminisms, and positionalities. I found work by Kaplan (1994), Basu (1995), Kondo (1999), Stasiulis (1999), King (2002), and Mohanty (2003) offered useful introductions to the complexities associated with the interplay of local social formations and transnationalism. In this regard, I added a session on geography and intersectionality using readings from Staeheli, Kofman, and Peake's (2004) edited collection *Mapping Women, Making Politics: Feminism and Political Geography.* In their essay in the book, Wastl-Walter and Staeheli (2004) argued:

> As social powers, territory and boundaries are ways of enforcing ideas about who and what belongs in particular places and the kinds of activities and practices that belong to a place or are seen as being appropriate; as such, questions of identity and difference are critical to the ways in which territory and boundaries are constructed. (p. 141)

Class member Jayme Schwartzman explained that "apparent in this assertion is the malleability of boundaries and territories depending upon one's social location and position in 'the state.'" Feminist social geographers offered another angle of vision on intersectionality that destabilizes essentialist notions of identity as well as that of place and space.

Queer intersectional analyses also proved productive in that they destabilize fixed or binary approaches to gender, sexuality, and the body. For this intervention, I included publications by Butler (1994) and Currah (2006) whose scholarship has been especially useful in this regard. Given my own research on sexuality and migration, I included a session on gender, race, sexualities, and migration that featured analyses by Luibhéid (1998), Cantú (2000, 2001), and Manalansan (2006). In our introduction to *The Sexuality of Migration: Border Crossings and Mexican Immigrant Men* (Cantú, 2009), Vidal-Ortiz and I (2009) explained how Cantú takes up the insights from theories of political economy and migration and places them in dialogue with feminist and queer theories to produce a new framework for understanding the immigration of Mexican men who have sex with men:

> He complicates analyses of sexuality and gender, not merely with a gesture towards intersectionality – the simultaneous study of gender, sexuality, race and class – but by intentionally illustrating how migration is constitutive of sexuality and how sexuality is constitutive of migration and as such, formulating a distinctive kind of analysis. He refers to his approach as a queer materialist paradigm and his goal, that of producing a queer political economy of immigration. (Naples & Vidal-Ortiz, 2009, p. 9)

Class member Miho Iwata found that "queering of and incorporating sexualities in transnational migration studies clearly has potential to provide yet another dimension to the analysis and production of critical intersectional understanding" that "also challenges researchers to broaden the scope of their research."

I concluded the course with a discussion of methodology, featuring Haraway (1991) and Sandoval (2000). We also read Ken's (2008) article that offered an innovative use of a culinary metaphor for intersectional analyses. In her final memo for the course, class member Nikki McGary wrote:

> Crenshaw once suggested that we envision a traffic intersection in order to see how gender, race, and class literally intersect on bodies and have very real affects in terms of lived experiences. I have carried that analogy with me all semester. And as our readings deepened my understanding of intersectionality, the traffic intersection became increasingly [too] simple . . . too one-dimensional . . . Ivy Ken's analogy of sugar, however, does take it a step further. By looking at food, especially sugar, we are able to see how it is grown, processed, manufactured, consumed, and recycled.

In terms of the embodied intersectionality of social categories and lived realities, the analogy is useful when considering how complex social power relations are taught, maintained, consumed in the market, internalized and perpetuated. However, this approach focuses on the body and does not focus so much on the intersectionality of methodology. Instead, imagine a multidimensional star, with lines that have no beginning and no end and that the point where they intersect is the point of focus. These lines could represent embodied social categories (gender, sexuality, race, class, ability, "etc . . . ") or social systems (education, the family, law, disciplinary practices . . .) or academic disciplines and theorists (cultural theory, racialization theory, poststructuralism, Foucault, Fanon, Butler . . .). But then imagine that the point of focus can slide endlessly along any part of any line, making an infinite number of possible foci for intersectional research. What lines are selected for examination, the boundaries between the lines, locating invisiblized lines and where the lines meet becomes the methodological point of departure.

In response to concerns raised by class member Barbara Gurr, whose research focuses on Lakota women's prenatal care and childbirth (Gurr, 2014), I wove in readings throughout the course by scholars who analyzed Indigenous or Native women's positionality and political activism. In her final memo for the course, Gurr commented on Ross's (2005) essay, "Personalizing Methodology: Narratives of Imprisoned Native Women," which we read for the concluding session:

Ross hints at the complexity of Native identity at several points in her essay; yet at the same time, she seems to find a sense of solidarity with the Native women prisoners she describes, despite the variable "states" of their Native-ness (for instance, reservation, off-reservation, and non-reservation). Thus there seems to be a unity forged among Native women in the face of a common "enemy" (White people? The prison system? Colonization?) The cultural and historical production of "Native-ness" shared by both Ross and the Native prisoners seems to create community between them those non-Native prisoners and staff members cannot (or do not) access. Is this sense of community amongst these Native women, similar perhaps to a common "Black" identity, forgeable only in the face of a common oppositional force?

Ideally, in my view, intersectional studies should link analyses across different fields (Greenwood, this volume). Few scholars discuss how to place different intersectional approaches in dialogue with one another. In fact, I wish more scholars who assert an intersectional analysis for their work would make their methodology explicit.

Smith's (2005) institutional ethnographic approach offers one of the most powerful methodologies for intersectional research. Smith's (1987, 1990, 2005) focus on reflection, action, and accountability formed a core component of what I have come to identify as a fifth approach to intersectionality, *intersectional feminist praxis*. This form of intersectionality foregrounds the ways activism or experience shapes knowledge, an insight often lost when theoretical approaches are institutionalized in the academy. It also reflects the feminist praxis that gave rise to the concept and honors the fact that theory develops in a dialogic fashion from practice. Intersectional analyses require crossing many different kinds of borders including those drawn between academic disciplines, between academic feminism and feminist activism, and between local and transnational politics. From the point of view of praxis it is necessary to create stronger links between local organizing and transnational politics and, in turn, translate the political strategies and organizing frames generated on the transnational political stage to benefit local social and economic justice movements.

Each approach to intersectionality we examined during the course offered a different angle of vision on the complex processes, relationships, and structural conditions that shape everyday life, relations of ruling, and the resistance strategies of diverse actors. But much has changed in the field since then including within my own work on intersectionality. For example, other scholars have developed typologies that more or less map onto my own. Knowledge generated through praxis continues to inform the feminist project both within and outside of the academy. The challenge is to keep the reflexive process alive through intersectional practice in different arenas. This includes attending to ways of knowing both within and outside of the academy. For example, Choo and Ferree (2010) considered the challenge in multiple approaches to intersectionality as "group-centered, process-centered, and system-centered" (p. 130). The first approach aligns with Strid, Walby, and Armstrong's (2012) attention to "giving voice to the oppressed" (Choo & Ferree, 2010, p. 131). The second mirrors my discussion of "analytic intersections" (Choo & Ferree, 2010, p. 131), or what I call the social structural approach, both approaches using McCall (2001, 2005) as an illustration. The third foregrounds the differences in the extent to which researchers do or do not "give *institutional primacy* to one or more sites for producing social inequalities" (Choo & Ferree, 2010, p. 131). Following an overview of the different approaches, Choo and Ferree concluded with a call for a complex intersectional approach.

Intersectional Feminist Praxis

In my review of different academic categorizations or differentiations of intersectionality, I was struck by the lack of attention to praxis as a central component. I then shifted attention to case studies informed by feminist praxis to explore the extent to which intersectionality was a central frame in the analysis.

Five dimensions surfaced in the shift from understanding intersectionality as an analytic framework to becoming more self-reflexively focused on social change. Some of these dimensions are evident in previously discussed approaches such as the embodied and relational approaches. The first dimension follows from the standpoint epistemological understanding that "the intersection of diverse social experiences . . . produce different ways of knowing" (Naples, 2013, p. 661). This also evokes a second dimension, the recognition that these knowledges are further deepened in community and dialogue.

Others dimensions are explicitly action-oriented such as "empowerment for activism" (Naples, 2013, p. 661), a third feature of intersectional feminist praxis. As I explained, "empowerment for activism underscores the significance of community and the availability of safe spaces for providing the context in which individuals can critically reflect on their experiences and political strategies in dialogue with others" (Naples, 2013, p. 661). This dimension of intersectional feminist praxis has a long history that evokes the work of Freire (1970/2000) and is evident in the feminist consciousness-raising groups of the 1970s. However, attention to race, class, and other structures of difference and power that Collins (2000) and Springer (2002) detailed in their Black feminist approaches were missing in these previous formulations.

A fourth dimension that informs intersectional feminist praxis is "placing in dialogue situated knowledges generated in multiple social locations by diverse social actors for generating collaborative strategies for action" (Naples, 2013, p. 662). This dimension captures the process by which local actors come into association with others who are, at times, far from their social positions and geographic locations (see also Young, 1990). In intersectional feminist praxis, the central role of the collaborative deliberative process of knowledge production is to generate strategies to inform collective active to challenge inequality and other social justice efforts. These actions are then reflected on though the participatory and deliberative process to inform subsequent social justice activism.

Collaborative deliberative practice is illustrated in Sharma's (2008) rich case study that demonstrated the challenges and possibilities of intersectional feminist praxis. Sharma's study brought the state back in and helped students understand the contradictions of feminist praxis as it engages with state-supported community action. The angle of vision offered by Sharma resurfaced a central concern of Crenshaw's (1989) in her analysis of Black women as plaintiffs in discrimination cases in the U.S. Using court cases, Crenshaw (1989) illustrated how race and gender were understood as separable facets of Black women's cases. Instead, she argued, an intersectional approach challenges the basic premise by which these cases are heard and resolved. Here it is important to point out the central goal of intersectional analyses, namely, to inform social activism and policy.

Strid et al. (2012) further examined the contradictory processes by which feminists engage with the state. They examined the extent to which multiple intersecting inequalities became visible in three different policy arenas: sexual violence, domestic violence, and forced marriage. Strid et al. (2012) conceptualized visibility of diverse inequalities ranging "from the simple naming of inequalities to a substantive recognition of intersectionality that has an effect on the policy outcome" (p. 565). The most robust inclusion of women's voices occurred in the construction of policy against forced marriage. Analysis of domestic violence policy also revealed a strong process of inclusion and increased visibility. Within the policy debates on sexual violence, intersectional inequalities were named but "the connection between inequalities and how they work structurally through intersecting fields and intersecting policy domains" remained invisible (Strid et al., 2012, p. 559). Strid and colleagues challenged "the assumption that visibility necessarily equates with recognition and voice, or that invisibility means a lack of inclusion and intersectionality" (p. 574). Strid et al. concluded that:

> For empirical analysis, the understanding that inequalities are interconnected but can simultaneously be named separately and distinguished is very important. This means that the relation between multiple inequalities is theorized as one that is mutually shaping rather than as either additive or mutually constituted. (p. 575)

Intersectional methodological practice is also a central concern of Choo and Ferree's (2010) analysis. Choo and Ferree argued for developing methods to study "multiple and intersection hierarchies more relationally . . . [and] call for critical understandings of the workings of the discourses and networks where power circulates throughout societal institutions at different 'scales'" (p. 147). Their goal was to promote a more robust intersectional sociological methodology. Although they did not start and end in praxis, implicit in their analysis was the goal of fostering research that provides better understanding of how inequality is produced and sustained. With such knowledge, it is possible to consider more effective interventions. In this way, Choo and Ferree shared an implicit praxis goal that Strid et al. (2012) made more explicit.

Conclusion

The institutionalization of intersectionality in the academy led to a displacement of praxis as the central force driving its articulation. However, intersectional feminist praxis continues to inform social justice activism and, in this way, has the potential to reinvigorate academic approaches (e.g., Dessel & Cordivae, this volume; Rios, Bowling, & Harris, this volume). Hewitt (2011) emphasized the importance of intersectional feminist praxis in transnational social justice activism. Feminist insights highlight the importance of generating processes to create and sustain "egalitarian, horizontal, and intersectional modes of working and thinking" (Hewitt, 2011, p. 88). Intersectional feminist praxis includes drawing insights from diverse social movements to further enrich complex under-standings of how power works and can be resisted in different contexts. As I noted, "lessons from anti-racist, anti-colonial, and anti-capitalist struggles and campaigns for LBGT and disabilities rights have been incorporated into intersec-tional feminist praxis and have also informed activism within these movements" (Naples, 2013, p. 674). For example, Crass (2013) analyzed the powerful soli-darity work of feminists and anti-racist organizers, Wappett (2002) detailed the significance of feminist praxis for disabilities rights activism, and Moghadam, Franzway, and Fonow (2011) explored the effective interventions of feminists and LGBT activists in the labor movement. Queer interventions have been especially powerful for interrupting the complacency of intersectional feminist approaches. For example, Currier (2012) demonstrated the importance of queer perspectives for intersectional feminist praxis. As I explained,

> Currier's rich historical and ethnographic comparative account cautions against positing intersectional feminist praxis as a decontextualized and abstracted political methodology, and, in and of itself, a solution to the contradictions and divisions that plague social justice organizing. (Naples, 2013, pp. 674–675)

Taken together, different intersectional approaches provide a powerful analytic lens through which scholars can uncover what Grewal and Kaplan (1994) termed the *scattered hegemonies* that differentially structure everyday lives. However, without making explicit its epistemological grounds, methodological strategies, and implications for praxis, feminist research will fail to achieve the promise of intersectionality. Feminist teachers have the opportunity to share the history, context, and complexity of intersectional approaches as they function within an ongoing feminist praxis designed to identify and challenge social inequalities and achieve social justice.

Note

1 A previous version of this chapter was published as: Naples, N. (2009). Teaching intersectionality intersectionally. *International Feminist Journal of Politics, 11*, 566–577. Reprinted by permission of the publisher (Taylor & Francis Ltd, www.tandfon line.com). The current version was altered to reflect APA style and formatting, update citations and information, and connect with the broader edited volume.

References

Abramovitz, M. (1988). *Regulating the lives of women: Social welfare policy from colonial times to the present*. Boston, MA: South End Press.
Anthias, F., & Yuval-Davis, N. (1983). Contextualizing feminism: Gender, ethnic, and class divisions. *Feminist Review, 15*, 62–75.

Anthias, F., & Yuval-Davis, N. (1992). *Racialized boundaries: Race, nation, gender, colour, and class and the anti-racist struggle.* London, UK: Routledge.

Basu, A. (1995). *The challenge of local feminisms: Women's movements in global perspective.* Boulder, CO: Westview Press.

Beckett, C. (2004). Crossing the border: Locating heterosexuality as a boundary for lesbian and disabled women. *Journal of International Women's Studies, 5*(3), 44–52.

Bettie, J. (2002). *Women without class: Girls, race, and identity.* Berkeley, CA: University of California Press.

Brah, A., & Phoenix, A. (2004). Ain't I a woman: Revisiting intersectionality. *Journal of International Women's Studies, 5*(3), 75–86.

Butler, J. (1990). *Gender trouble: Feminism and the subversion of identity.* New York, NY: Routledge.

Butler, J. (1994). More gender trouble: Feminism meets queer theory. *Differences: A Journal of Feminist Cultural Studies, 6,* 1–26.

Cantú, L. (2000). Entre hombres/between men: Latino masculinities and homosexualities. In P. Nardi (Ed.), *Gay masculinities* (pp. 224–246). Thousand Oaks, CA: Sage.

Cantú, L. (2001). A place called home: A queer political economy of Mexican immigrant men's family experiences. In M. Bernstein & R. Reimann (Eds.), *Queer families, queer politics: Challenging culture and state* (pp. 112–136). New York, NY: Columbia University Press.

Cantú, L. (2009). *The sexuality of migration: Border crossings and Mexican immigrant men.* N. A. Naples & S. Vidal Ortiz (Eds.). New York, NY: New York University Press.

Case, K. A. (this volume). Toward an intersectional pedagogy model: Engaged learning for social justice. In K. A. Case (Ed.), *Intersectional pedagogy: Complicating identity and social justice* (pp. 1–24). New York, NY: Routledge.

Choo, H. Y., & Ferree, M. M. (2010). Practicing intersectionality in sociological research: A critical analysis of inclusions, interactions, and institutions in the study of inequalities. *Sociological Theory, 28*(2), 129–149.

Chun, J. J., Lipsitz, G., & Shin, Y. (2013). Intersectionality as a social movement strategy: Asian immigrant women advocates. *Signs, 38*(4), 917–940.

Collins, P. H. (1998). It's all in the family: Intersections of gender, race and nation. *Hypatia, 13*(3), 62–82.

Collins, P. H. (2000). *Black feminist thought: Knowledge, consciousness, and the politics of empowerment* (2nd ed.). New York, NY: Routledge.

Combahee River Collective. (1997). A Black feminist statement. In L. Nicholson (Ed.), *The second wave: A reader in feminist theory* (pp. 63–70). New York, NY: Routledge. (Original work published in 1977)

Cooper, B. (2015). Intersectionality. In L. Disch & M. Hawkesworth (Eds.), The *Oxford handbook of feminist theory.* doi:10.1093/oxfordhb/9780199328581.013.20

Crass, C. (2013). *Towards collective liberation: Anti-racist organizing, feminist praxis, and movement building strategy.* Oakland, CA: PM Press.

Crenshaw, K. (1989). Demarginalizing the intersection of race and sex: A Black feminist critique of antidiscrimination doctrine, feminist theory, and antiracist politics. *University of Chicago Legal Forum, 1989,* 139–167.

Crenshaw, K. (1991). Mapping the margins: Intersectionality, identity politics, and violence against women of color. *Stanford Law Review, 43*(6), 124–199.

Currah, P. (2006). Gender pluralisms under the transgender umbrella. In P. Currah, R. M. Juang, & P. S. Minter (Eds.), *Transgender Rights* (pp. 3–31). Minneapolis, MN: University of Minnesota Press.

Currier, A. (2012). *Out in Africa: LGBT organizing in Namibia and South Africa*. Minneapolis, MN: University of Minnesota Press.

Davis, A. (1983). *Women, race, and class*. New York, NY: Random House.

Davis, K. (2008). Intersectionality as buzzword: A sociology of science perspective on what makes a feminist theory successful. *Feminist Theory, 9*, 67–85.

Dessel, A., & Corvidae, T. (this volume). Experiential activities for engaging intersectionality in social justice pedagogy. In K. A. Case (Ed.), *Intersectional pedagogy: Complicating identity and social justice* (pp. 214–231). New York, NY: Routledge.

Fenstermaker, S., & West, C. (2002). *Doing gender, doing difference: Inequality, power, and institutional change*. New York, NY: Routledge.

Freire, P. (1970/2000). *Pedagogy of the oppressed*. New York, NY, USA: Continuum.

Glenn, E. N. (1992). From servitude to service work: Historical continuities in the racial division of paid reproductive labor. *Signs, 18*(1), 1–43.

Glenn, E. N. (2004). *Unequal freedom: How race and gender shaped American citizenship and labor*. Cambridge, MA: Harvard University Press.

Glenn, E. N., Chang, G., & Forcey, L. R. (Eds). (1994). *Mothering: Ideology, experience, and agency*. New York, NY: Routledge.

Greenwood, R. (this volume). Intersectionality foundations and disciplinary adaptations: Highways and byways. In K. A. Case (Ed.), *Intersectional pedagogy: Complicating identity and social justice* (pp. 27–45). New York, NY: Routledge.

Grewal, I., & Kaplan, C. (Eds). (1994). *Scattered hegemonies: Postmodernity and transnational feminist practices*. Minneapolis, MN: University of Minnesota Press.

Grzanka, P. (this volume). Undoing the psychology of gender: Intersectional feminism and social science pedagogy. In K. A. Case (Ed.), *Intersectional pedagogy: Complicating identity and social justice* (pp. 63–81). New York, NY: Routledge.

Gurr, B. (2014). *Reproductive justice: The politics of health care for Native American women*. New Brunswick, NJ: Rutgers University Press.

Haraway, D. (1991). *Simians, cyborgs and women: The revinvention of nature*. London, UK: Free Association Books.

Hewitt, L. (2011). Framing across differences, building solidarities: Lessons from women's rights activism in transnational spaces. *Interface: A Journal for and about Social Movements, 3*(2), 65–99.

James, S. M., & Busia, A. P. A. (1993). *Theorizing Black feminism: The visionary pragmatism of Black women*. New York, NY: Routledge.

Kaplan, C. (1994). The politics of location as transnational feminist critical practice. In I. Grewal & C. Kaplan (Eds.), *Scattered hegemonies: Postmodernity and transnational feminist practices* (pp. 137–152). Minneapolis, MN: University of Minnesota Press.

Ken, I. (2008). Beyond the intersection: A new culinary metaphor for race-class-gender studies. *Sociological Theory, 26*(2), 152–172.

King, K. (2002). "There are no lesbians here": Lesbianisms, feminisms, and global gay formations. In A. Cruz-Malave & M. F. Manalansan (Eds.), *Queer globalizations: Citizenship and the afterlife of colonialism* (pp. 33–48). New York, NY: New York University Press.

Kondo, D. (1999). Fabricating masculinity: Gender, race, and nation in a transnational frame. In C. Kaplan, N. Alarcon, & M. Moallem (Eds.), *Between woman and nation: Nationalisms, transnational feminisms, and the state* (pp. 296–319). Durham, NC: Duke University Press.

Luibhéid, E. (1998). "Looking like a lesbian": The organization of sexual monitoring at the United States-Mexican border. *Journal of the History of Sexuality, 8*(3), 477–506.

Manalansan, M. F. (2006). Queer intersections: Sexuality and gender in migration studies. *International Migration Review, 40*(1), 224–249.

Maynard, M. (1994). "Race," gender, and the concept of "difference" in feminist thought. In H. Afshar & M. Maynard (Eds.), *The dynamics of race and gender* (pp. 9–25). London, UK: Taylor & Francis.

McCall, L. (2001). *Complex inequality: Gender, class, and race in the new economy.* New York, NY: Routledge.

McCall, L. (2005). The complexity of intersectionality. *Signs, 30*(3), 1771–1800.

Moghadam, V. M., Franzway, S., & Fonow, M. M. (Eds.). (2011). *Making globalization work for women: The role of social rights and trade union leadership.* Albany, NY: State University of New York Press.

Mohanty, C. T. (2003). *Feminism without borders: Decolonizing theory, practicing solidarity.* Durham, NC: Duke University Press.

Naples, N. A. (1992). Activist mothering: Cross-generational continuity in the community work of women from low-income communities. *Gender & Society, 6*(3), 441–463.

Naples, N. A. (1998). *Grassroots warriors: Activist mothering, community work, and the war on poverty.* New York, NY: Routledge.

Naples, N. A. (2003). *Feminism and method: Ethnography, discourse analysis, and activist research.* New York, NY: Routledge.

Naples, N. A. (2013). Sustaining democracy: Localization, globalization, and feminist praxis. *Sociological Forum, 28*(4), 657–681.

Naples, N. A., & Vidal-Ortiz, S. (Eds.). (2009). Introduction. In L. Cantú, *The sexuality of migration: Border crossings and Mexican immigrant men* (pp. 1–20). N. A. Naples & S. Vidal-Ortiz (Eds.). New York, NY: New York University Press.

Nash, J. C. (2008). Re-thinking intersectionality. *Feminist Review, 89,* 1–15.

Prins, B. (2006). Narrative accounts of origins: A blind spot in the intersectional approach? *European Journal of Women's Studies, 13*(3), 227–290.

Rios, D., Bowling, M., & Harris, J. (this volume). Decentering student "uniqueness" in lessons about intersectionality. In K. A. Case (Ed.), *Intersectional pedagogy: Complicating identity and social justice* (pp. 194–213). New York, NY: Routledge.

Ross, L. (2005). Personalizing methodology: Narratives of imprisoned Native women. In I. Hernandez-Avila, J. Barker, G. Bird, V. Bomberry, M. C. Churchill, E. Cook-Lynn, . . . H. J. Tsinhnahjinnie, (Eds.), *Reading Native American women: Critical/creative representations* (pp. 39–62). Lanham, MD: AltaMira Press.

Sandoval, C. (2000). *Methodology of the oppressed.* Minneapolis, MN: University of Minnesota Press.

Sharma, A. (2008). *Logics of empowerment: Development, gender, and governance.* Minneapolis, MN: University of Minnesota Press.

Smith, D. E. (1987). *The everyday world as problematic: A feminist sociology.* Toronto, Canada: University of Toronto Press.

Smith, D. E. (1990). *The conceptual practices of power: A feminist sociology of knowledge.* Boston, MA: Northeastern University Press.

Smith, D. E. (2005). *Institutional ethnography: A sociology for people.* Lanham, MD: AltaMira Press.

Smith, B. G., & Hutchison, B. (2004). *Gendering disability.* New Brunswick, NJ: Rutgers University Press.

Springer, K. (2002). Third wave Black feminism? *Signs, 27*(4), 1059–1082.

Staeheli, L. A., Kofman, E., & Peake, L. (Eds). (2004). *Mapping women, making politics: feminism and political geography.* New York, NY: Routledge.

Stasiulis, D. K. (1999). Relational positionalities of nationalisms, racisms, and feminisms. In C. Kaplan, N. Alarcon, & M. Moallem (Eds.), *Between woman and nation: Nationalisms, transnational feminisms, and the state* (pp. 182–218). Durham, NC: Duke University Press.

Stephan, N. L. (1996). Race and gender: The role of analogy in science. In E. F. Keller & H. E. Longino (Eds.), *Feminism and science* (pp. 121–136). Oxford, UK: Oxford University Press. (Original work published in 1986)

Strid, S., Walby, S., & Armstrong, J. (2012). Intersectionality and multiple inequalities: Visibility in British policy on violence against women. *Social Politics, 20*(4), 558–581.

Wappett, M. (2002). Self-determination and disability rights: Lessons from the women's movement. *Journal of Disability Policy Studies, 13*(2), 119–124.

Wastl-Walter, D., & Staeheli, L. A. (2004). Territory, territoriality, and boundaries. In L. A. Staeheli, E. Kofman, & L. Peake (Eds.), *Mapping women, making politics: Feminism and political geography* (pp. 141–152). New York, NY: Routledge.

Wiegman, R. (2012). *Object Lessons.* Durham, NC: Duke University Press.

Young, I. M. (1990). The ideal of community and the politics of difference. In L. J. Nicholson (Ed.), *Feminism/postmodernism* (pp. 300–323). New York, NY: Routledge.

Yuval-Davis, N. (2006). Intersectionality and feminist politics. *European Journal of Women's Studies, 13*(3), 193–209.

7

TEACHING INTERSECTIONAL PSYCHOLOGY IN RACIALLY DIVERSE SETTINGS

Kim A. Case and Michele K. Lewis

Teaching "lesbian, gay, bisexual and transgender" (LGBT) psychology using an intersectional pedagogical approach provides several advantages to enhance student learning. This reflection[1] documents the benefits and challenges of critical liberatory feminist pedagogy and the intersectional framework used in teaching two courses: (a) Black Issues in LGBT Psychology and (b) Psychology of Gender, Race, and Sexuality. Taught in the context of a historically Black university (originally developed for disenfranchised people of African descent in the United States; see Hall, this volume) and a Hispanic-serving institution (universities with 25% or more Hispanic student population and officially recognized by the Hispanic Association of Colleges and Universities), respectively, the intersectional theoretical approach offered integration of students' privileged and marginalized identities with their learning about LGBT psychology.

Critical Liberatory Feminist Pedagogy

Developed by Paulo Freire (1970/2000), critical consciousness (or *conscientização*) produces "deepening of the attitude of awareness" (p. 109) as the oppressed recognize their own abilities as social change agents. Further popularized by priest and scholar Ignacio Martin-Baro (1996) within a framework of liberation psychology, critical consciousness motivates people into action against oppressive forces within their lives stemming from an increased awareness and understanding of the negative and limiting social factors within a community. Within the classroom, this approach promotes a learning process that encourages students' critical analysis of multiple realities as well as co-creation of knowledge. Expanding on Freire's concept, Lather (1998) described critical pedagogy as emphasizing empowerment of marginalized student populations including antiracist, feminist, and queer pedagogies. Critical theory acknowledges that educational systems, the process of knowledge building, and knowledge itself can never achieve objectivity, but instead are social constructions "deeply rooted in a nexus of power relations" (McLaren, 2003, p. 72).

Critical feminist pedagogical research examines an assortment of classroom strategies and innovations, developed within historic sites of oppression from around the world, to promote transformational learning (Bohmer, 1998; Deay & Stitzel, 1998; Hase, 2002; Maher, 1998; McKenna, 2003; Naples, 2002; Sanchez-Casal, 2002; Short, 2002; Sinacore & Boatwright, 2005) appropriate for application to teaching LGBT psychology. In addition, Moane (2003), writing within and about the Irish context of both conflict and colonialism, cites concentration on the collective, emphasis on structural levels of oppression, and analysis of internalized oppression as benefits of liberation psychology. Given the emphasis of feminist, critical, and liberation pedagogies on asymmetrical power, empowerment, structural change, and reflection, we incorporated these approaches, labeled by Case, Kanenberg, Erich, and Tittsworth (2012) as "critical liberatory feminist psychology," into designing LGBT psychology courses taught at a historically Black university and a Hispanic-serving institution with a racially diverse student population.

Learning through an Intersectional Lens

Work by Greene (2000, 2005), Sue (1996), and Sue and Sue (2008) not only called for culturally competent clinical practices and transformative curricular content, promoting such competencies within counseling programs, but also influenced psychology education more broadly. In terms of curriculum design, psychology as a field now typically includes courses focused on "women" or "gender" as well as race, nationality, and ethnicity, usually labeled as "multicultural" or "cross-cultural" psychology. With the widespread addition of gender-focused courses, the psychology curriculum began to challenge the traditional androcentric models in favor of incorporating women's lived experience and voices that were previously neglected into course materials. Much less common are courses or infused curricular content devoted to sexual orientation, gender identity, or both (Case, Stewart, & Tittsworth, 2009; Goldfried, 2001; Greene & Croom, 2000; Neumann, 2005; Simoni, 2000; Weinstock, 2003). Within psychology programs offering such courses, common titles such as LGBT Psychology and The Psychology of Sexual Orientation indicate a targeted focus on LGBT content. As more psychology courses focus on LGBT content, the marginalized group's experience becomes the central focus of the curriculum and assumptions of heteronormativity are challenged. Although entire courses devoted to LGBT psychology provide space for advancing student learning in a neglected area of psychology, teaching LGBT psychology from an intersectional framework offers pedagogical avenues for complicating dichotomous notions and assumptions (Case, this volume; Rivera, this volume). As noted by Greene (2000), "heterosexism is not a singular or isolated experience" (p. 2) and must be studied with attention to the complexities of sexism, race, class, and other influential aspects of identity. Use of an intersectional pedagogical design is supported by research that extensively examined intersectional invisibility as manifest within multiple subordinate group identities (Purdie-Vaughns & Eibach, 2008). This provides rationale for teaching LGBT psychology with an aim of reducing common perceptions such as gay individuals being predominantly White and male-identified (Bérubé, 2001; Rivera, this volume).

Application of Intersectional Critical Liberatory Feminist Pedagogy

In developing and teaching the two courses described here, each instructor made pedagogical decisions through an intersectional and critical liberatory feminist lens. Black Issues in LGBT Psychology, an undergraduate course at a historically Black university, provided students with LGBT content while connecting identity intersections such as their own racial backgrounds. A graduate-level course at a Hispanic-serving institution, Psychology of Gender, Race, and Sexuality, required students from diverse backgrounds to connect personal identity intersections with LGBT psychology. Reflecting on the student learning successes and obstacles within the two courses, the instructors considered the implications of using intersectional pedagogy for enhancing LGBT psychology courses among marginalized and privileged student populations.

University and Sociocultural Context

Research documenting the experiences of Black and Hispanic students at historically Black, Hispanic-serving, tribal (developed by and for indigenous peoples in the United States and built on culturally relevant curriculum and pedagogy), and majority of White universities (numerical majority of the student population is White) emphasize student success rates and call for further investigation of the factors affecting academic achievement (Allen, 1992; Crosnoe, 2005; Cross & Astin, 1981; Kim & Conrad, 2006). Scholars have also called for culturally relevant curricular developments (Cole, 2006) and attention to intersectional perspectives such as Bonner's (2001) study of gender at historically Black colleges and universities. This research focuses on culturally relevant, intersectional LGBT psychology at a historically Black university and a Hispanic-serving institution.

Winston Salem State University (WSSU) has an active student advocacy organization which focuses on LGBT and allied concerns that was formed in 2008. The university also included non-discrimination against sexual minorities in its policy as of 2009. However, at the time of the course offering discussed here, neither WSSU nor any other historically Black university in the United States had offered a course examining LGBT issues from an intersectional approach or otherwise. Due to staunch religiosity within the geographical region and the relative lack of open engagement of LGBT issues within the university and among the area's Black community, documenting the successes and failures of the pedagogy and content of a Black LGBT focused seminar is significant.

Black Issues in LGBT Psychology, as a cultural study in liberation psychology, developed as an undergraduate liberal learning seminar to teach critical thinking and critical reading within a cultural context of limited open and formal discussion of such issues. The hypothesis was that critical consciousness or conscientization would be enhanced among the students concerning marginality for same gender loving and gender non-conforming people of African descent.

The University of Houston-Clear Lake (UHCL) adapted the university non-discrimination statement to include sexual orientation in the mid-1990s, but not gender identity. This meant that discrimination based on sexual orientation was banned at the university, protecting LGB students and employees, without the same policy protections for transgender individuals. A student-centered advocacy campaign to add gender identity to that policy passed through shared governance and student council, and was eventually approved by the President in 2006. After years of advocacy work (Case, Kanenberg, et al., 2012), in 2013, the university system added gender identity and expression to the non-discrimination statement. The campus also offers several LGBT-affirming programs and resources. The "gay-straight alliance" student organization was founded in 1993 and continues to grow. In 2009, the university hired a staff member to coordinate women's and LGBT resources programming. An active "Safe Zone" program provides training and safe space posters on office doors. The goal of the program is to educate campus staff, faculty, administrators, and students about the concerns of LGBT students and create a more welcoming educational environment. The program coordinator also supplies the campus culture with speakers, programs, and displays for National Coming Out Day, the Transgender Day of Remembrance, the Day of Silence, and many more annual events. Therefore, the university culture provides many welcoming and affirming cues to LGBT students.

Despite the resources, programs, and Safe Zone success, the curricular landscape continues to face challenges. Although courses with an exclusive focus on sexual orientation, gender identity, or a combination of LGBT issues have yet to be taught, several faculty in human sciences, humanities, and education incorporate LGBT content into both core and diversity courses. Given that Texas is well-known as a conservative state, legislation often threatens to limit the effectiveness of higher education to raise awareness of LGBT issues. For example, the 2011 state legislature attempted to pass a law limiting each state university's ability to fund LGBT resource centers unless they provide equal funding to "traditional and family values" centers.

Complicating Identity Assumptions: Course Pedagogical Structure

Black Issues in LGBT Psychology

Principles of critical consciousness and liberation psychology were used in the pedagogy for delivering a liberal learning seminar (Garnett, 2009). The subject matter of the seminar focused on the relative invisibility of Black LGBT people. A goal was to develop students' critical consciousness regarding LGBT marginalization within their cultural context. Students were provided access to reading and audio-visual materials and expected to challenge assumptions, ask questions, and express academic freedom in the pursuit of their learning, which was to be free from criticism, intimidation, or ridicule from the professor and others in the class (Garnett, 2009). Although critical thinking and critical reading were student learning goals, I (Michele) also expected that conscientization would be achieved with students via the various assignments.

Students were not to be assessed on their learning of course content, but instead their progress in critical thinking and critical reading using LGBT people of African descent as the focus. The learning outcomes for the Black Issues in LGBT Psychology seminar were assessed by students' performance on four short reports: (1) the concept of liberation psychology, (2) their analyses of theoretically relevant poetry, narratives, and websites, (3) students' brief campus research studies, and (4) designing a short assessment about gender conformity. The students were also expected to demonstrate progress in critical thinking and critical reading via their writing of two major reports after: (1) listening to an in-class panel discussion and (2) designing questions based on the content of a 27-minute independent film shown in class. Research has highlighted the relationship between reading comprehension, critical thinking, and cognitive ability in first-year students (Farley & Elmore, 1992). Assignments also related to an initial assigned reading about liberation psychology (Moane, 2003). All assignments related to the culture, marginalization, oppression, or invisibility of Black LGBT persons. Table 7.1 provides a few examples of class exercises.

Fifteen first-year students were enrolled in the semester-long seminar. All of the students racially self-identified as African American, with one of them additionally identifying as African American of Hispanic ethnicity. Of the original students, 14 identified as female and one as male. The majority of the students identified as heterosexual women. The four students who did not identify as heterosexual identified as lesbian, bisexual (female), and gay (male). None of the students identified as transgender. Students enrolled from a diverse range of majors including economics, social work, mass communications, psychology, business, chemistry, rehabilitation studies, and exercise science. One female student ceased attending the seminar by mid-semester. The course fulfilled general education requirements for first-year students.

TABLE 7.1 Sample Activities and Assignments from Black Issues in LGBT Psychology

Type	Description
Reading and group skit	Paul Laurence Dunbar's poem "We Wear the Mask" (Dunbar, 1944) was assigned for critical reading, including analysis and development of a skit to convey its meaning; the skits were performed by three groups of five students.
Reading and guest speaker panel	A journal article on religion and spirituality (Buchanan, Dzelme, Harris, & Hecker, 2001) of lesbians and gays was assigned for reading prior to an in-class panel discussion on the issue; the panel that visited the seminar comprised a Black transman, a Black woman who identified as queer, a Black gay male, and two Black persons who identified as allies (1 male, 1 female). The Black male ally was also a local pastor, and the Black queer woman was partnered with the Black transman. After hearing the panelists address questions from the instructor, the students asked questions and/or made comments.
Quote analysis	Students were asked to interpret a quote from Audre Lorde, "When I dare to be powerful, to use my strength in the service of my vision, then it becomes less and less important whether I am afraid," as cited in Battle, Cohen, Warren, Fergerson, and Audam (2002); this and other excerpts from the survey report were presented to the students to document their critical thinking during survey interpretation and discussion. See Hall (this volume) for another example.
Critical thinking exercise	Students were asked to complete a critical thinking exercise requiring them to interpret what is meant by heterosexism = sexism = classism = racism.
Video analysis	An 8-minute YouTube video entitled "Lesbians corrective rape in South Africa" (www.youtube.com/watch?v=vBXBtC-5Eko), which originally aired via Channel 4 news in the UK, was shown to students as a critical thinking exercise. Following the video, students were asked to offer analysis of the behavior based on statements made in the video by some of the male perpetrators of the crime.
Film and discussion question assignment	Students viewed Pariah (Rees, 2011), a 27-minute independent film about a Black lesbian teenager who struggles with juggling her multiple identities to avoid being rejected by her family and friends. This was shown as part of a critical thinking assignment in which students had to develop discussion questions based on their viewing the film.

Media images data collection activity	Gender nonconformity was assigned as a short research assignment topic. Students collectively selected media images of well-known African Americans (irrespective of sexual identity) in which the same individual publicly appeared feminine in appearance or masculine in appearance, irrespective of his or her biological sex. Students found both masculine and feminine images of Prince, Queen Latifah, RuPaul, Da Brat, Sylvester, and Caster Semenya. The images were rated by the students as likable or not likable, and the students showed the images to random members of the university community during class period. The students obtained responses from members of the university community regarding likability of the two images for each public figure.

Psychology of Gender, Race, and Sexuality

Using a co-intentional education model (Freire, 1970/2000) to create knowledge, four graduate students and I (Kim) developed a student-faculty collaboration and designed the course to infuse intersectionality throughout the LGBT psychology readings, assignments, activities, and assessment process (Case, Miller, & Jackson, 2012). At each step of curriculum design, critical liberatory feminist pedagogy (Case, Kanenberg, et al., 2012) informed reading choices, assignment learning goals and instructions, creation and facilitation of in-class exercises, and assessment of student outcomes. Learning goals included articulating an understanding of the matrix of privilege and oppression, application of intersectional theory to LGBT psychology in real-world contexts, and facilitation of public education with regard to intersectionality.

The first reading assignment provided a solid foundation for intersectional theory from Dill and Zambrana (2009). Textbooks for the course included:

- *Race, Class, and Gender: An Anthology* (Andersen & Collins, 2010);
- *Colonize This! Young Women of Color on Today's Feminism* (Hernandez & Rehman, 2002);
- *As Nature Made Him: The Boy Who Was Raised as a Girl* (Colapinto, 2006); and
- *Global Woman* (Ehrenreich & Hochschild, 2002).

In these intersectionally focused texts, students read, for example, "browngirlworld: queergirlofcolor organizing, sistahood, heartbreak" by Piepzna-Samarasinha (2002) that required critical intersectional analysis during the in-class discussion of LGBT psychology.

Two assignments emphasized learning about intersectionality: a photography project and a public education campaign. For the photovoice (Case & Rios, this volume; Chio & Fandt, 2007; Wang, 1999) assignment, students spent several weeks taking photos that illustrated and helped explain intersectionality as a concept or their personal social identity intersections. The intersectionality project asked students to apply what they learned about intersectionality to raise public awareness of intersectionality in people's lives (for variations, see Case & Rios, this volume; Rios, Bowling, & Harris, this volume). Students could address public education through a variety of creative means such as online videos, facilitating workshops, or designing and providing brochures. Both assignments prompted students to educate their classmates and the broader community while applying intersectional theory to their own social locations.

Developing a culture of student engagement came with challenges, given that many students in the class expected to face the front and listen to lectures. However, class exercises were developed to increase student engagement, support a community learning experience, and enhance comprehension and application of intersectional theory to LGBT psychology. The activities, as well as explicit expectations of participation and peer support, created a space for co-intentional learning for exploration of LGBT psychology. Class activities and exercises are included in Table 7.2.

TABLE 7.2 Sample Activities and Assignments from Psychology of Gender, Race, and Sexuality

Type	Description
Reading and concept brainstorm activity	After reading Dill and Zambrana's (2009) chapter on intersectional theory, students brainstormed words associated with intersectionality for 60 seconds then spent 5 minutes with a partner explaining the words' connections with theory. In the end, the entire class wrote the associated words on the board and discussed emerging patterns for deeper comprehension of abstract concepts.
"Grab bag" activity	"Grab Bag" activity: students reached into a bag and chose one item. Once all students had an object, they took 3 minutes to connect the item and some concept or theory from the assigned readings or specifically intersectional theory. Students then paired up for support from a partner to practice their explanations for the items. For example, when a key was pulled from the bag, the student described its representation of access automatically afforded to privileged groups, such as Whites and heterosexuals, while marginalized groups face locked doors.

Sharing cultural backgrounds	Students brought objects to the class that represented their social identities or cultural heritage. Several weeks later, this show-and-tell exercise was repeated with food items from each student's cultural background. A Filipino student provided the class with a batch of rice muffins and a working-class White female brought fried potato cakes. Both activities required students not only to articulate the connection to social identity, but also to explicitly link the item or food to assigned readings and concepts learned in the course.
Film and discussion	After reading *As Nature Made Him* (Colapinto, 2006), students viewed *Sex: Unknown* (Cohen & Sweigart, 2001), a film documenting the life of David Reimer, the boy who was raised as a girl. Through discussion of the book and film, students addressed the restrictions of dichotomous gender-conforming norms, gender identity struggles, and the oppression faced by transgender people.
Group workshop development exercise	Students participated in a small group activity and developed a workshop to educate the public on intersectional components of LGBT psychology. Each group received a setting and target audience context from the instructor, wrote workshop goals related to course readings and concepts, and designed an activity they would facilitate to reach those goals. This group exercise gave them a chance to practice application of theory and course content in the form of public education.

Fourteen Master's students enrolled in the course as an elective. In terms of racial and ethnic background, students self-identified as Latino, Filipina, African American, biracial (Black and White), White, Italian, Chinese, Native American, and unknown (due to her mother's adoption). Three students identified as male and 11 as female. Although the majority identified as heterosexual, some students identified in class as bisexual (female), lesbian, gay (male), or fluid in their sexuality. The lesbian student also later indicated some identification with the transgender community in terms of perceptions of her as a masculine female. Socioeconomic status of the students present ranged from previously homeless to working-class to middle- and upper-middle class backgrounds. Of those who disclosed religious identification, students represented Atheist, Jewish, and Christian viewpoints. The 14 enrolled students also joined the class from a variety of social science Master's programs: general psychology, family therapy, clinical psychology, sociology, and cross-cultural studies. Three White female students dropped the course before the mid-semester.

Instructor Reflections on Intersectional LGBT Psychology Student Learning Goal Success

Black LGBT Psychology

Conscientization, to the degree that it was reached, was primarily achieved through the semester-long dialogues about the seminar content (Martin-Baro, 1996). As reported by the students, I (Michele) was able to maintain dialogue and student interest by arranging seating in a circle during each class meeting, whether students were viewing media or responding to questions that I posed. Examples of some degree of critical consciousness being reached were that students began the seminar as either neutral regarding Black LGBT liberation or as open-minded or "not bothered" by LGBT persons. None of the students initially identified with use of the term "ally," though by the end of the semester (i.e., after hearing life experiences of two of the panelists) several students embraced usage of this term to refer to themselves. They were eager to begin using the term to identify themselves, and several stated that they could envision themselves being activists supporting liberation for LGBT persons.

The students were enthusiastic and engaged for the skit assignment based on the Dunbar (1944) poem, "We Wear the Mask." The expressions of their understanding of the meaning of the poem reflected successful critical reading and interpretation of the poem's meaning regarding the stress of oppression. They performed skits in which they portrayed the silencing of victims of racism or heterosexism.

When the students were asked to complete a critical thinking exercise requiring them to interpret what is meant by: Heterosexism = sexism = classism = racism, they were able to achieve this with prompting, not spontaneously. After prompting them to look at the "equal" symbol among the words, I had expected them to state that the terms were equal due to all being oppressions. However, as with the reading exercises, we had to dissect and examine each word individually and separately. This allowed the students to create examples for each term. They gave the following relevant examples for the terms: someone being anti-gay marriage (heterosexism); differences among students in disposable income for non-essential shopping (classism); a person who would feel uncomfortable being treated by a Black physician (racism); and someone opposing racism but not outraged by domestic violence against a woman (sexism). Though the students grasped the meaning of the exercise, not all fully accepted a worldview of no hierarchy of oppressions. Specifically, there were a few students who insisted that racism is to be prioritized above other oppressions such as sexism, classism, or heterosexism. For students who have elected to attend a historically Black university, the greater significance of race for them may be intuitive. Also, the students were relatively underexposed to academic discourse on LGBT oppression within their racial/ethnic cultural context.

Psychology of Gender, Race, and Sexuality

Students demonstrated, within their critically reflective response papers and in-class discussions of the readings, the development of critical consciousness (Freire, 1970/2000) with regard not only to LGBT psychology but also intersections with sex, race, class, ability, religion, and citizenship. For example, a gay African American man in the class reported that the essay by a gay Asian man (Han, 2010) provided an innovative viewpoint for him that complicated both heterosexism and racism as systems of oppression. By making connections between lived experiences of the oppressed and the content chosen to promote student learning, students drew upon their own expertise that carved out spaces for practical application of theory. This pedagogical strategy led to co-intentional education in which both faculty and students unveil oppression and create "knowledge of reality through common reflection and action" (Freire, 1970/2000, p. 69). The grab bag exercise positioned each student to think critically about intersectionality, concepts, and readings in ways that would enhance learning for the broader community of learners in the course. The activity resulted in successful student application of feminist, queer, and critical race theories to the items chosen and the course readings. A student identified the cassette tape as representative of ways that history gets recorded from the privileged group's perspective which Takaki (2010) describes in "A Different Mirror." Another student described the ball of rubber bands pulled from the bag as a network of social locations within the matrix of oppression, each band imagined as a particular identity category. The class expanded this metaphor to recognize heterosexual and gender-conforming identities as centralized (center of the ball) and normative versus LGBT identities as marginalized (outer edges of the ball) by systematic privilege and oppression. The class "show and tell" days when students and I (Kim) brought in objects or food representing our own privileged and oppressed identities allowed the group to form a community and establish complex theoretical ties to the real world while analyzing meaning through each individual's cultural heritage.

Photovoice assignment

Given Freire's "insistence that the oppressed engage in reflection on their own concrete situation" (1970/2000, p. 66), students conducted intentional and critical reflection on their own social identities within the matrix of oppression and privilege within the photovoice project. One female student, who identified as biracial (Black and White), bisexual, and tri-cultural (including Latina identification as a result of her neighborhood growing up), created a crossword puzzle to encompass all of her intersecting identities in one powerful visual aid. This crossword illustrated her realization that her unique social location allows her to more effectively bridge traditionally separated social groups, such as heterosexuals and LGB people. Choosing to focus on the concept of intersectionality, rather than personal identity, a White female student transformed popular board games into teaching tools. She used Risk, Scrabble, Life, and Monopoly to raise awareness of intersections of socially constructed identity categories that influence lived experiences. Another female student presented her identity as a lesbian and masculine female to the class, providing a deconstruction of heteronormativity and gender-conforming norms. Overall, the students reported that the photovoice presentations enabled their own critical analysis of intersections, the matrix of social locations, and application of LGBT psychology to individual identity and experience. By systematically reflecting on personal identities and the impact of race, gender, class, gender identity, and religion on sexuality (and vice versa), they successfully incorporated an intersectional lens into their own individualized theoretical frameworks for critical analyses.

Intersectionality Public Education Project

The major final project challenged students to develop and carry out a strategy for public education. The project would educate others with regard to a specified identity intersection. Nervous at first about how to invent a public education plan, students ultimately created innovative projects and exceeded my expectations as an instructor. The varied public education campaigns and workshops that resulted targeted a wide range of audiences as chosen by each student. For example, a Filipina student directed a complex video documentary deconstructing media representations of sexuality, race, and gender in popular films. A student with a privileged social location created a brand new board game that effectively taught players about oppression, privilege, and intersectionality. She then gathered several community groups and facilitated their discussion of the matrix of privilege and oppression as they played. One male student developed a relationship with a non-profit organization and created workshops for boys in the juvenile justice system on masculinity, homophobia, and human trafficking. He facilitated the workshop with juvenile detention officers and then with the boys after our course ended. Through their efforts to take action and educate the public about some aspect of intersectionality, students applied their own learning to real-world problems. This project allowed them to recognize and develop new pathways to create change through empowerment and application of liberatory psychology. See Case and Rios (this volume) for more details on this project and altering the assignment for the undergraduate level.

Learning Goal Challenges and Obstacles

Black LGBT Psychology

Critical reading as a learning objective was challenging to achieve with this group of first-year students. This was somewhat anticipated. To be proactive, I (Michele) attempted to compensate for this by choosing from a broad variety of disciplinary writings to focus on marginalization and related social justice issues among people of African descent. This was necessary because the LGBT psychology literature is not yet intersectionally diverse enough to perhaps be viewed as relevant to the group of students in the seminar. The readings were chunked in order to motivate the students to read. Thus, the pre-selected journal articles were not read in their entirety, although this had been the intention when I designed the seminar. Though the students were attentive and engaged for the guest panel discussion, again the accompanying related reading assignment given before the panel was not read in entirety by the students. Excerpts from the article had to be assigned to be read during class as a brief reading period prior to the panel day. Students were, however, able to read in entirety brief news articles assigned during the semester from the website, Behind the Mask: The Voices of Africa's LGBTI Community. Most of the stories from this site are the equivalent of two pages or less.

For first-year students who may be inexperienced with reading longer scholarly articles, it may be necessary to select short pieces or select excerpts only for critical examination and comprehension. It is plausible that the students of the seminar had not had adequate training experiences in scholarly reading comprehension prior to entering the university. All but one of the students in the seminar shared during the course that they perceived their high schools to be academically inadequate. Based upon the assignments that were designed for the seminar, future offerings of the seminar should include assessment or knowledge of enrolled students' reading comprehension levels as well as progressively longer, graded, reading-based assignments, leading up to the longer academic readings. On a related note, the poems used in the seminar were short, so they were more effective for critical reading and critical thinking exercises. These could be built upon in terms of using them for teaching critical thinking. Also, students did less well interpreting a Langton Hughes poem, "Democracy" (Hughes, 1949), relative to the Dunbar (1944) poem, "We Wear the Mask." This may have been a result of differences in the reading comprehension difficulty of the poem. Both poems were short in length.

The independent film exercise was not successful with respect to its intended objective to stimulate critical thinking based in critical consciousness. Though the students were attentive to the film, and they empathized with the oppression of the main character (Black lesbian teen), they were unsuccessful in developing critical thought questions that could be used to guide a discussion group about the film. Using the short film *Pariah* (Rees, 2011), students were requested to write questions based on the movie; however, the questions were to be written as intended for a fictitious community group of parents. Generally, students were unable to produce questions that reflected critical thought in which they demonstrated the ability to anticipate substantive questions that might be asked by religious parents who are stressed by having a lesbian teenage daughter.

The independent film exercise could likely be more effective with moderated dialogue before asking students to write their questions. In future efforts,

I (Michele) would spend one entire class session to show the film and discuss it, then during a second meeting have students think and write questions prompted by our discussion, while viewing the film a second time (27-minute film). It is likely that a similar explanation applies to the challenges with the film exercise as with the reading exercises, suggesting greater need for cognitive ability enhancement among this group of first-year students (Farley & Elmore, 1992). More focused attention on critical thinking and critical reading assignments that become progressively more challenging may be necessary with first-year students, particularly if they are underprepared from their secondary education. Black Issues in LGBT Psychology as an example of a cultural study in liberation psychology can provide substantive material for teaching general education skills to first-year students. Adequate forethought must be given to progressively challenging graded assignments with regular feedback and ongoing discussion.

Acceptance of gender non-conformity was limited among the students in the Black Issues in LGBT Psychology seminar. This may relate to "secondary marginalization," which employs rhetoric and blame that is directed at the most stigmatized and vulnerable who exist within the generally marginalized community (in this case, gender non-conforming Black males) of African Americans (Cohen, 1999). Only one student was completely accepting of an imagined gender non-conforming male child to the degree that she would be comfortable, for example, with her young son wearing pink nail polish. When students rated Black male and female images as likable or not likable, most selected the gender-conforming images as more appealing. University community respondents were similar in opinion, such that others in the culture of the university seem to expect gender conformity, particularly for Black males. One exception was in the case of celebrity personality, Prince. Students and other members of the community were more accepting of his femininity.

Overall, for the liberatory issue of genderism, much more work is needed. The students were most rejecting of femininity in male-bodied persons, suggesting strong identification with distinct boundaries of Blackness and masculinity for Black men (Cohen, 1999). They also voiced more rejection of bisexual behavior in men relative to women, which again may be based upon more rigid gender role and expression rules for Black men. It should be noted that the seminar students were overwhelmingly heterosexual-identified women, and thus perhaps for selfish reasons, they could not embrace ideas of potential boyfriends behaving bisexually or demonstrating feminine characteristics. Such views could also reflect their underexposure to substantive open discussion and experience with the issues.

Psychology of Gender, Race, and Sexuality

Although this is a graduate course, only one student had previous exposure to intersectional theory. Therefore, tackling Dill and Zambrana (2009) as the first reading assignment presented challenges to the majority of the students, which Case and Rios (this volume) also describe. In fact, they struggled for several weeks to grasp the main tenets of the theory and to comprehend that particular reading. In future iterations of this course, advance preparation of the students before they read Dill and Zambrana (2009) could include advice to take careful notes and to expect some new concepts and perspectives. In addition, re-assigning the reading before the mid-semester followed by a second-class discussion may aid student development. This would also provide the instructor with information as to how the students progressed from week 1 to the mid-semester in their comprehension of intersectional theory.

The small group activity to create a workshop for public education seemed to flounder. Students struggled at each step to articulate goals for the imaginary workshop and to connect the workshop goals and content to course readings, concepts, and theories. One way to improve this in-class activity would be to provide a well-conceived public education workshop with each component clearly explained before the students begin considering their own. In addition, the instructor could provide more details in the written scenarios that set up each group's workshop context.

Another challenge in this class came in the form of three White heterosexual females dropping the course just before the mid-semester exam. These students indicated to peers in the class that the decision to drop the course was based on the fear of getting an A- final grade rather than an A. On the other hand, student resistance to course content and expectations for student performance may also influence student withdrawal from courses addressing LGBT psychology.

Of course, completion of the course did not equate to comprehension of LGBT psychology or intersectional theory. One White, Christian, upper-middle-class female student attended class, completed assignments, and participated (with the exception of the day the transgender guest speaker led discussion). Then on the last day of class, she expressed her views that (1) gay individuals should simply ignore discrimination, and (2) those who avoid flaunting their sexuality will not face discrimination. These comments created a storm of visibly upset LGBT and ally students in the class, followed by an intense student-led discussion to challenge her views. Although faculty may experience such student resistance as pedagogical failure, these challenges may function as a necessary developmental stage of the learning process (Tatum, 1992).

Implications for the Pedagogy of LGBT Psychology

As Naples (this volume) describes, instructors often struggle to identify effective ways to move students beyond the additive model of oppression and identity. Psychology courses typically cover issues of oppression within distinct diversity courses that maintain traditional categorical boundaries between identity groups, for example, as Case (this volume) taught gender

144 Kim A. Case and Michele K. Lewis

and race separately within the same course (Bargad & Hyde, 1991; Chang, 2002; Henderson-King & Kaleta, 2000; Henderson-King & Stewart, 1999; Katz, Swindell, & Farrow, 2004; Kernahan & Davis, 2007; Stake & Hoffman, 2001; Waterman, Reid, Garfield, & Hoy, 2001). Teaching the two courses described here benefited from an intersectional framework to supplement and strengthen critical liberatory feminist pedagogy. Teaching and learning about LGBT psychology through an intersectional lens allows students from a variety of backgrounds to connect seemingly irrelevant systems of oppression and privilege to their own social identities and social locations. For traditionally marginalized student populations (e.g., students of color, poor and working-class students, or students identified with non-Christian religions or no religion), approaching LGBT psychology intersectionally promotes application of complex analysis to both privileged and oppressed identities. For example, a heterosexual and gender-conforming Latina student may advance her understanding of LGBT oppression by reading and applying critical liberatory feminist analysis (Case, Kanenberg, et al., 2012) to the experiences of a Mexican American bisexual woman describing her daily encounters with racism and heterosexism. At the same time, students with privileged identities benefit from intersectional pedagogy as it aids deconstruction of assumptions about LGBT people and also complicates categorical identities. In other words, privileged and marginalized students apply intersectional analysis to discover that LGBT people of color exist despite common cognitive schemas of the LGBT community as White (and as middle-class U.S. citizens). By applying this intersectional lens, students with both privileged and oppressed identities learn to deconstruct artificial categorization of social identity in favor of the matrix of oppression that highlights the infinite complexity of identity (Case, this volume; Grzanka, this volume).

As psychology programs infuse more LGBT content across the curriculum, both within diversity courses and across core and additional elective courses (Case et al., 2009; Neumann, 2005; Waterman et al., 2001), implementation of an intersectional theoretical framework to develop student learning goals, develop assignments, and assess student outcomes will strengthen student comprehension of LGBT psychology. This intersectional attention to LGBT inclusion not only expands psychology students' knowledge of diverse populations but also provides the field of psychology innovative avenues for decreasing marginalization within both teaching and research (Cole, 2009). Although the use of an intersectional pedagogical approach is particularly relevant when teaching LGBT psychology within colleges and universities that serve large numbers of students of color, teaching LGBT psychology intersectionally enhances student learning regardless of student social location. In other words, students from privileged backgrounds with privileged social identities also benefit from intersectional LGBT psychology through increased awareness of the matrix of privilege and oppression.

The infusion of an intersectional theoretical lens into LGBT psychology courses, as well as more common diversity courses in psychology emphasizing gender (Grzanka, this volume) and race, benefits both faculty and students by providing avenues for complicating social identity. As students become more aware of the complex social locations within the matrix of privilege and oppression, intersectional understanding reduces the tendency to generalize stereotypical characterizations to entire social categories and identities (Case, this volume; Collins, 1990; Dill, 2009; Dill & Zambrana, 2009). A psychology curriculum enhanced by intersectional theory may also broaden perspectives to include and value structural and institutional components of oppression, as opposed to the field's emphasis on generalizable findings that often reinforce social identity categorization.

Note

1 A previous version of this chapter was published as: Case, K. & Lewis, M. (2012). Teaching intersectional LGBT psychology: Reflections from historically Black and Hispanic-serving universities. *Psychology and Sexuality, 3,* 260–276. Reprinted by permission of the publisher (Taylor & Francis Ltd, www.tandfonline.com).The current version was altered to reflect standard American English spelling, APA style and formatting, update citations and information, and connect with the broader edited volume.

References

Allen, W. (1992). The color of success: African American college student outcomes at predominantly White and historically Black public colleges and universities. *Harvard Educational Review, 62,* 26–45.

Andersen, M. L., & Collins, P. (Eds.). (2010). *Race, class, and gender: An anthology* (7th ed.). Belmont, CA: Wadsworth.

Bargad, A., & Hyde, J. S. (1991). Women's studies: A study of feminist identity development in women. *Psychology of Women Quarterly, 15,* 181–201. doi:10.1111/J.14716402.1991.tb00791.x

Battle, J., Cohen, C., Warren, D., Fergerson, G., & Audam, S. (2002). *Say it loud: I'm Black and I'm proud: Black pride survey 2000.* New York, NY: The Policy Institute of the National Gay and Lesbian Task Force.

Bérubé, A. (2001). How gay stays White and what kind of White it stays. In B. B. Rasmussen, E. Klinenberg, I. J. Nexica, & M. Wray (Eds.), *The making and unmaking of whiteness* (pp. 234–265). Durham, NC: Duke University Press.

Bohmer, S. (1998). Resistance to generalizations in the classroom. In G. E. Cohee, E. Daumer, T. D. Kemp, P. M. Krebs, S. A. Lafky, & S. Runzo (Eds.), *The feminist teacher anthology: Pedagogies and classroom strategies* (pp. 61–69). New York, NY: Teachers College Press.

Bonner, F. B. (2001). Addressing gender issues in the historically Black college and university community: A challenge and call to action. *Journal of Negro Education, 70,* 176–191. doi:10.2307/3211209

Buchanan, M., Dzelme, K., Harris, D., & Hecker, L. (2001). Challenges of being simultaneously gay or lesbian and spiritual and/or religious: A narrative perspective. *The American Journal of Family Therapy, 29,* 435–449. doi:10.1080/01926180127629

Case, K. A. (this volume). Toward an intersectional pedagogy model: Engaged learning for social justice. In K. A. Case (Ed.), *Intersectional pedagogy: Complicating identity and social justice* (pp. 1–24). New York, NY: Routledge.

Case, K., Kanenberg, H., Erich, S., & Tittsworth, J. (2012). Transgender inclusion in university non-discrimination statements: Challenging gender-conforming privilege through student activism. *Journal of Social Issues, 68,* 145–161. doi:10.1111/j.1540-4560.2011.01741. x

Case, K., Miller, A., & Jackson, S. B. (2012). "We talk about race too much in this class!" Complicating the essentialized woman through intersectional pedagogy. In C. Banks & S. Pliner (Eds.), *Teaching, learning, and intersecting identities in higher education* (pp. 32–48). New York, NY: Peter Lang.

Case, K. A., & Rios, D. (this volume). Infusing intersectionality: Complicating the Psychology of Women course. In K. A. Case (Ed.), *Intersectional pedagogy: Complicating identity and social justice* (pp. 82–109). New York, NY: Routledge.

Case, K., Stewart, B., & Tittsworth, J. (2009). Transgender across the curriculum: A psychology of inclusion. *Teaching of Psychology, 36,* 117–121. doi:10.1080/0098628 0902739446

Chang, M. J. (2002). The impact of an undergraduate diversity course requirement on students' racial views and attitudes. *Journal of General Education, 51,* 21–42. doi: 10.1353/jge.2002.0002

Chio, V., & Fandt, P. (2007). Photovoice in the diversity classroom: Engagement, voice, and the 'eye/I' of the camera. *Journal of Management Education, 31,* 484–504. doi: 10.1177/1052562906288124

Cohen, A. (Director), & Sweigart, S. (Director). (2001). *Sex: Unknown* [film]. United States: NOVA.

Cohen, C. J. (1999). *The boundaries of Blackness: AIDS and the breakdown of Black politics.* Chicago: University of Chicago Press.

Colapinto, J. (2006). *As nature made him: The boy who was raised as a girl.* New York, NY: Harper.

Cole, E. (2009). Intersectionality and research in psychology. *American Psychologist, 64,* 170–180. doi:10.1037/a0014564

Cole, W. (2006). Accrediting culture: An analysis of tribal and historically Black college curricula. *Sociology of Education, 79,* 355–387. doi:10.1177/003804070607900404

Collins, P. H. (1990). *Black feminist thought: Knowledge, consciousness, and the politics of empowerment.* New York, NY: Routledge.

Crosnoe, R. (2005). The diverse experiences of Hispanic students in the American educational system. *Sociological Forum, 20,* 561–588. doi:10.1007/s11206-005-9058-z

Cross, P., & Astin, H. (1981). Factors influencing Black students' persistence in college. In G. Thomas (Ed.), *Black students in higher education* (pp. 76–90). Westport, CT: Greenwood Press.

Deay, A., & Stitzel, J. (1998). Reshaping introductory women's studies course: Dealing upfront with anger, resistance, and reality. In G. E. Cohee, E. Daumer, T. D. Kemp, P. M. Krebs, S. A. Lafky, & S. Runzo (Eds.), *The feminist teacher anthology: Pedagogies and classroom strategies* (pp. 87–97). New York, NY: Teachers College Press.

Dill, B. T. (2009). Intersections, identities, and inequalities in higher education. In B. T. Dill & R. E. Zambrana (Eds.), *Emerging intersections: Race, class, and gender in theory, policy, and practice* (pp. 229–252). New Brunswick, NJ: Rutgers.

Dill, B. T., & Zambrana, R. E. (Eds.). (2009). Critical thinking about inequality: An emerging lens. In B. T. Dill & R. E. Zambrana (Eds.), *Emerging intersections: Race, class, and gender in theory, policy, and practice* (pp. 1–21). New Brunswick, NJ: Rutgers.

Dunbar, P. L. (1944). *The complete poems of Paul Laurence Dunbar.* New York, NY: Dodd, Mead and Company.

Ehrenreich, B., & Hochschild, A. R. (Eds.). (2002). *Global woman: Nannies, maids, and sex workers in the new economy.* New York, NY: Henry Holt & Co.

Farley, M. J., & Elmore, P. B. (1992). The relationship of reading comprehension to critical thinking skills, cognitive ability, and vocabulary for a sample of underachieving college freshmen. *Educational and Psychological Measurement, 52,* 921–931. doi:10.1177/0013164492052004014

Freire, P. (1970/2000). *Pedagogy of the oppressed.* New York, NY: Continuum.

Garnett, R. F. (2009). Liberal learning as freedom: A capabilities approach to undergraduate education. *Studies in Philosophy and Education, 28,* 437–447. doi:10.1007/s11217-009-9126-6

Goldfried, M. R. (2001). Integrating gay, lesbian, and bisexual issues into mainstream psychology. *American Psychologist, 56,* 977–988. doi:10.1037//0003-066X.56.11.977

Greene, B. (2000). Beyond heterosexism and the cultural divide. In B. Greene & G. L. Croom (Eds.), *Education, research, and practice in lesbian, gay, bisexual, and transgendered psychology: A resource manual* (pp. 1–45). Thousand Oaks, CA: Sage.

Greene, B. (2005). Psychology, diversity, and social justice: Beyond heterosexism and across the cultural divide. *Counseling Psychology Quarterly, 18,* 295–306. doi:10.1080/0951 5070500385770

Greene, B., & Croom, G. L. (Eds.). (2000). *Education, research, and practice in lesbian, gay, bisexual, and transgendered psychology: A resource manual.* Thousand Oaks, CA: Sage.

Grzanka, P. (this volume). Undoing the psychology of gender: Intersectional feminism and social science pedagogy. In K. A. Case (Ed.), *Intersectional pedagogy: Complicating identity and social justice* (pp. 63–81). New York, NY: Routledge.

Hall, N. (this volume). Quotes, blogs, diagrams, and counter-storytelling: Teaching intersectionality at a minority-serving institution. In K. A. Case (Ed.), *Intersectional pedagogy: Complicating identity and social justice* (pp. 150–170). New York, NY: Routledge.

Han, C. (2010) Darker shades of queer: Race and sexuality at the margins. In M. L. Andersen & P. H. Collins (Eds.), *Race, class, and gender: An anthology* (7th ed., pp. 255–262). Belmont, CA: Wadsworth.

Hase, M. (2002). Student resistance and nationalism in the classroom: Reflections on globalizing the curriculum. In A. A. MacDonald & S. Sanchez-Casal (Eds.), *Twenty-first-century feminist classrooms: Pedagogies of identity and difference* (pp. 87–107). New York: Palgrave MacMillan.

Henderson-King, D., & Kaleta, A. (2000). Learning about social diversity: The undergraduate experience and intergroup tolerance. *Journal of Higher Education, 71,* 142–164. doi:10.2307/2649246

Henderson-King, D., & Stewart, A. J. (1999). Educational experiences and shifts in group consciousness: Studying women. *Personality and Social Psychology Bulletin, 25,* 390–399. doi:10.1177/0146167299025003010

Hernandez, D., & Rehman, B. (2002). *Colonize this! Young women of color on today's feminism.* CA: Seal Press.

Hughes, L. (1949). *Democracy.* Retrieved from www.americanpoems.com/poets/Langston-Hughes/

Katz, J., Swindell, S., & Farrow, S. (2004). Effects of participation in a first women's studies course on collective self-esteem, gender-related attitudes, and emotional well-being. *Journal of Applied Social Psychology, 34,* 2179–2199. doi:10.1111/j.1559-1816.2004. tb02696.x

Kernahan, C., & Davis, T. (2007). Changing perspective: How learning about racism influences student awareness and emotion. *Teaching of Psychology, 34,* 49–52. doi:10. 1080/00986280709336651

Kim, M. M., & Conrad, C. F. (2006). The impact of historically Black colleges and universities on the academic success of African-American students. *Research in Higher Education, 47,* 399–427. doi:10.1007/s11162-005-9001-4

Lather, P. (1998). Critical pedagogy and its complicities: A praxis of stuck places. *Educational Theory, 48,* 487–497.

Maher, F. A. (1998). My introduction to "Introduction to Women's Studies:" The role of the teacher's authority in the feminist classroom. In G. E. Cohee, E. Daumer, T. D. Kemp, P. M. Krebs, S. A. Lafky, & S. Runzo (Eds.), *The feminist teacher anthology: Pedagogies and classroom strategies* (pp. 24–30). New York: Teachers College Press.

Martin-Baro, I. (1996). *Writings for a liberation psychology.* Cambridge, MA: Harvard University Press.

McKenna, T. (2003). Borderness and pedagogy: Exposing culture in the classroom. In A. Darder, M. Baltodano, & R. Torres (Eds.), *The critical pedagogy reader* (pp. 430–439). New York: RoutledgeFalmer.

McLaren, P. (2003). Critical pedagogy: A look at the major concepts. In A. Darder, M. Baltodano, & R. Torres (Eds.), *The critical pedagogy reader* (pp. 69–96). New York, NY: RoutledgeFalmer.

Moane, G. (2003). Bridging the personal and political: Practices for a liberation psychology. *American Journal of Community Psychology, 31,* 91–101. doi:10.1023/A:1023026 704576

Naples, N. (2002). Teaching community action in the introductory women's studies classroom. In N. A. Naples & K. Bojar (Eds.), *Teaching feminist activism: Strategies from the field* (pp. 71–94). New York, NY: Routledge.

Naples, N. A. (this volume). Pedagogical practice and teaching intersectionality intersectionally. In K. A. Case (Ed.), *Intersectional pedagogy: Complicating identity and social justice* (pp. 110–128). New York, NY: Routledge.

Neumann, S. L. (2005). Creating a "safe zone" for sexual minority students in the psychology classroom. *Teaching of Psychology, 32,* 121–123. doi:10.1207/s15328023top3202_8

Piepzna-Samarasinha, L. L. (2002). browngirlworld: queergirlofcolor organizing, sistahood, heartbreak. In D. Hernandez & B. Rehman (Eds.), *Colonize this! Young women of color on today's feminism* (pp. 3–16). Emeryville, CA: Seal Press.

Purdie-Vaughns, V., & Eibach, R. P. (2008). Intersectional invisibility: The distinctive advantages and disadvantages of multiple subordinate-group identities. *Sex Roles, 59,* 377–391. doi:10.1007/s11199-008-9424-4

Rees, D. (Director). (2011). *Pariah.* [film]. United States: Focus Features.

Rios, D., Bowling, M., & Harris, J. (this volume). Decentering student "uniqueness" in lessons about intersectionality. In K. A. Case (Ed.), *Intersectional pedagogy: Complicating identity and social justice* (pp. 194–213). New York, NY: Routledge.

Rivera, D. P. (this volume). Revealing hidden intersections of gender identity, sexual orientation, race, and ethnicity: Teaching about multiple oppressed identities. In K. A. Case (Ed.), *Intersectional pedagogy: Complicating identity and social justice* (pp 173–193). New York, NY: Routledge.

Sanchez-Casal, S. (2002). Unleashing the demons of history: White resistance in the U.S. Latino studies classroom. In A. A. MacDonald & S. Sanchez-Casal (Eds.), *Twenty-first-century feminist classrooms: Pedagogies of identity and difference* (pp. 59–85). New York, NY: Palgrave Macmillan.

Short, K. (2002). Global feminism and activism in a women's studies practicum. In N. A. Naples & K. Bojar (Eds.), *Teaching feminist activism: Strategies from the field* (pp. 123–137). New York, NY: Routledge.

Simoni, J. M. (2000). Confronting heterosexism in the teaching of psychology. In B. Greene & G. L. Croom (Eds.), *Education, research, and practice in lesbian, gay, bisexual, and transgendered psychology: A resource manual* (pp. 74–90). Thousand Oaks, CA: Sage.

Sinacore, A. L., & Boatwright, K. J. (2005). The feminist classroom: Feminist strategies and student responses. In C. Z. Enns & A. L. Sinacore (Eds.), *Teaching and social justice: Integrating multicultural and feminist theories in the classroom* (pp. 109–124). Washington, DC: American Psychological Association.

Stake, J. E., & Hoffman, F. L. (2001). Changes in student social attitudes, activism, and personal confidence in higher education: The role of women's studies. *American Educational Research Journal, 38*, 411–436. doi:10.3102/00028312038002411

Sue, D. (1996). Multicultural counseling: Models, methods, and actions. *Counseling Psychologist, 24*, 279–284. doi:10.1177/0011000096242008

Sue, D., & Sue, D. (2008). *Counseling the culturally diverse: Theory and practice* (5th ed.). Hoboken, NJ: Wiley.

Takaki, R. T. (2010). A different mirror. In M. L. Andersen & P. H. Collins (Eds.), *Race, class, and gender: An anthology* (7th ed., pp. 49–60). Belmont, CA: Wadsworth.

Tatum, B. D. (1992). Talking about race, learning about racism: The application of racial identity development theory in the classroom. *Harvard Educational Review, 62(1)*, 1–25.

Wang, C. (1999). Photovoice: A participatory action research strategy applied to women's health. *Journal of Women's Health, 8*, 185–192. doi:10.1207/S15328023TOP2801_05

Waterman, A. D., Reid, J. D., Garfield, L. D., & Hoy, S. J. (2001). From curiosity to care: Heterosexual student interest in sexual diversity courses. *Teaching of Psychology, 28*, 21–26. doi:10.1207/S15328023TOP2801_05

Weinstock, J. S. (2003). Lesbian, gay, bisexual, transgender, and intersex issues in the psychology curriculum. In P. A. Bronstein & K. Quina (Eds.), *Teaching gender and multicultural awareness: Resources for the psychology classroom* (pp. 285–297). Washington, DC: American Psychological Association.

8

QUOTES, BLOGS, DIAGRAMS, AND COUNTER-STORYTELLING

Teaching Intersectionality at a Minority-Serving Institution

Naomi M. Hall

As a Master's student in a Public Health program in San Diego in the mid-1990s, I was not familiar with the concept of intersectionality, but understood the premise of intersecting aspects of the self based on my educational and personal experiences. I was one of a handful of Black women in the graduate program and remember very vividly enduring uncomfortable classroom discussions about the differences in birth outcomes between Black,[1] White, and Latina women. Numerous faculty members in the program presented statistics that told the story of how low-income Black women without insurance did not get prenatal care and essentially presented for the first time at the hospital to give birth. Many of these births produced low birth weight babies. The information was presented as a simple addition problem:

poor + Black + no insurance = low birth weight.

I recall statements such as "Black women have poor birth outcomes" and "poor people don't go to the doctor." I remember thinking this explanation was too simplistic for me to accept. My advisor, the only Black faculty member in the program, encouraged students to think deeper about how race, social class, and environment interact to produce these less than optimal outcomes. She did not use the term *intersectionality*, but clearly tried to get students to think deeper about the multifaceted relationships, practices, and structural conditions that create lived experiences.

Fast forward to the mid-2000s when I was a doctoral student in an applied social psychology program researching social and cultural factors impacting health disparities among Black men and women. Again, I was presented with an additive model to explain the disproportionate rates of certain diseases and disorders within the Black community. Intuitively I knew that something critically important was missing, but I still lacked the theory and terminology.

My research agenda is fueled by my desire to understand the complicated, reciprocal relationships between social and cultural factors that influence behavior, and subsequently, health outcomes. When a wonderful mentor talked to me about the importance of intra- and inter connected relationships that contribute to experiences and outcomes, my research was forever changed. I began to read more about intersectionality as a methodological and analytical strategy in research. Like many instructors, particularly those in social sciences, the struggle of moving beyond the traditional additive model from my training has been difficult. Singular and categorical identity variables are viewed as "cleaner" and "easier" to explain. However, Cole (2009) wrote that researchers should be "increasingly concerned with the effects of race/ethnicity, gender, social class, and sexuality on outcomes such as health and well-being, personal and social identities, and political views and participation" (p. 170). Strangely enough, even after re-focusing my research to integrate tenets of intersectionality, it took me a few years to incorporate intersectionality into my courses.

Below, I focus on the importance of integrating an intersectional framework into teaching and learning opportunities for undergraduates. I begin with a brief overview of intersectionality and its use as a pedagogical foundation. I share my perspective on incorporating intersectionality into undergraduate classes, while focusing on the importance of including issues such as diversity, power, and privilege. The next section focuses on key activities I found to effectively demonstrate the importance and complexities of incorporating an intersectional framework. These activities, which can be integrated across disciplines and within various types of institutions, include *Quote Analysis, Reaction Blogs, Autobiographical Diagrams,* and *Counter-Storytelling.* I conclude with successes and challenges I encountered through this ongoing process and provide suggestions for infusing intersectionality into the curriculum with students, as well as integration of intersectionality across various disciplines and institution types.

My Pedagogical Perspective

I believe a culturally centered pedagogy that takes into consideration the historical, political, social, and cultural backgrounds of the student population is critical and non-negotiable. My perspective and experience is that of a Black, female professor at a minority-serving institution (MSI),[2] more specifically, a Historically Black College/University (HBCU). This context holds significance for four important reasons:

- The discussion on diversity within the HBCU context is overwhelmingly about African Americans, other people of color, and their experiences navigating white environments (Closson & Henry, 2008). However, HBCUs consistently admitted racially and ethnically diverse students, staff, and faculty since their inception (Closson & Henry, 2008). In fact, Slater (1993) noted that significant diversity among faculty in the U.S. exists only within HBCUs.
- HBCUs maintain a unique cultural milieu, and the ways the critical dialogue and practice of utilizing an intersectional approach may be different than in predominately White institutions (PWIs).
- I teach primarily Black/African American students, and issues around marginalization and oppression based on race abound in discussions.
- Much of the literature about teaching intersectionality, or teaching and learning from an intersectional perspective, highlights course development and application in PWIs (Lee, 2012; Sharp, Bermudez, Watson, & Fitzpatrick, 2007).

HBCUs functioned as key institutions in the social, political, and economic development of the African American community since the 1830s (Jewell, 2002). Therefore, my illustrative examples and commentary reflect my social location, an HBCU in the southeastern part of the United States. However, I want to reiterate that the key activities and recommendations can be altered and framed for use within any discipline or educational environment.

Laying the Groundwork for Intersectionality

Rooted in Black feminism and critical race theory (CRT), intersectionality is a term used to describe an analytical approach reflecting on meanings and consequences of holding membership in several social groups simultaneously (Carbado, Crenshaw, Mays, & Tomlinson, 2013; Cole, 2009). Scholars often recognize Kimberlé Crenshaw (1991) for the term *intersectionality*. However, the ideas and work of other scholars also focused on the limitations of analyses employing only one aspect of identity (Collins, 1990, 2009; hooks, 1984). Early iterations of intersectionality focused on the experience of holding multiple disadvantaged social identities for individuals. More recent work (Crenshaw, 1991; Museus & Griffin, 2011) illustrated that individuals who hold marginalized social identities (e.g., woman, Black) may concurrently hold privileged identities (e.g., middle-class, heterosexual). The idea of concurrently holding disadvantaged and advantaged group membership needs deeper exploration, especially when identity often receives central focus of the course or discipline (e.g., African American studies, Chicano/a studies, women's studies, sexuality studies, psychology).

Banks and Pliner (2012) posited that all institutions of higher learning need to be mindful of the ways intersectionality and structures of privilege and oppression enter into educational settings. Traditionally, faculty and researchers hesitated to integrate intersectionality into their work because of the difficulty in explaining and empirically testing questions generated from this framework (McCall, 2005; Nash, 2008). As a social psychologist, I am acutely aware that my primary discipline has not customarily emphasized the intersection of identities to the extent of other disciplines (e.g., gender studies). In fact, scholars noted that psychology, specifically social psychology, tended to minimize the ways multiple identities relate to each other (Goff & Kahn, 2013). Throughout its long history and today, psychology typically discusses race, gender, social class, age, and sexual identity as separate, non-overlapping constructs (Case, this volume; Cole, 2009; Goff & Kahn, 2013; Purdie-Vaughns & Eibach, 2008; Shields, 2008). My psychology training taught me to believe stratification occupies an important space in research and statistical comparisons. I now know that the lived experiences of individuals indicate that social identities are mutually constructed, not mutually exclusive. Even though social psychology arguably focuses on race/ethnicity, sex/gender, prejudice, discrimination, and oppression the most within the psychological sciences, yet too few social psychologists understand the problems associated with simply focusing on the conjunction *and* to connect complicated identities together. Spelman (1998) called this emphasis the *ampersand problem*.

Intersectionality's movement within and across various disciplines facilitated the building of interdisciplinary bridges and hopefully more discussion about the importance and utilization of the framework (Carbado et al., 2013). As more undergraduate programs increased the number of courses focused on race, gender, and culture in the curriculum and attracted more diverse students, it became imperative to explore intersectionality in the classroom. By implementing the framework of intersectionality, scholars and instructors reduced over-emphasizing any single characteristic or quality in their understanding of individual realities (Dill & Zambrana, 2009) and turned their focus to examination of social locations with respect to privilege and oppression (Case, this volume; Cole, 2009).

Intesectionality in the Classroom: From Theory to Practice

Intersectionality provides an analytic framework for critically examining transecting social identities such as race, ethnicity, sexual identity, gender, ability, religion, nationality, and social class in an academic context. Jones and Wijeyesinghe (2011) posited that application of theory to practice represents a fundamental principle of intersectionality. I teach courses that appeal to a diverse group of undergraduate majors, but most students in my courses major in one of the social or health sciences. When designing courses, I incorporated Dill and Zambrana's (2009) four theoretical classroom interventions of intersectionality: (1) centering the experiences of people of color; (2) complicating identity; (3) unveiling power in interconnected structures of inequality; and (4) promoting social justice and social change. The use of the term *intervention* by Dill and Zambrana (2009) should be highlighted because it conveys the importance of *doing,* which underlies intersectionality (Case, this volume; Jones & Wijeyesinghe, 2011). As an applied social psychologist, a framework that focuses on application appeals to me. Infusing Dill and Zambrana's (2009) interventions of intersectionality requires educators to understand and acknowledge that race, ethnicity, gender, social class, sexual identity, and power occupy the core of inequality among people of color in the U.S. In HBCUs, issues of race, ethnicity, and culture often occupy the forefront of course development and instruction. Pedagogy centered on identity and history are considered vital to understanding oneself and others (Nahal, 2009), and HBCU students often expect to discuss these topics within courses. The mission of HBCUs inherently includes a social justice perspective (McMickens, 2012) because the institutions were created to address inequality and oppression. This framework focused on transforming the ways people create and transfer knowledge to create social change, not simply theorizing about what could or should be done.

Infusing Intersectionality into Undergraduate Courses

As the core of diversity, intersectionality should be at the core of diversity courses. Unfortunately, integration of intersectionality into diversity courses remains rare (Case, this volume; Dill, 2009). The number of racial/ethnic groups present often defines and represents diversity in educational settings (Museus & Griffin, 2011). In contrast, minority-serving institutions (MSIs), such as HBCUs, by definition must maintain a certain percentage of racial/ethnic groups for federal designation. However, focusing only on these elements (race and ethnicity) perpetuates the belief that groups of people, specifically people of color, are monolithic. This can also inhibit the student's ability to consider how other cultural variables and backgrounds are essential to human functioning (Lee, 2012). Intersectionality, which promotes social justice and diversity, provides an important strategy toward achieving social justice (Jones, 2006).

The push for inclusion of diversity courses within institutions of higher education took place over four decades ago (Butler, 2014; Cole, Case, Rios, & Curtin, 2011; Jones, 2006). Diversity courses were designed to introduce and/ or immerse students into discourse about race, gender, class, age, physical ability, religion, and sexuality. Case (this volume) notes that haphazardly designed and one-dimensional courses often failed to acknowledge multiple interrelated areas of oppression or privilege. Poorly designed courses can incorrectly lead students to believe that diversity and cultural integration are only important in certain topic areas and/or disciplines, but not relevant throughout all areas of discussion. Much like the foundation of intersectionality, the integration of diversity transcends any particular course or discipline. Diversity has the ability to raise awareness of the importance of understanding oneself as well as others in ways counter to stereotypes or categorization. Diversity is empowering and essential to knowledge acquisition and transfer in all areas of study (Lee, Poch, Shaw, & Williams, 2012). Gurin, Nagda, and Lopez (2004) noted the fostering of meta-cognition and cognitive growth when students are presented with information or situations unfamiliar to them and must work to comprehend and understand this material.

The mere inclusion of works from people of color does not constitute "diversity" or cultural responsiveness. Transformative thinking cannot occur by adding readings from scholars of color to a course. Creating diversity cannot be achieved with a one-time addition or discussion of information, but involves a more holistic approach to inclusion. Faculty must dedicate themselves to creating opportunities for students to learn and experience diversity. With more inclusion comes more integration of critical identities into the curriculum and subsequent courses.

Exploring Power and Privilege in Undergraduate Courses

Power and privilege are foundational to intersectionality (Case, this volume) and integral to discourse in all areas of study. Beginning the dialogue about power and privilege, especially as it relates to specific identities, can be difficult. Blumenfeld and Jaekel (2012) noted that inexperienced students may be hesitant to talk about issues related to social inequities, including disparities in power. Additionally, talking about how power and privilege impact both education opportunities and experiences and overall societal outcomes may be challenging. Race, ethnicity, and sexual identity seem to be especially difficult as some students, and faculty, are apprehensive about appearing as racist, "close-minded," or homophobic. This trepidation can prevent honest and sincere dialogue. The environment created within the classroom can either promote candid, empowering dialogue or make people feel powerless and unheard (Quaye, 2012). Dill and Zambrana (2009) provided a helpful guide for faculty to discuss four interrelated domains of power in the classroom as a way of addressing the construction and maintenance of oppression and privilege through concurrent convergence of identity characteristics.

McIntosh (1988) defined privilege as unearned benefits based on social identity. These unearned advantages manifest in the form of economic, social, and political power of White people and of men. Two categories, race (Case, Iuzzini, & Hopkins, 2012) and gender (Shields, 2008), receive the most attention within discussions about privilege. Using an intersectional framework means moving beyond these domains as the only ones where privilege deserves deconstruction (Case et al., 2012). Other social identity indicators such as sexual orientation, social class, and religion are important and significant in the lives of students.

Case (2013; this volume) explored best practices for engaging college students about privilege and outlined a pedagogical model for an intersectional approach to teaching and learning about privilege. Although specific individuals receive privileges, classroom discussions should really focus on the societal and structural privileges given to social groups and not to others. This represents a social justice approach to teaching intersectionality. Faculty must be willing to analyze and potentially deconstruct privilege with students in order for them to understand how privilege can create and maintain marginalization of those not in those dominant groups. For instance, many of my students came from low-to-middle-income environments and grew up with one parent or extended family in the home. I acknowledged my privileged position of growing up in a two-parent, middle-income environment. I talked to students about the obliviousness of my privilege well into my adult years. Something unearned, like privilege, often remains invisible until someone or something brings it to your attention.

Unique Qualities of Power and Privilege on HBCU Campuses

Scholars who researched power and privilege noted that White, heterosexual men traditionally get labeled as the standard or norm (Case, 2013; Case et al., 2012; Johnson, 2006; McIntosh, 1988). However, White men represent a relatively small population with no visible power or privilege on HBCU campuses. Scholars consider White men "temporary minorities" (Hall & Closson, 2005) without structural power at HBCUs. Power changes in different cultural contexts and locations (Weber, 2010). As previously mentioned, students need to understand that they can experience oppression related to identity (e.g., Black) while simultaneously experiencing privilege (e.g., heterosexual) related to another identity. Black women usually outnumber Black men on most HBCU campuses and theoretically experience the greatest privilege and power based on numerical majority. However, on many HBCU campuses, identifying as a Black, heterosexual male affords you certain privileges and power not granted within most PWIs or broader society. Since Black, heterosexual men are a smaller percentage of the population, their power and privilege in areas such as dating and partner selection increases based on their social location.

Another identity that represents privilege and power on many HBCU campuses centers on religion, specifically Christianity. The geographical location of most HBCUs is in the southern part of the United States which is informally referred to as "The Bible Belt." This reference denotes the strong, often conservative as well as religious, social, and political views of those who live in this region. In fact, many HBCUs were established in conjunction with church denominations and/or mission societies (Closson & Henry, 2008). Understanding the importance of religious identity to many people of color supports a more effective classroom learning environment (Stewart & Lozano, 2009). In these settings,

Christian power and privilege are considered the norm (Blumenfeld & Jaekel, 2012; Case, McMullen, & Hentges, 2013). Talking about Christian privilege and the ways race, ethnicity, sexual identity, and religious denomination facilitate oppression and privilege can be extremely uncomfortable for some students and professors. However, discussions of Christian privilege signify a significant step in acknowledging bias and how these biases may continue to provide opportunity for some and constrain others.

Designing Course Content

Although courses may be designed in a plethora of ways, my experience dictated that students needed help understanding intersectionality, its relevance, and its importance upfront. To do this, I provided foundational readings at the beginning of the course to help ground them in the framework and its applications. Beginning in week 2 students read "Mapping the Margins: Intersectionality, Identity Politics, and the Violence against Women of Color" (Crenshaw, 1991) and "Intersectionality and Research in Psychology" (Cole, 2009). Additionally, early class discussions included the matrix of domination (Collins, 1990) along with examples of how the matrix manifests in students' lives. The matrix of domination includes both social positions of power and privilege and marginalization and oppression. The students and I spent three class periods talking about intersectionality and grappling with the following three questions:

- How do you explain it?
- How do you measure it?
- How does one experience multiple identities simultaneously?

Beginning each course with select empirical and in some cases non-empirical literature on intersectionality worked well for grounding students in the foundation for the framework with support via real-world examples. The most meaningful activities allowed students to examine their own lived experiences. Real-world application, such as integrating various speakers throughout the course who discussed how social identities and locations impact their lives, aided students' critical examination of the material while also understanding the lived experiences of the transections of oppressive and privileged identities. Scholars continue to grapple with the seemingly infinite complexity of intersectionality. Integrating intersectionality into the classroom is difficult and takes quite a bit of forethought. I taught in both traditional and non-traditional focused programs at various universities and noticed that understanding intersectional theory appears to be more difficult for younger students. Additionally, it appeared to be extremely difficult for students to understand and apply the framework to their lives and the activities and assignments within class without guidance.

Much like Rios, Bowling, and Harris (this volume), the following interactive activities were designed to challenge students to identify their privileged and oppressed entities as well as conceptualize their understanding of each in relation to specific contexts (group, institutional, and societal) and other persons who are more or less privileged and oppressed. Since I am a faculty member at an HBCU, centering the experiences of people of color, the first intervention of intersectionality (Dill & Zambrana, 2009), was integral to all activities. These pedagogical strategies can be used in all disciplines, not just the social and health sciences. Faculty may tailor each activity to a particular discipline or topic. I included illustrative examples and student feedback, both positive and negative, to demonstrate how students received and experienced the activity.

Quote Analysis

I used quote analysis as a pedagogical strategy in all of my courses to assist students in learning about intersectionality. A quote can begin the classroom discussion on a particular topic, reading, or the overall focus of the course. There are different ways to approach the utility of quotes in the classroom setting (see Case & Lewis, this volume, for an alternative example). Depending upon the structure of the course (once a week course versus multiple days), I used either "Quote of the Day" or "Quote of the Week." Students needed a solid foundation in using an intersectional framework to appropriately analyze the quotes. Therefore, quotes were not introduced until weeks 4 or 5 (of a 16-week semester) after students read and discussed the foundational articles on intersectionality.

All quotes utilized in my courses are either about people of color or written by people of color. One of my favorite quotes to use in the classroom is by W. E. B. Du Bois (1903) and states, "To the real question, how does it feel to be a problem? I answer seldom a word" (p. 1). I gave students 5–7 minutes to do two things: (1) write down any information they can recall about the author; and (2) analyze the quote as if someone was speaking directly to them. To do this, students must interpret what aspects of their identity could be considered a "problem" and by whom. At this point, students identified both their privileged and marginalized identities. Students usually identified one or more interrelated oppressed/marginalized identities as the "problem." Sometimes, students selected a problem related more specifically to the focus of the course. For example, when I taught Human Sexuality, students identified sexual minorities or gender nonconforming individuals as problems. In other courses, students named various groups of people as problems: youth, people of color (specifically Black men), low-income mothers, etc. One of the most interesting interpretations of a problem I encountered was written by a young woman in my Social Psychology course who identified with the hip-hop culture:

I am seen as a problem to mainstream society because I support this art form which many say demeans my very being. I don't agree. I see hip-hop as a form of cultural resistance against the inequitable society I was born into. Being a young Black woman in hip-hop is not a problem. Being a young Black woman in hip-hop that won't let you exploit her is a problem. That's why I don't respond.

Once students completed their initial quote analyses, intense classroom conversations often focused on the students' interpretations and thoughts, the critical elements represented in the quotes, and how this connects to the bigger societal and structural systems of oppression and privilege. The classroom conversation stemming from the quote above focused on the intersection between race, gender, social class, age, sexism, and popular culture. Additionally, this student identified the media and the recording industry as the "you" in her quote which provided an opportunity to connect institutional power structures to individual characteristics. In my experience with this, and similar exercises, students need assistance connecting their experiences with larger institutional, systemic, and structural policies and practices. This exercise provided an excellent segue into discussions about power structures as outlined by Collins (2009) and Dill and Zambrana (2009). Quotes such as the one by W. E. B. Du Bois can be used to discuss various cross-cutting interdisciplinary topics in a variety of courses. For instance, those recognized as the "problem" in education may be different than the perceived "problem" in a business classroom. Identifying "problems," across disciplines provides fodder for discussion among students and faculty about groups identified as oppressed and privileged and how the inequalities between the groups can be eradicated (Jones & Wijeyesinghe, 2011).

Reaction Blogs

Reaction blogs provided an effective avenue to encourage students to share their thoughts, "speak" about topics, and reach an audience for their work. I presented students with readings and/or videos related to specific topics or course material and asked students to post their reaction online (through our course management system). Blogs, especially when open to everyone in the classroom, encouraged students to develop critical thinking skills about what to write and how to express themselves (Rahman Sidek & Yunus, 2012). Reaction blogs offered students the opportunity to explore situations using a framework which considers overlapping identities and their inextricable links to each other and are strategically integrated into the course three to four times per semester. Most of the reaction blogs were based on timely and/or emerging issues going on around the world. I also experienced great success with a particular TED talk by Michelle Alexander (2013) entitled, "The Future of Race in America." I used this video regularly in my Black Psychology, Social Psychology, and

Forensic Psychology courses. I typically made this the first reaction blog because the video sets the tone for helping students understand how individual social identities intersect with structural power to create systemic issues that help facilitate unearned social benefits (privilege) for some groups and the marginalization of other groups in society. This 24-minute video focused on racial bias within the criminal justice system. In particular, Alexander (2013) addressed mass incarceration of young Black men and how the criminal justice system functions structurally, in her opinion, like a "caste" system.

Students watched the video at home and provided a 400–500 word reaction that included attention to intersections of privilege and marginalization relative to race, ethnicity, gender, sexual identity, and social class in a criminal justice context. The assignment required students to post their responses by a certain day of the week to provide ample opportunity to comment on the blogs of at least two other students. For example, I asked students to post by Thursday night and respond to classmates by Sunday night. I engaged the class in discussion about the video and their responses the following week. Students provided favorable reviews of this video and reaction blogs as helping them learn more about an intersectional framework. One young man, who identified as White, wrote within his reaction blog:

> I see Black men get arrested on the news all of the time. I never really thought too much about it until last week I was pulled over for speeding. I was riding in the car with my friend, who is Black, and the officer asked my friend to get out of the car and put his hands on the car. I was confused because I was driving. My friend was frisked and asked a series of questions about drugs and weapons. I secretly felt relieved because I wasn't the one being harassed, but I also felt sad. My friend is from a good home, never does anything wrong, but he was targeted. All I can think of is because he is Black and I'm White.

Although the young man did not want to be identified in class (I always ask first), he agreed for his blog to become a discussion starter. Using his words garnered a wide variety of reactions and opportunities to discuss intersectionality within the criminal justice, and subsequent social justice, perspective. As another benefit of this assignment, students archived their experiences, thoughts, and voices over the course of the semester. This allowed both the instructor and the student the opportunity to explore the language used, perspectives taken, and knowledge acquired and shared about topics throughout the semester. Blogs are dynamic and can be integral to the intersectional framework learning process.

For my students at an HBCU, the "caste" system that Alexander (2013) spoke of often sparked discussion about colorism. Colorism refers to the discriminatory and hierarchical system of skin tone preference (Maxwell, Brevard,

Abrams, & Belgrave, 2015). Preference and privilege given to lighter-skinned African Americans began in slavery and the effects are still felt today (Hunter, 2007). Faculty working with African American students must understand and acknowledge how race, gender, and skin tone interact within and across different dimensions of their lives. Educators must know and understand the historical context that dictated certain privileges given to those who have physical features closer to those of European descent. Those with darker skin are subjugated and marginalized in many areas. In fact, research indicates that darker African Americans experience more racial discrimination, and in terms of the criminal justice system, receive harsher legal punishment (Blair, Judd, & Chapleau, 2004; Eberhardt, Davies, Purdie-Vaughns, & Johnson, 2006).

Autobiographical Diagrams

In the autobiographical diagram assignment, students created a visual tool that considered themselves as the "center" of their diagram. Students brainstormed and identified different identities/aspects (e.g., race, sexual orientation) of themselves which they deem important to the experiences they embody. I find that students identified more salient identities quickly, usually within 10 minutes. Afterwards, students paired up with classmates, discussed their diagrams, and shared with the entire class. This process was very similar to the Think-Pair-Share technique (Millis & Cottell, 1998). I found this approach did not afford students the opportunity to think critically about these identities, nor did it provide students with the experience I wanted for them. Students were producing a basic Venn diagram that did not meet my learning goals of critical and intersectional analysis.

In order to facilitate critical analysis, I altered the assignment and gave students three non-consecutive class periods to finalize their diagram. On day one, students turned in their initial diagram, and we moved to other course content. Over the next few class periods, we covered other topics that illuminate different ways to identify oneself and incorporate various identities. For example, I noticed that my local students (i.e., from North Carolina) seldom associate geography with their identity because they represent the assumed norm. Conversely, students from other states and countries often identified location and/or nationality as very salient in their initial diagram. Students received their initial diagrams and were asked to add any additional identities or aspects of their identity they did not include before. We repeated this sequence a couple of weeks later so students could revise the diagram one last time. A great example of the autobiographical diagram came from an international student from Liberia versus a student raised in the U.S. Both students consider themselves Black but lived experiences were often very different, and the diagrams illustrated the nature of identity as more complex than just a shared racial/ethnic heritage. This exercise combatted the misperception that people of color, particularly those attending MSIs, are homogenous and lacking diversity in racial, social, economic, and other lived experiences.

With this assignment and all others, I reinforced to students that individuals maintain multiple identities that intersect, and thinking critically and reflectively about one's own identity allows insight into unexplored facets of the self. I began with the individual and then expanded to larger macro structures in society: group-level, institutional/organizational-level, and societal level. At each level, students engaged in conversation about the interrelated aspects of these identities and systemic structures. This approach may appear to run counter to a number of activities that start with bigger structural aspects and filter down to the individual level. However, I found either approach perfectly acceptable as long as students maintain the focus on the intersectional framework

Alejano-Steele et al. (2011) used a similar activity called the Multicultural Circles Exercise. Autobiographical Diagrams and Multicultural Circles Exercise focused on the student's (or participants') identification of in-group and out-group memberships, perceived positives and negatives of those memberships, and how those memberships influence the student at the center of the circles. For example, discussions of race as a monolithic experience offer limited value, and one cannot simply add the Black experience to women's experience to understand Black women's experiences (Alejano-Steele et al., 2011).

As a model for students, I created an autobiographical diagram, along with students, and shared mine first as a way of "breaking the ice." I attributed my ability to connect with students to the belief that sharing relevant personal experiences with them promotes for bidirectional learning. As I reflected on my diagrams, I explained to students that the salience of particular identities fluctuates with contextual factors (Ellemers, Spears, & Doosje, 2002). I warned them to expect to keep growing and discovering new aspects of themselves over time in changing contexts. I also talked to students about the changes that occurred since my first years at the university and now. When I first began teaching at the university, I was single, in my 30s, childless, and a recent transplant from southern California. My most recent diagram reflected who I am now: married, in my 40s, mother to a toddler, and acclimated to "southern culture." As new identities emerged, I incorporated them into how I see myself and approach certain issues. This allowed me to ground students in understanding that social identities are in a perpetual state of motion and will change.

Counter-Storytelling

Storytelling represents a rich oral tradition and integral part of the African American experience. Centering the experiences of multiple marginalized groups gives voice to the students themselves, often drawing upon a critical race theory (CRT) methodology known as counter-storytelling (Connor, 2006). A story becomes a counter-story when it incorporates the five elements of CRT

(Solórzano & Yosso, 2002): (1) intercentricity of race/racism with other forms of subordination; (2) challenges the dominant ideology; (3) commitment to social justice; (4) centrality of experiential knowledge; and (5) transdisciplinary perspective. Central to CRT are the issues of race and racism. Given that intersectionality is imbedded in CRT, both contend that race, gender, and class must be integrated into simultaneous discourses (Delgado, 1989). In my courses, I assigned personal narratives which describe an individual's experiences with various forms of oppression (e.g., racism and sexism). Personal narratives also challenged stereotypical or historical narratives that subjugate groups and position the students' experiences within the context of larger structural systems. This activity helped to promote social justice by personalizing the information and teaching others about social realities rarely heard or acknowledged.

After difficulty implementing counter-storytelling within lower-level courses, I decided to use it only with senior-level courses. I usually introduced this activity toward the end of the semester after students read the foundational literature on intersectionality, participated in discussions about intersectional frameworks, and completed relevant assignments.

Much of the published discourse about counter-storytelling described students' perspectives on their academic experiences (Archer, 2003; Connor, 2006). I encouraged students to think about their personal narratives and how they can create counter-stories from a variety of lived experiences. The prompts for stories can come from diverse sources. For example, Asimeng-Boahene (2010) used quotes and proverbs, and Stinson (2008) asked students, "How do you define success?" I achieved pedagogical success with both strategies. Students also used stories from news headlines, stereotypes (e.g., women are not good in math), and theories (e.g., acting white theory; Fordham & Ogbu, 1986) as prompts.

As they learned to reflect on counter-stories, students needed time to think about the dominate narrative and how their experience ran counter to mainstream discourse. Early feedback from students indicated that I did not provide enough time for students to sufficiently think about their stories. Based on this, I suggest allowing students to think about their counter-story for at least a weekend rather than during limited class time because most have never identified these narratives. Students created counter-stories in three phases. In Phase I, students received guiding questions to create their initial counter-story: (1) What factors/identities do you attribute to the dominant perspective? (2) What factors/identities do you attribute to your counter-story? and (3) How do/did they negotiate these factors/identities?

After students identified their initial counter-story, they identified data on the dominant narrative to support their assertion in Phase II. Students compiled, summarized, and analyzed the data as if they were creating a literature review. Unlike a standard literature review, students made connections between their personal experiences and the data. I found that giving students at least a week, after the data had been compiled and analyzed, to complete their counter-story provided sufficient time. Phase III consisted of students ensuring the five elements of CRT were represented in the counter-story. Students emphasized the intersectionality of experiences with oppression, privilege, and in many cases, resistance and resilience in the final rewrite. Class discussion ensued after students received feedback on their counter-stories.

One of the most powerful counter-stories came from an openly gay Black Christian male student who wrote about acceptance in the Black church and his family. His narrative challenged the dominant story that the Black church and Black families are homophobic and reject those who do not identify as heterosexual. The class discussion helped students analyze his story, and their own, on various levels. Not only were the stories important individual testimonies, but they provided critical information for understanding and extending the conversation of how oppression and privilege operate structurally. The counter-stories were quite transformative and added pedagogical value in the connection between individual, institutional, and societal levels of knowledge acquisition and transfer (Merriweather Hunn, Guy, & Manglitz, 2006; Scheurich & Young, 2004).

Challenges to Applying Intersectionality in Undergraduate Courses

The three main challenges I encountered in my quest to integrate intersectionality into my classroom were: (1) the push for operationalization; (2) recognizing the impact of positionality; and (3) increasing student engagement. A foundational aspect of my primary discipline of psychology is defining or operationalizing constructs for analysis, which counters the main tenets of intersectionality. To address positionality, educators must critically reflect on their own social locations within the classroom and ask themselves the following:

- Am I positioning myself as the content expert who imparts knowledge to students through traditional routes such as lectures and readings?
- Or am I positioning myself as a reciprocal learner, who happens to have subject matter expertise, but remains actively engaged in discussion and activities so that intersectional knowledge is obtained from both the students and me?

Using a dynamic style in the classroom helps make students comfortable and facilitates active discussion between faculty and students (Closson & Henry, 2008). By strategically drawing upon a range of approaches, faculty can work at becoming more culturally responsive to students' intersectional identities on an ongoing basis and across disciplinary boundaries. Finally, a recurring theme for faculty engaged in teaching intersectionality is the difficulty of engaging students in this type of thought-process. I found the topic of intersectionality complex and difficult for many students. Faculty often struggle with how to explain simultaneous membership in groups and how these memberships impact lived experiences. I discovered students are more engaged and interested when I participate in activities and think through the explanations and experiences with them. Sometimes these activities are complicated and a bit thorny. Difficult yet necessary discussions about race/ethnicity, diversity, power, and privilege are necessary to truly and fully engage in teaching and learning from an intersectional perspective.

Concluding Thoughts

As more institutes of higher education focus on internationalization of their curriculum and concentrate on general education courses, professors are encouraged to think about the importance of infusing intersectionality into their curricula. Much like Case and Lewis (this volume) report, intersectionality allows diverse students to identify the associations between their own social identities and locations to seemingly unrelated systems of oppression and privilege. Using an intersectional approach enables the identification of categorical differences that may help facilitate coalition building within and across disciplines while acknowledging differences and promoting commonalities (Roberts & Jesudason, 2013). An earlier example contrasted the experiences of African Americans and those from Black international students. Although the countries of origin differ, using tenets of intersectionality illuminated the commonality between slavery and colonialism and how students can work together to create a social justice movement that promotes social change.

Culturally Appropriate and Responsive Pedagogy

Intersectionality elucidates the need for faculty, researchers, and scholars to address social identities and locations and their impact, or relationship with, perceptions and lived experiences. There is a need in the U.S. to move toward an educational system that embraces culturally appropriate and responsive pedagogy that prepares all students by developing their sensitivity, acknowledgment, and appreciation for diversity and equity (Asimeng-Boahene, 2010). This paradigm shift benefits students attending all universities, including HBCUs, as well as the faculty, and translates into culturally relevant and timely research and scholarship. As hooks (1994) noted, educators must embrace struggle and sacrifice to transform the academy into a place where cultural diversity is integrated into every facet of learning.

   The creation of a culturally responsive pedagogy helps to foster critical consciousness, encourage peer and community engagement, and focus on social justice issues related to their lived environments (Grant & Zwier, 2013). Faculty members, irrespective of identity, must be knowledgeable and comfortable with theories and issues of identity to be effective in teaching and learning environments (Alejano-Steele et al., 2011). Culturally connected teachers seek to gain a better understanding of their own cultures, their students' cultures, and the historical relationships among them (Irizarry, 2007). For those teaching in higher education, knowledge acquisition and transfer cannot be from only one tradition. By presenting one cultural model, educators perpetuate the notion that, for example, the White middle-class experience in America is the only important experience and all other experiences provide only interesting anecdotes (Alejano-Steele et al., 2011). People of color are part of the story, and without their voices, the story is incomplete.

Finally, there is a continuing dialogue about the current relevance of MSIs. All institutions of higher education face challenges and MSIs are no different. As MSIs such as HBCUs celebrate the spirit of a shared cultural identity, the notion of highlighting diversity within the community offers an exciting and enriching opportunity for students to better understand the contours and unlimited possibilities of identity through intersectionality (Greenfield, Innouvong, Aglugub, & Yusuf, 2015). Freire (1970/1993) articulated that education offers a path toward liberation in which people become aware of their social positions, and through praxis (reflection and action), transform the world. Educators must be self-reflective to understand personal motives, privileges, biases, strengths, and limitations. Intersectionality matters both inside and outside of the academy because lived experiences and everyday life are the primary domains grounding the conceptualization and understanding of multiple intersecting identities (Dill & Zambrana, 2009).

Notes

1 Throughout the chapter, Black is a term used to include all people of African descent. The terms Black and African American will be used interchangeably based on what term was used in the source cited.
2 MSI designations for academic establishments are based on enrollment criteria, typically the percentage of minorities enrolled at a particular school. The federally recognized categories of MSI based on racial/ethnic enrollment (usually at least 25% of total undergraduate enrollment) are: HBCUs, Hispanic-serving institutions, Asian-serving institutions (includes Asian Americans and Pacific Islanders), and tribal colleges and universities.

References

Alejano-Steele, A., Hamington, M., MacDonald, L., Potter, M., Schafer, S., Sgoutas, A., & Tull, T. (2011). From difficult dialogues to critical conversations: Intersectionality in our teaching and professional lives. *New Directions for Teaching and Learning, 125*, 91–100. doi:10.1002/tl.436

Alexander, M. (2013, October 17). *The future of race in America: Michelle Alexander at TEDxColumbus* [Video]. Retrieved from tedxtalks.ted.com/video/

Archer, L. (2003). *Race, masculinity, and schooling: Muslim boys and education.* Maidenhead, UK: Open University Press.

Asimeng-Boahene, L. (2010). Counter-storytelling with African proverbs: A vehicle for teaching social justice and global understanding in urban, U.S. schools. *Equity & Excellence in Education, 43*(4), 434–445. doi:10.1080/10665684.2010.518878

Banks, C. A., & Pliner, S. M. (2012). Introduction. In S. M. Pliner & C. A. Banks (Eds.), *Teaching, learning, and intersecting identities in higher education* (pp. 1–14). New York, NY: Peter Lang.

Blair, I. V., Judd, C. M., & Chapleau, K. M. (2004). The influence of Afrocentric facial features in criminal sentencing. *Psychological Science, 15,* 674–679. doi:10.1111/j.0956-7976.2004.00739.x

Blumenfeld, W. J., & Jaekel, K. (2012). Exploring levels of Christian privilege awareness among preservice teachers. *Journal of Social Issues, 68*(1), 128–144. doi:10.1111/j.1540-4560.2011.01740.x

Butler, J. E. (2014). Replacing the cracked mirror: The challenge for diversity and inclusion. *Diversity and Democracy, 17(4).* Retrieved from www.aacu.org/diversity-democracy/

Carbado, D. W., Crenshaw, K. W., Mays, V. M., & Tomlinson, B. (2013). Intersectionality: Mapping the movements of a theory. *Du Bois Review, 10*(2), 303–312. doi:10.1017/S174 2058X13000349.

Case, K. (2013). Beyond diversity and whiteness: Developing a transformative and intersectional privilege studies pedagogy. In K. Case (Ed.), *Deconstructing privilege: Teaching and learning as allies in the classroom* (pp. 1–14). New York, NY: Routledge.

Case, K. A. (this volume). Toward an intersectional pedagogy model: Engaged learning for social justice. In K. A. Case (Ed.), *Intersectional pedagogy: Complicating identity and social justice* (pp. 1–24). New York, NY: Routledge.

Case, K., Iuzzini, J., & Hopkins, M. (2012). Systems of privilege: Intersections, awareness, and applications. *Journal of Social Issues, 68,* 1–10. doi:10.1111/j.1540-4560.2011.01732.x

Case, K., & Lewis, M. (this volume). Teaching intersectional psychology in racially diverse settings. In K. A. Case (Ed.), *Intersectional pedagogy: Complicating identity and social justice* (pp 129–149). New York, NY: Routledge.

Case, K., McMullen, M., & Hentges, B. (2013). Teaching the taboo: Walking the tightrope of Christian privilege. In K. Case (Ed.), *Deconstructing privilege: Teaching and learning as allies in the classroom* (pp. 188–206). New York, NY: Routledge.

Closson, R. B., & Henry, W. J. (2008). Racial and ethnic diversity at HBCUs: What can be learned when Whites are in the minority? *Multicultural Education, 15(4),* 15–19. doi:10.1353/csd/0.0036

Cole, E. R. (2009). Intersectionality and research in psychology. *American Psychologist, 64,* 170-180. doi:10.1037/a0014564

Cole, E. R., Case, K. A., Rios, D., & Curtin, N. (2011). Understanding what students bring to the classroom: Moderators of the effects of diversity courses on student attitudes. *Cultural Diversity and Ethnic Minority Psychology, 17(4),* 397–405. doi:10.1037/a0025433

Collins, P. H. (1990). *Black feminist thought: Knowledge, consciousness, and the politics of empowerment.* Boston, MA: Unwin Hyman.

Collins, P. H. (2009). Emerging intersections: Building knowledge and transforming institutions. In B. T. Dill & R. E. Zambrana (Eds.), *Emerging intersections: Race, class, and gender in theory, policy, and practice* (pp. vii-xiii). New Brunswick, NJ: Rutgers University Press.

Connor, D. J. (2006). Michael's story: "I get into so much trouble just by walking": Narrative knowing and life at the intersections of learning disability, race, and class. *Equity & Excellence in Education, 39*, 154–165. doi:10.1080/10665680500533942

Crenshaw, K. (1991). Mapping the margins: Intersectionality, identity politics, and the violence against women of color. *Stanford Law Review, 43*, 1241–1299.

Delgado, R. (1989). Storytelling for oppositionists and others: A plea for narrative. *Michigan Law Review, 87*(8), 2411–2441.

Dill, B. T. (2009). Intersections, identities, and inequalities in higher education. In B. T. Dill & R. E. Zambrana (Eds.), *Emerging intersections: Race, class, and gender in theory, policy, and practice*. New Brunswick, NJ: Rutgers University Press.

Dill, B. T., & Zambrana, R. E. (2009). Critical thinking about inequality: An emerging lens. In B. T. Dill & R. E. Zambrana (Eds.), *Emerging intersections: Race, class, and gender in theory, policy, and practice*. New Brunswick, NJ: Rutgers University Press.

Du Bois, W. E. B. (1903). *The souls of Black folk*. Chicago, IL: A.C. McClurg & Co.

Eberhardt, J. L., Davies, P. G., Purdie-Vaughns, V. J., & Johnson, S. L. (2006). Looking death worthy: Perceived stereotypicality of Black defendants predicts capital sentencing outcomes. *Psychological Science, 17*, 383–386. doi: 10.1111/j.1467-9280.2006.01716.x.

Ellemers, N., Spears, R., & Doosje, B. (2002). Self and social identity. *Annual Review of Psychology, 53*, 161–186. doi:10.1146/annurev.psych.53.100901.135228

Fordham, S., & Ogbu, J. U. (1986). Black students' school success: Coping with the "burden of 'acting White.'" *Urban Review, 18*(3), 176–206.

Freire, P. (1970/1993). *Pedagogy of the oppressed*. New York, NY: Continuum.

Goff, P. A., & Kahn, K. B. (2013). How psychological science impedes intersectional thinking. *Du Bois Review, 10*(2), 365–384. doi:10.1017S1742058X13000313

Grant, C. A., & Zwier, E. (2013). Intersectionality and student outcomes: Sharpening the struggle against racism, sexism, classism, ableism, heterosexism, nationalism, and linguistic, religious, and geographical discrimination in teaching and learning. *Multicultural Perspectives, 13*(4), 181–188. doi:10.1080/15210960.2011.616813

Greenfield, D. F., Innouvong, T., Aglugub, R. J., & Yusuf, I. A. (2015). HBCUs as critical context for identity work: Reflections, experiences, and lessons learned. *New Directions for Higher Education*, (170), 37–48. doi:10.1002/he.20130

Gurin, P., Nagda, B., & Lopez, G. (2004). The benefits of diversity in education for democratic citizenship. *Journal of Social Issues, 60*, 17–34. doi:10.1111/j.0022-4537.2004.00097.x

Hall, B., & Closson, R. (2005). When the majority is the minority: White graduate student social adjustment at an HBCU. *Journal of College Student Development, 46*(1), 28–41. doi:10.1353/csd.2005.0004

hooks, b. (1984). *Feminist theory: From margin to center*. Boston, MA: South End Press.

hooks, b. (1994). *Teaching to transgress: Education as the practice of freedom*. New York, NY: Routledge.

Hunter, M. (2007). The persistent problem of colorism: Skin tone, status, and inequality. *Sociology Compass, 1*(1), 237–254. doi:10.1111/j.1751-9020.2007.00006.x

Irizarry, J. G. (2007). Ethnic and urban intersections in the classroom: Latino students, hybrid Identities, and culturally responsive pedagogy. *Multicultural Perspectives, 9*(3), 21–28. doi: 10.1080/15210960701443599

Jewell, J. O. (2002). To set an example: The tradition of diversity at historically Black colleges and universities. *Urban Education, 37(1),* 7–21.

Johnson, A. G. (2006). *Privilege, power, and difference* (2nd ed.). New York, NY: McGraw-Hill.

Jones, C. (2006). Falling between the cracks: What diversity means for Black women in higher education. *Policy Futures in Education, 4(2),* 145–159. doi:10.2304/pfie.2006. 4.2.145

Jones, S. R., & Wijeyesinghe, C. L. (2011). The promises and challenges of teaching from an intersectional perspective: Core components and applied strategies. *New Directions for Teaching and Learning, 125,* 11–20. doi:10.1002/tl.429

Lee, M. R. (2012). Teaching gender and intersectionality: A dilemma and social justice approach. *Psychology of Women Quarterly, 36,* 110–115. doi:10.1177/036168431142612 9

Lee, A., Poch, R., Shaw, M., & Williams, R. (2012). Engaging diversity in undergraduate classrooms: A pedagogy for developing intercultural competence. *ASHE Higher Education Report, 38(2).* Hoboken, NJ: John Wiley & Sons, Inc.

Maxwell, M., Brevard, J., Abrams, J., & Belgrave, F. (2015). What's color got to do with it? Skin color, skin color satisfaction, racial identity, and internalized racism among African American college students. *Journal of Black Psychology, 41*(5), 438–461. doi:10.1177/00 95798414542299

McCall, L. (2005). The complexity of intersectionality. *Signs, 30,* 1771–1800. doi:10. 1086/426800

McIntosh, P. (1988). *White privilege and male privilege: A personal account of coming to see correspondences through work in women's studies* (Working Paper No. 189). Wellesley, MA: Wellesley Centers for Women.

McMickens, T. L. (2012). Running the race when race is a factor. *Phi Delta Kappan, 93*(8), 39–43. doi:10.1177/003172171209300809

Merriweather Hunn, L. R., Guy, T. C., & Manglitz, E. (2006). Who can speak for whom? Using counter-storytelling to challenge racial hegemony. In M. Hagen & E. Goff (Eds.), *The many faces of adult education: Proceedings of the 47th Annual Adult Education Research Conference, May 18–21,* (pp. 244–250). Minnesota, MN: University of Minnesota.

Millis, B. J., & Cottell, P. G., Jr. (1998). *Cooperative learning for higher education faculty.* American Council on Education Oryx Press Series on Higher Education. Phoenix, AZ: Rowman & Littlefield.

Museus, S. D., & Griffin, K. A. (2011). Mapping the margins in higher education: On the promise of intersectionality frameworks in research and discourse. *New Directions for Institutional Research, 151,* 5–14. doi: 10.1002/ir.395

Nahal, A. (2009). Tending to diversity at an HBCU. *Diverse Issues in Higher Education, 26*(20), 24.

Nash, J. C. (2008). Re-thinking intersectionality. *Feminist Review, 89,* 1–15. doi:10.1057/ fr.2008. 4

Purdie-Vaughns, V., & Eibach, R. P. (2008). Intersectional invisibility: The distinctive advantages and disadvantages of multiple subordinate-group identities. *Sex Roles, 59(5–6), 377–391.* doi:10.1007/s11199-008-9424-4.

Quaye, S. J. (2012). Think before you teach: Preparing for dialogues about racial realities. *Journal of College Student Development, 53*(4), 542–562. doi:101353/csd.2012.0056

Rahman Sidek, E. A., & Yunus, M. M. (2012). Students' experiences on using blog as learning journals. *Procedia-Social and Behavioral Sciences, 67,* 135–143. doi:10.1016/j. sbspro.20 12.11.314

Rios, D., Bowling, M., & Harris, J. (this volume). Decentering student "uniqueness" in lessons about intersectionality. In K. A. Case (Ed.), *Intersectional pedagogy: Complicating identity and social justice* (pp. 194–213). New York, NY: Routledge.

Roberts, D., & Jesudason, S. (2013). Movement intersectionality. *Du Bois Review, 10*(2), 313–328. doi:10.1017/S1742058X13000210

Scheurich, J. J., & Young, M. (2004). Coloring epistemologies: Are our research epistemologies racially biased? *Educational Researcher, 26(4),* 4–16.

Sharp, E. A., Bermudez, J. M., Watson, W., & Fitzpatrick, J. (2007). Reflections from the trenches: Our development as feminist teachers. *Journal of Family Issues, 28,* 529–548. doi:10.1177/0192513X06297473

Shields, S. (2008). Gender: An intersectionality perspective. *Sex Roles, 59,* 301–311.

Slater, R. B. (1993). White professors at Black colleges. *Journal of Blacks in Higher Education, 1*(1), 67–70.

Solórzano, D. G., & Yosso, T. J. (2002). Critical race methodology: Counter-storytelling as an analytical framework for education research. *Qualitative Inquiry, 8*(1), 23–44. doi: 10.1177/107780040200800103

Spelman, E. V. (1998). Gender and race: The ampersand problem in feminist thought. In S. Ruth (Ed.) *Issues in feminism: An introduction to women's studies,* 4th ed. (pp. 22–34). Mountain View, CA: Mayfield.

Stewart, D. L., & Lozano, A. (2009). Difficult dialogues at the intersection of race, culture, and religion. *New Directions for Student Services, 125,* 23–31. doi:10.1002/ss.304

Stinson, D. W. (2008). Negotiating sociocultural discourses: The counter-storytelling of academically (and mathematically) successful African American male students. *American Educational Research Journal, 45(4),* 975–1010. doi: 10.3102/0002831208319723

Weber, L. (2010). *Understanding race, class, gender, and sexuality: A conceptual framework* (2nd ed.). New York: Oxford University Press.

PART III

Intersectional Pedagogy for Social Justice

9

REVEALING HIDDEN INTERSECTIONS OF GENDER IDENTITY, SEXUAL ORIENTATION, RACE, AND ETHNICITY

Teaching about Multiple Oppressed Identities

David P. Rivera

A student walked into his first diversity course, "Multiculturalism in America." The student reviewed the syllabus and noticed topics such as "Asian Americans," "American Indians," "Black Americans," "Latina/o Americans," "Women," "Disability," "LGBTQ," and "Religion," as well as a few other social and cultural identity classifications. The student felt excited to learn about different cultural groups. At the end of the semester, he left the course with more knowledge about the histories and lived experiences of a variety of social and cultural groups plus an unintended lesson. This student, who was actually me, left with the idea that identity can be represented by a pie chart. In other words, each sociocultural identity occupies its own separate space and does not overlap or influence any of the other identities. While not the intention of my professor, this influenced my conceptualization of identity and how I understood my own sense of self.

In my graduate courses, I learned about race, cultures, societies, and institutions while exploring and processing myself as a cultural being. Although these courses deepened my understanding of the distinct, individual aspects of identity that formed me as a person, the "pie chart" notion that each identity functions independently of others stayed with me. While I recognized the importance of comprehending individual aspects of identity as unique constructs, introspective processing often left me feeling fragmented, frustrated, and confused about who I was and how I fit into society. These experiences left me pondering, "How can I understand one aspect of my identity without considering how it relates to other aspects of my identity, as well as society and context?" Case (this volume) criticizes this additive approach to teaching about identity and intersectionality that most likely leaves many students struggling with the same question.

Ideas of intersectionality came to me later in my graduate studies. While I appreciated an intersectionality framework, instructors often included it as a curricular afterthought. The main emphasis remained on individual aspects of identity, most often based on race and ethnicity. An intersectional lens for understanding oppression existed as a mere "add-on." This marginal mention of intersectionality left me confused about how to make sense of identity, including my own. Additionally, the focus on race and ethnicity, although extremely significant social constructs, left me wondering what to do about my other identities that had a salient impact on my reality. As a Latino, the focus on racial and ethnic identity sent me the indirect message that my other identities, such as my sexual orientation, were less important to process and comprehend. I soon learned that this conundrum was quite common for queer[1] people of color. This group often endures an internal struggle when it comes to aligning with either sexual identity or racial and ethnic identities due to the false assumption that categories of the self operate as mutually exclusive. This dilemma can be even more pronounced and intense for women, transgender, and gender non-conforming people with a long history of intersectional invisibility. Three factors significantly influence this identity tug-of-war: (a) the absence or minimization of an interactive intersectionality framework influences people to conceptualize identity as segmented; (b) the hierarchical positioning of social and cultural identities elevates race above gender identity and sexual orientation, sending an implicit message about the greater importance of race; and (c) for some people of color, opposing cultural values between an individual's racial or ethnic group and their queer sexual orientation identity and gender identity suggest the person must choose a side, thus denying some aspect of the self.

The conceptualizations and strategies discussed below draw from my experiences as a student, teacher, researcher, and practitioner who made the journey from viewing identity as a pie chart to understanding identity as synergistic and interactively intersectional in nature. My perspective relies on theoretical frameworks and empirical studies related to identity. Below, I make the case for applying an intersectional theory to conceptualize intersections, specifically the often marginalized intersections of gender identity, sexual orientation, ethnicity, and race. I elucidate concepts that inform emerging best practices for engaging learners in an intersectional framework. Given the dearth of knowledge about applying intersectionality theory to practice, I close with recommendations for future directions.

Making the Invisible Visible: Giving Voice to the Oppressed

Situating identity within the dynamic of privilege and oppression (Case, this volume) represents a focal point of intersectional theory. This system of privilege and oppression impacts every aspect of the lived experience, from the societal level to the intrapersonal level, and causes social inequalities and disparities as well as the internalized oppressions that disrupt an individual's sense of self and lead to psychological dysfunction (David, 2013). People typically accept the privileged norms of society as status quo. For example, privilege overshadows the marginalized via overrepresentation of White, cisgender (gender identity privileged), heterosexual, middle-class, able-bodied, Christian experiences in nearly every facet of life. Case (this volume) illustrates this dynamic in Figure 1.2. Given this stark imbalance, experiences of the oppressed must move to the forefront when considering an intersectional approach for teaching about sexual orientation, gender identity, race, and ethnicity. This does not mean that the privileged identities get ignored, but an overt and intentional emphasis needs to be placed on the marginalized as a way to create more visibility of the oppressed experiences. Additionally, people living at the intersections of several marginalized groups, such as at the intersections of their gender identity, sexual orientation, ethnicity, and race, attribute microaggressions to the combination of their identities (Bowleg, 2013; Nadal et al., 2015). Given common silencing of the voices of the oppressed and that individuals with multiple marginalized identities experience various forms of oppression and microaggressions, educators must intentionally elevate these experiences in the curriculum.

Instructor Social Location Considerations

Given the politicized nature of gender identity, sexual orientation, race, and ethnicity (e.g., Logan, 2014; Randall & Waylen, 1998; Whisman, 1996), teaching about these particular topics presents unique challenges. Additionally, students often view overt discussion of these identities as taboo which can further complicate effective pedagogy in the classroom (Eliasoph, 1999; Sue, 2013). Instructor accounts of their teaching experiences illuminated a number of these challenges and suggested qualitative and quantitative differences in the teaching dynamic between instructors with overt privileged identities (e.g., White men) and instructors with overt marginalized identities (e.g., queer women of color) (Sue et al., 2011; Sue, Torino, Capodilupo, Rivera, & Lin, 2009). When considering how to incorporate intersectionality in teaching about gender identity, sexual orientation, race, and ethnicity, recognition of these challenges and the classroom reality for instructors with marginalized identities must occur so that educators can modify their teaching strategies.

Teachers of courses focusing on social justice and multiculturalism report that the curriculum sometimes leads to student resistance (Asher, 2007; Case & Cole, 2013; Reynolds, 2011). This resistance may present itself through surface-level discussions, minimal student involvement in class activities, challenging the instructor's credibility, and dismissing course content (Reynolds, 2011). Resistance may result from inadequate institutional support for social justice education, unacknowledged microaggressions in the classroom, privileged students dominating discussions, and teaching techniques that isolate students (Sensoy & DiAngelo, 2014). Therefore, instructors must acknowledge and address potential sources of resistance as a means of reducing the negative impact on students' engagement with the course material and productive interaction with each other.

Another significant challenge relates specifically to educators with marginalized identities. However, little documentation exists on the experiences of instructors teaching multicultural or social justice courses. Perhaps unsurprisingly many of them come from socially marginalized backgrounds (Gorski, 2012). The majority of women's studies faculty are women, ethnic studies faculty are people of color, and queer studies faculty identify as transgender, queer, bisexual, lesbian, or gay. Similarly, many teachers of multicultural or social justice courses in departments of psychology, sociology, education, history, English, etc., also belong to socially marginalized groups. Given that instructors of social justice courses identify with marginalized groups, the impact of these instructor social locations on teaching dynamics must be considered (Ladson-Billings, 1996). Case's (this volume) pedagogical model for intersectionality stresses the importance of teacher reflection on the ways their identities impact the learning milieu. This may be especially important for educators whose marginalized identities overlap with course topics (e.g., a lesbian instructor teaching about sexual orientation).

Educators of social justice and multicultural courses report that they witness a form of resistance characterized by students accusing the instructor of pushing "a political agenda" that infringes on student rights (Case, 2013; Reynolds, 2011). Even though same-sex marriage earned federal recognition, this issue remains contentious in the classroom and across the U.S. as certain jurisdictions have attempted to defy the Supreme Court ruling. In 2015, state legislators introduced more than 100 anti-LGBT (lesbian, gay, bisexual, transgender) bills (McCarty, 2016). As an example of the supposed hidden agenda, the aforementioned lesbian instructor might be accused of trying to sway her students to support marriage equality. While instructors from privileged backgrounds may also be accused of pushing a political agenda, they likely receive less resistance and criticism. Due to their identity being perceived as disconnected from the course material, students may judge them as less biased (Ladson-Billings, 1996; Sensoy & DiAngelo, 2014). This qualitative difference needs to be incorporated into the instructor's approach to the course and how they engage the students with course material. In addition, institutions must acknowledge this difference given that resistance based on instructor social location may lower student evaluations (Case, this volume; Huston, 2006; Merritt, 2008; Nast, 1999).

Teaching Intersectionality of the Oppressed

By acknowledging the experiential realities of students and faculty, educators include the necessary ingredients for competently incorporating an intersectionality framework into pedagogies (Case, this volume). Many students enter the classroom with a fragmented and simplistic conceptualization of identity that ignores structural and institutional influences. Because many educators learned from the pie chart perspective, they often reinforce this construction of identity in their instructional practices even when they aim to incorporate an intersectional framework. Instructors from marginalized groups report a qualitatively different experience in teaching social justice content than their more privileged counterparts (Sue, Torino, et al., 2009; Sue et al., 2011). In light of these realities, educators may use this information to form the foundation of their pedagogies for navigating intersectionality in the classroom.

Laying the Foundation for Teaching Intersectionality of the Oppressed

Other contributors to this volume elucidate on the main theoretical and philosophical underpinnings that influenced the formation of intersectional theory (Case, this volume; Greenwood, this volume; Grzanka, this volume; Kurtis & Adams, this volume; Naples, this volume). Notably, women of color called for intersectional theorizing of their lived experiences that differed from the primarily White, middle-class women that led the mainstream feminist movement (Crenshaw, 1989). The work of Crenshaw (1989) and others contributed an important step toward examining the synergistic relationship between various aspects of identity as situated in social context. Additionally, the writings of the Combahee River Collective (1977/2007), a group of Black lesbian feminists, provided some of the first arguments for taking an intersectional approach to systems of privilege and oppression relating specifically to the intersections of gender, sexual orientation, and race. These scholars called for feminists to abandon their singular, generalized focus on women and move toward exploring how gender interlocks with sexuality, class, and race. Incorporating this philosophy into teaching gender identity, sexual orientation, race, and ethnicity honors the work of these luminaries in the intersectionality movement.

Two additional theories informed my intersectional pedagogy for teaching gender identity, sexual orientation, race, and ethnicity: critical race theory (CRT; Delgado & Stefancic, 2012) and queer theory (Sullivan, 2003). Both theories call for analyses of the oppression/privilege relationship from a structural level and an elevation of people of color and queer voices in understanding phenomena related to these identities, consistent with the Case (this volume) pedagogical model emphasis on marginalized experiences. While each focuses on a particular social identity category, both theoretical perspectives call for the inclusion of intersectionality for complicating the dynamic nature of racial and queer identities. In this section, I expand on the main tenets of these theories that inform the teaching strategies recommended below.

CRT offers a number of tenets that inform intersectionality pedagogies. As with any theoretical perspective, CRT lacks complete applicability to every situation and context. Therefore, CRT's application to the intersectionality framework that I advocate for comes with caveats. CRT may covertly lead one to believe that race represents the single most important social force in society. Although some scholars argued this perspective, CRT theorists more commonly endorse an intersectional approach to race and racial dynamics and articulate inarguable differences between the lived experiences based on the various social identities (Crenshaw, 1991; Delgado & Stefancic, 1993; Ladson-Billings & Tate, 1995; Roberts, 1995). CRT also posits that while those from marginalized groups share the experience of being oppressed, the quality of this shared oppression differs based on the respective intersectional identities and occupied social context (Delgado & Stefancic, 1993). Finally, the emphasis on storytelling and counter-storytelling (Hall, this volume) as methods for elevating the voices of the oppressed in understanding their realities highlights the necessity to focus on often silenced and invisible intersections, such as queer people of color (Solorzano & Yosso, 2001, 2002). I further expand on storytelling and counter-storytelling as a teaching technique for exploring the intersections of race, ethnicity, sexual orientation, and gender identity.

Rooted in critical theory (Sullivan, 2003; Turner, 2000), queer theory provides a perspective that challenges and moves away from a focus on rigid and binary notions of sexuality (e.g., heterosexual vs. gay and lesbian) toward an inclusion of all sexualities and gender experiences, making it a fitting ally to intersectional perspectives. Given that academic and popular discourse misunderstand and inappropriately conflate aspects of sexual orientation and gender identity, a foundation in queer theory helps avoid these pitfalls. Queer theory also argues for the deconstruction of labels used for sexual orientation and gender identity by positing that these identities are not static, but rather dynamic in nature and exist in concert with the array of identities (Luhmann, 1998; Sullivan, 2003). I further argue that the indiscriminate application of labels can be inadvertently reductive and negate the intersectional nature of identity. For example, when the term *gay* serves as an umbrella term for all same-sex attractions, this action invalidates the diversity of experiences and helps maintain the invisibility of many intersections.

Since queer theory suggests a deconstructionist perspective to understanding sexuality and gender identity, this perspective supports conceptualizations and applications of intersectionality. Informed by this deconstructionist lens, educators participating in a *revaluation* of words update the meanings attributed to these words and add value to historically devalued identities. For example, the term *gay* evolved over time in reference to identity, at first, uniformly applied to same-sex attracted men and later describing same-sex attraction regardless of sex and gender identity. However, the meaning embedded within the term may not necessarily capture the experiences of every person with same-sex attractions. For example, some people of color may attribute the term *gay* to the experiences of White people. Thus, revaluation of the term to acknowledge these differences enacts intersectionality as encouraged by Case's (this volume) call to make hidden intersections visible.

Strategies for Incorporating Intersectionality in the Classroom

A counseling psychologist by training, whose doctoral education centered on issues of cultural competency, I learned to infuse multiculturalism and social justice into my professional practices including teaching. Recognizing and honoring cultural competency as a lifelong journey, I intentionally sought out experiences to enhance my professional development. This involved using my teaching experiences across several disciplines (e.g., psychology, counselor education, and higher education student affairs) as personal learning opportunities. The courses I taught facilitated learning about diverse topics as well as traditionally multicultural content, such as Cross-Cultural Psychology (undergraduate). I also taught graduate-level courses where students assumed issues of multiculturalism and social justice were less relevant, such as Theories of Group Counseling, Lab in Group Counseling, Career Counseling Theory and Practice, and Student Development Theory. Most of my instructional experiences occurred within urban, public university settings with diverse students in terms of race, ethnicity, religion, and social class, and, to a lesser extent, gender identity and sexual orientation. These experiences and contexts shaped my role in the classroom where I incorporated principles of intersectionality by utilizing a number of instructional techniques shared below.

Strategy 1: Meaning What You Say

Queer theory calls for a deconstructionist framework that includes a revaluation of words (Sullivan, 2003). This revaluation process examines the meaning attributed to words and also the value applied to words. When teaching about multiple oppressed identities via an intersectionality framework, the instructor must develop intentionality in both the pedagogical strategies and in the very words chosen to talk about intersectionality. In terms of the vernacular of social justice work, many educators know the appropriate words to avoid. Regardless, I observed teachers continuing to use outdated or offensive terms. For example, many know that the term *homosexual* should be avoided. For this term in particular, the origins of the term assigned pathology as a mental illness, and the medical diagnosis was removed from the American Psychiatric Association's *Diagnostic and Statistical Manual for Mental Disorders* (Drescher, 2015) in 1973. Same-sex attracted people currently prefer other terms such as bisexual, demisexual, gay, lesbian, pansexual, queer, etc. (for terminology definitions see Killerman, 2015). Similarly, some outdated terms connote a certain level of derogation, such as *colored people*. Used quite frequently until the 1970s, scholars now consider the term colored people outdated and offensive because of its history as a racial slur (Malesky, 2014). In contrast, reference to a specific group (e.g., American Indian, Asian, Black, Latino, Multiracial, etc.) or *person of color* provides a more respectful word choice. However, as with any umbrella term, person of color risks rendering various intersections invisible.

Language intentionality recommends that educators remain deliberate in not only word choice, but also grammatical structure, such as word order. When discussing various identity classifications, word order may send implicit messages that certain identities or social groups carry more value than others. In essence, by not challenging this social hierarchy of identity, instructors add to the maintenance of this hierarchy and the invisibility of various intersections. For example, when instructors first introduce race, ethnicity, sexual orientation, and gender identity in multicultural or diversity courses, they often present terms in this very same order in the syllabus schedule. In addition, they commonly list these identities in the same order, with race mentioned first, during lectures and discussions. Educators and students alike expect race will be discussed before issues of sexual orientation. These unconscious practices imply that race deserves attention before sexual orientation (i.e., race is more important) and that sexual orientation deserves exploration before gender identity. The common acronym *LGBTQ* (lesbian, gay, bisexual, transgender, and queer) communicates a hierarchy of sexual orientation first and gender identity last. The current configuration, which may function as a form of microaggression, also suggests that binary sexual orientations (same-sex vs. heterosexual) are viewed as more important than non-binary sexuality (e.g., bisexual, asexual) and gender identity.

For me, the instructional practice of being intentional about word usage and placement served two purposes. First, this practice provided effective modeling for students in terms of how to discuss issues of social justice and intersectionality, especially when discussing multiple oppressed identities. Careful attention to word usage and terminology order also reinforced the message that students do not have to choose one identity over another. For example, in the classroom, I utilized the previously described language intentionality strategy and explained to my students the reasons I chose certain words and language structures. Hopefully, explanations of language influenced what terms and phrases students took with them and used in their daily lives. Second, by leveling the artificial social hierarchy of marginalized identities, students with competing identities may have struggled less with the psychological tug-of-war and feeling that they must choose one identity over another. This practice helped students conceptualize their identities as synergistic rather than mutually exclusive and provided support in teaching about multiple marginalized identities of sexual orientation, gender, race, and ethnicity. Language intentionality is recommended across the teaching experience and can be applied to any pedagogical framework or academic discipline.

Strategy 2: Connecting Structural Forces and Individual Identity

Learning about identity all too often begins with learning about specific sociocultural groups or reflecting upon one's own specific sociocultural identities. As presented earlier, instructors often arrange syllabi according to sociocultural groups or forms of oppression (e.g., Asian Americans, Black Americans, women, religion, disability, social class). Similarly, discussions of various levels of oppression (societal, institutional, group, individual) often occur within the context of specific sociocultural identity groups or categories (e.g., institutionalized racism, gender inequality, heterosexism, health disparities for transgender individuals). Both of these approaches run counter to intersectional theory by focusing on one specific sociocultural identity at a time. The main focus on individual identity also negates the societal and institutional factors integral to intersectionality theory (Case, this volume; Rios, Bowling, & Harris, this volume). To address this pitfall, I employed the *recursive funnel approach* when introducing the topic of identity.

Using the recursive funnel approach, I began the discussion with a focus on the broader societal context, followed by institutional, then group, and finally, individual context. Within this approach, each subsequent context linked back to the broader levels. For example, a conversation about institutional oppression directly and overtly connected back to the relevant societal issues. Similarly, individual issues directly and overtly connected back to the relevant group, institutional, and societal levels. By applying this recursive funnel approach, students recognized individual-level issues as systematically embedded in and connected to group, institutional, and societal issues. I found this approach helpful as students often expressed the most difficulty understanding the nature of structural (societal and institutional) issues and their interrelatedness with individual lived experiences.

The recursive funnel approach proved effective in teaching about the connection between various marginalized identities and structural issues. For example, a discussion of a broader societal issue, health disparities, illuminated how these issues create and maintain the marginalization of transgender women of color, thus affecting their compromised health outcomes (Hughto, Reisner, & Pachankis, 2015; Jefferson, Neilands, & Sevelius, 2013). A discussion of health disparities inevitably revealed how institutional issues, such as adequate access to culturally competent healthcare, and the group-level outcomes of gender, gender identity, race, and social class impact health disparities. Also, by focusing on the broader topic of health disparities first, I maintained an emphasis on the complexity of the issue. In other words, studying health disparities required moving beyond one particular group-level issue (e.g., race, gender, gender identity, social class) to complex intersectional analysis.

The previous example of incorporating the recursive funnel approach to teaching about health disparities from an intersectional framework can be applied to nearly any academic topic in developing class activities and assignments. For example, the following pedagogical steps outline an assignment that incorporates the recursive funnel approach:

1. Choose and assign a reading applicable to the course material from an academic journal or from print or online media. The use of current events can be especially accessible for students in bolstering their ability to grasp complex intersectionality issues. Given the health disparities example, the reading by Jefferson et al. (2013) on transgender women of color and mental health outcomes will be used to illustrate this assignment.
2. Instruct students to identify and be mindful of the primary societal issues that impact the content while they are reading the article.
3. Begin in-class discussion of the reading with the societal issues students identified in the reading. As the instructor, offer additional societal issues not yet identified by the students. In this example, health disparities would be identified as a main societal issue and would be defined.
4. Following the recursive funnel approach, ask students to identify the institutional issues that impact health disparities. For this part of the activity, separate students into dyads or triads depending on the size of the class. Provide some examples of societal-level institutions (e.g., education, healthcare system, labor/workforce, financial, legal). The class then discusses the relationship between institutional policies and social problems. In this example, the class would discuss how various institutional forces, such as lack of access to culturally competent healthcare, educational opportunities, and economically sustainable employment, influence health disparities.
5. Next, fold sociocultural group perspectives into the discussion. In this example, ask students "What are the specific institutional barriers faced by transgender women of color?" and "How are racial health disparities and gender-identity health disparities connected?" In this way, students begin directly linking group-level issues to structural issues.
6. Examples of individual transgender women of color can be used to further illustrate the health disparities they experience. However, when addressing the individual level, the discussion must intentionally be guided by the instructor to incorporate the group, institutional, and societal issues that impact the individual.

The recursive funnel approach contrasts the typical approach of learning about individual groups of identity that can give the impression, for example, that racial health disparities are not connected to health disparities experienced by transgender people.

Strategy 3: Incorporating Context and History

In line with the recursive funnel approach, this strategy recommends persistent inclusion of the immediate social and educational context when teaching about intersectionality. Maintaining a focus on the local social and educational context helps ensure that instructors do not minimize the significance of structural issues that maintain the recursive funnel approach and reduce the tendency for students to get stuck in their own uniqueness (Rios et al., this volume). This strategy calls for the use of specific examples that are easily accessible to students rather than relying on generalizations that may seem abstract or disconnected from students. Use of this strategy encourages students to locate themselves in a social system that directly influences their lived experiences. Providing examples that relate to the immediate social context also decreases the intellectualization that often dominates social justice conversations and improves the balance between the cognitive and affective components for effective facilitation of social justice-oriented discussions (Sue, Lin, Torino, Capodilupo, & Rivera, 2009; Sue, Rivera, Capodilupo, Lin, & Torino, 2010; Sue et al., 2011; Sue, Torino, et al., 2009).

To highlight history and location, I contextualized social issues within the immediate milieu of the students as much as possible. I often began discussion on a time-relevant issue, for instance, federal laws meant to promote inclusion of people from marginalized backgrounds in various social institutions, such as education and the workplace. Rather than leave the discussion at the federal level, which might not be as accessible to students and may paint a picture that is too general, I introduced the treatment of federal laws at the local level, including within the educational institution. This analysis compared and contrasted the differences and similarities between the laws and policies to reveal discrepancies in workplace protections. For example, this analysis revealed that workplace protections at the federal level for women do not necessarily apply to all women at the local level where state anti-discrimination laws fail to protect transgender women. Using this analysis, students illuminated a disparity at the intersection of gender and gender identity and participated in more nuanced discussions via intersectional theory.

Contextualization should also incorporate the historical context. Focusing too much on the current context when discussing social justice leads to a dilution or oversimplification of the issue. For example, highly inaccurate rhetoric created the "post-racial" movement that denies the historical legacy of racial inequalities in present day oppression and represents one justification for infusing historical context into discussions (Wise, 2013). Similarly, an inclusion of the historical context reveals that educational protections for White women and many people of color did not occur at the same time across all educational contexts. A historical review of the university where one teaches might reveal that Black Americans were allowed to attend that particular college before women and that both groups attend the university well before the establishment of a comprehensive federal student aid program. If class discussion focuses attention to race and then to gender as distinct categories, students miss awareness of Black women's exclusion even after Black men were accepted which highlights the intersectional disparities created by institutional policy. Further, without consideration of issues that impact social class, such as the availability of federal student aid, students lose sight of the poor who continued to be denied access to higher education. By attending to the specific institutional and historic context, instructors highlight intersectionality. Present day students then situate their experiences within their accessible local contexts and apply historical and contextual analyses to learning how social and institutional level forces impact their lived experiences.

Strategy 4: Sharing Instructor Personal Experiences

Student resistance frequently creates a negative impact on the learning dynamic in social justice education (Asher, 2007; Case, this volume; Case & Cole, 2013; Reynolds, 2011). As mentioned earlier, students might perceive the instructor as promoting a hidden or political agenda behind their focus on social justice issues, and therefore, become resistant in response to this perception. Resistance may even be especially heightened when teaching about sexual orientation, gender identity, and race as these identities carry long histories of being highly politicized. To alleviate this response, principles and techniques from the practice of psychotherapy may transfer to preventing and addressing student resistance behaviors.

In a therapeutic context, forms of resistance may occur due to transference and countertransference. Racker (1968) described transference as faulty feelings and associations that the client projects onto the therapist that originated in formative interpersonal associations (e.g., transferring anger onto the therapist originally associated with the client's withdrawn father). Racker (1968) defined countertransference as feelings and associations the therapist projects onto the client either in reaction to the client's transference or the therapist's unconscious feelings ignited by the therapist-client interaction. Ethnocultural transference and countertransference (Comas-Diaz & Jacobsen, 1991) may occur within the context of teaching and learning about sociocultural identities. In particular, ethnocultural transferences and countertransferences relate to an individual's conscious and unconscious associations with various sociocultural group categories such as those based on race, gender identity, ethnicity, and sexual orientation. In a teaching context, ethnocultural transference may surface as a White, heterosexual, middle-class, male student discounting verified statistics given to the class about societal-level health disparities experienced by Latina/o Americans from their Latina professor. Ethnocultural transference in the classroom may also manifest as a religiously orthodox, heterosexual student reflexively agreeing with the comments and ideas of the instructor that appear to be in favor of same-sex marriage as a way to mask their contradicting beliefs that same-sex marriage is immoral. In both scenarios, the ethnocultural transference will most likely lead to lost learning opportunities if not effectively addressed.

Several techniques may prove useful to effectively address potential ethnocultural transferences directed at the professor from students. First, awareness of transference and countertransference buffers any harmful emotions (e.g., anger, resentment, or disdain) produced by ethnocultural transferences. Essentially, the professor's knowledge of these concepts may serve to decrease the likelihood of internalizing the feelings and resistant reactions of the student. Second, the framework of ethnocultural transference informs the instructor's strategy for responding to the student. This strategy might include educating students about resistance often experienced when learning about social justice issues (Jackson, 1999). The professor might assign a journal article that discusses this phenomenon and lead a discussion examining similar dynamics present in the classroom (Jackson, 1999). Given the common occurrence of resistance (Asher, 2007; Reynolds, 2011), scheduling this article and discussion about resistance early in the semester may circumvent a portion of this resistance. Overall, unresolved resistance that may impede student learning must be appropriately facilitated by the instructor.

Additionally, therapeutic concepts of transparency and self-disclosure transferred for pedagogical use may minimize the occurrence of ethnocultural transference in the classroom. Self-disclosure, a form of transparency, may positively impact student learning (Sorensen, 1989). As professors share more information about themselves and demystify the teaching process, they become more "real" in the eyes of students. This might result in fewer opportunities for students to misdirect previously held ethnocultural associations onto the professor because they begin to perceive a less stereotypical person. However, just as in therapeutic practice, the professor should exercise prudence when deciding what personal information to disclose to their students. In general, self-disclosures made in the classroom must contribute positively to the course material and be relevant to the context. In teaching intersectionality, an instructor might share examples from personal experiences that demonstrate the process of developing insight concerning the various tenets of an intersectional framework. For example, an effective instructor self-disclosure in a conversation about heterosexual identity, biases, and intersections might play out like this:

> Coming from a very religious Catholic family, heavily influenced by machismo cultural values from my Mexican heritage, and situated in a rural, low-income setting, I had negative attitudes related to what it meant

to be gay or lesbian. In my community, there were no openly out gays or lesbians. As a child and well into my teenage years, I would commonly put down boys who appeared more feminine using derogatory slurs. It was not until I went to college and became exposed to ways of living beyond what I was exposed to in my community of origin that some of these harsh biases began to soften. It took several years and the development of meaningful relationships with gay men and lesbians for me to lose most of these biases that I had accepted as truths. I still have some shame about who I was growing up, but I try not to let this shame negatively impact my present day living that embraces difference. At the same time, I acknowledge that some of these biases are still alive and that my heterosexual identity and conservative upbringing still play a role in the injustices experienced by gay men and lesbians.

In this example, self-disclosure of an issue that the professor successfully navigated revealed a complexity to intersectional identities and the synergistic relationship between the self, others, and structural issues. Effective self-disclosures must be as honest and realistic as possible. Instructor disclosure of challenges associated with a privileged social location serves as a crucial part of effective modeling for students. These types of disclosures also highlight the lifelong commitment to unlearning biases that come with acknowledging privilege.

Strategy 5: Navigating Difficult Dialogues

Teaching about multiple marginalized identities inevitably involves difficult dialogues in the classroom. Studies on the manifestation and dynamics of conversations about race revealed these dialogues often include microaggressions that may trigger difficult tensions (Sue, Lin, et al., 2009; Sue et al., 2010; Sue et al., 2011; Sue, Torino, et al., 2009). Furthermore, students suggested that instructors do not always effectively facilitate these interactions (Sue, Lin, et al., 2009; Sue, Torino, et al., 2009). These studies also revealed a number of strategies that faculty and students believe aid the effective facilitation of difficult dialogues. While these studies focused on race, many of the lessons learned transfer to discussions of sexual orientation, gender identity, and other social identity groups. Drawing from this scholarship, the next section covers ways to transfer these findings for use in discussions of intersectionality in the classroom.

Dialogues often become challenging because of the highly charged emotions evoked by the topics. Difficulty emerges when differing worldviews collide among students or between student(s) and instructor. This clash of worldviews is inevitable because every person brings a unique perspective created by the composite of their identities and life experiences. The emotions attached to these conversations often get ignored or invalidated (Sue, Lin, et al., 2009). Invalidating the emotional experiences of the participants causes an unproductive dialogue characterized by ambivalence, resistance, and withdrawal from the learning experience (Sue, 2015). Given that most instructors completed no training in the practice of acknowledgment and processing of affective experiences, emotions in the classroom rarely receive proper attention. However, even those without the skills of a trained psychotherapist can be effective at recognizing and negotiating emotions in the classroom. Tenets of affective learning support development of these skills among educators, especially for teaching and learning about topics that include an evaluation of values and attitudes (Shephard, 2008).

Two basic strategies help me ensure that emotions receive appropriate acknowledgment. When I first notice an emotional reaction to the discussion, I acknowledge the emotional experience by reflecting it back to the student as a check of the reaction. For example, "Angelica, it looks like it is upsetting for you to talk about the confusion you experience when trying to make sense of how you occupy positions of power and oppression because of your identity." In this example, the instructor attended to both the cognitive and emotional aspects of the student's learning experience. Next, I try to avoid dismissing or minimizing the emotional experiences of their students. An instructor might inadvertently minimize the emotional experience of a student who they believe is "making too much out of the issue" or "making a mountain out of a mole hill." This may relate to the instructor's own discomfort regarding expressions of certain feelings such as anger or sadness. This component of the strategy prevents further harm to people from marginalized backgrounds with an historical legacy of emotional and experiential invalidation. In reflecting feelings back to students, the instructor honors the intensity of the emotions being expressed and refrains from any attempts to minimize that experience. Reflecting feelings back to students and validating the students' emotional experiences builds understanding and creates an environment conducive to effective processing of identities that might clash on intrapersonal and interpersonal levels.

Studies of difficult dialogues found that students become keenly aware of their instructor's comfort levels in these dialogues (Sue, Lin, et al., 2009; Sue et al., 2010) and even base their participation levels on these assessments. For example, if I express hesitancy in talking about sexual orientation, gender identity, race, or ethnicity, my students may refrain from fully participating in these discussions. In the classroom, an instructor's hesitancy may manifest in the form of ignoring or stuttering over certain words like "lesbian," "Black," and "transgender." In essence, this instructor sends an implicit message marking discussions of gender identity, sexual orientation, and ethnicity as taboo and uncomfortable. Additionally, this same educator may exhibit difficulty in discussing structural issues including health disparities, workplace discrimination, and educational access. To increase the comfort level of students in these dialogues, I work to demonstrate comfort in discussing various identity issues or approach my discomfort with transparency. In line with the previous strategy encouraging self-disclosure, the uncomfortable educator might share with the class:

I am not an expert in the areas of gender identity and race, and I might make mistakes when discussing these issues. However, these issues are important for our class discussions, and I will do my best to incorporate these areas to the best of my ability. This is a learning experience for us all, and I encourage you to take risks in sharing your experience with the course material. Also, I welcome your feedback when you believe I have misspoken.

Statements like this strengthen the student-instructor teaching alliance, a necessary component in an effective educational process (Estrada, 2015). Additionally, this communication models how to navigate difficult topics related to intersectionality.

Where Do We Go From Here?

The concept of intersectionality, while not necessarily considered a new phenomenon, still needs development and further implementation in pedagogical practices (Case, this volume). As other chapters in this volume emphasize, a contemporary conceptualization of intersectionality theory includes all identities, reaching beyond the initial focus on race and gender (e.g., Case & Lewis, this volume; Hall, this volume; Kurtis & Adams, this volume). Similarly, I advocate for a specific focus on the intersections of the marginalized identities inherent in sexual orientation, gender identity, race, and ethnicity in the context of social and institutional systems of oppression and privilege. Despite the availability of theoretical frameworks and best practices supported by the existing literature, relatively little is known about specific paradigms and practices that most effectively facilitate student learning concerning intersectionality.

In future development of pedagogies that focus on teaching about the intersections of marginalized identities, more empirical research is needed to investigate the intersections of gender identity, sexual orientation, race, and ethnicity (Parent, DeBlaere, & Moradi, 2013). Given that applying an intersectionality framework to the teaching of multiple marginalized identities remains relatively new, qualitative methods of inquiry might be helpful in revealing more about effective practices in the classroom. For example, qualitative research can help answer questions such as:

- Which philosophies influence instructors who incorporate an intersectionality framework in their teachings?
- What are the challenges instructors encounter when teaching about intersectionality and multiple marginalized identities?
- Which strategies prove most effective in this type of instruction?
- How does the instructor's unique social location impact their ability to effectively teach about intersections of multiple marginalized identities?

Another future direction focuses on the institutional dynamic regarding the social justice paradigm and its interconnections with tenets of intersectionality. Of course, what happens in the classroom correlates with institutional-level issues, such as teaching-oriented resources, student evaluation processes, and tenure and promotion procedures. Just as in society and non-academic institutions, people typically assume that procedures and policies operate as fair and equitable (Castilla & Benard, 2010). However, proponents of intersectional theory and analysis critique this assumption and recognize that disparities based on social identities exist across all institutions and social systems (e.g., Case, this volume; Crenshaw, 1991; Delgado & Stefancic, 2012; Sue, 2010). Given this reality, institutions must recognize and ameliorate the institutional-level disparities in policies and resources that impede optimal development and inclusion of intersectionally orientated academic programs and classroom instruction. For example, supervisors and evaluators must understand possible disparities in teacher evaluations for educators teaching social justice orientations and those who do not. Research by Nast (1999) suggested evaluations might be lower for instructors who base their pedagogies on social justice philosophies and instructors from socially marginalized backgrounds. This type of backlash might also be experienced by those advocating for a framework inclusive of intersectionality throughout their institutions. Since student evaluations often influence the tenure and promotion process, institutions must recognize these potential disparities and develop policies to address any inadvertent negative ramifications to these instructors (Case, this volume). Additionally, as educators teaching via intersectional pedagogies, instructors benefit from working within institutions that overtly support this perspective at all levels (Ukpodoku, 2007).

Final Thoughts

The previously described approaches for addressing the intersections of gender identity, sexual orientation, race, and ethnicity apply to a variety of disciplines at the undergraduate and graduate levels. Based on foundational intersectionality theories and philosophies, the pedagogies shared here were influenced by the scholarship of Crenshaw (1989), the Combahee River Collective (1977/2007), and the more recent scholarly frameworks of critical race theory (e.g., Delgado & Stefancic, 1993, 2012) and queer theory (e.g., Sullivan, 2003). As these theoretical and philosophical perspectives stress, the voices and lived experiences of marginalized people connect to a long history of silence and oppression which impacts the present day lived experiences of these groups (Delgado & Stefancic, 2012; Sullivan, 2003). An intersectionality approach to teaching about identity must intentionally elevate the voices of the oppressed and recognize the synergistic relationships between societal, institutional, group, and individual systems of oppression (Case, this volume). The approaches illustrated above form a basis for honoring this premise. Utilizing these approaches in teaching about the intersections of gender identity, sexual orientation, ethnicity, and race assists instructors in avoiding the pitfalls that impede student learning about the inter-relatedness of identity, privilege, oppression, and structural inequalities.

Note

1 For ease of reading, the term *queer* is used as an umbrella term for all non-heterosexual sexual orientations.

References

Asher, N. (2007). Made in the (multicultural) U.S.A.: Unpacking tensions of race, culture, gender, and sexuality in education. *Educational Researcher, 36*(2), 65–73. doi:10.3102/0013189X07299188

Bowleg, L. (2013). "Once you've blended the cake, you can't take the parts back to the main ingredients": Black gay and bisexual men's descriptions and experiences of intersectionality. *Sex Roles, 68*(11–12), 754–767. doi:10.1007/s11199-012-0152-4

Case, K. A. (Ed.). (2013). *Deconstructing privilege: Teaching and learning as allies in the classroom*. New York, NY: Routledge.

Case, K. A. (this volume). Toward an intersectional pedagogy model: Engaged learning for social justice. In K. A. Case (Ed.), *Intersectional pedagogy: Complicating identity and social justice* (pp. 1–24). New York, NY: Routledge.

Case, K. A., & Cole, E. R. (2013). Deconstructing privilege when students resist: The journey back into the community of engaged learners. In. K. A. Case (Ed.), *Deconstructing privilege: Teaching and learning as allies in the classroom* (pp. 34–48). New York, NY: Routledge.

Case, K. A., & Lewis, M. (this volume). Teaching intersectional psychology in racially diverse settings. In K. A. Case (Ed.), *Intersectional pedagogy: Complicating identity and social justice* (pp 129–149). New York, NY: Routledge.

Castilla, E. J., & Benard, S. (2010). The paradox of meritocracy in organizations. *Administrative Science Quarterly, 55*(4), 543–676. doi:10.2189/asqu.2010.55.4.543

Comas-Diaz, L., & Jacobsen, F. M. (1991). Ethnocultural transference and countertransference in the therapeutic dyad. *American Journal of Orthopsychiatry, 61*(3), 392–402.

Combahee River Collective. (2007). A Black feminist statement. In E. B. Freedman (Ed.), *The essential feminist reader* (pp. 325–330). New York, NY: Modern Library. (Original work published 1977).

Crenshaw, K. (1989). Demarginalizing the intersection of race and sex: A Black feminist critique of antidiscrimination doctrine, feminist theory, and antiracist politics. *University of Chicago Legal Forum, 1989,* 139–167.

Crenshaw, K. W. (1991). Mapping the margins: Intersectionality, identity politics, and violence against women of color. *Stanford Law Review, 43,* 1241–1299.

David, E. J. R. (2013). *Internalized oppression: The psychology of marginalized groups.* New York, NY: Springer Publishing Company.

Delgado, R., & Stefancic, J. (1993). Critical race theory: An annotated bibliography. *Virginia Law Review, 79*(2), 461–516.

Delgado, R., & Stefancic, J. (2012). *Critical race theory: An introduction.* New York, NY: New York University Press.

Drescher, J. (2015). Queer diagnoses revisited: The past and future of homosexuality and gender diagnoses in DSM and ICD. *International Review of Psychiatry, 27*(5), 386–395.

Eliasoph, N. (1999). "Everyday racism" in a culture of political avoidance: Civil society, speech, and taboo. *Social Problems, 46*(4), 479–502.

Estrada, F. (2015). The teaching alliance in multicultural counseling course education: A framework for examining and strengthening the student-instructor relationship. *International Journal for the Advancement of Counselling, 37*(3), 233–247. doi:10.1007/s10447-015-9240-9

Gorski, P. C. (2012). Instructional, institutional, and sociopolitical challenges of teaching multicultural teacher education courses. *The Teacher Educator, 47*(3), 216–235. doi:10.1080/08878730.2012.660246

Greenwood, R. (this volume). Intersectionality foundations and disciplinary adaptations: Highways and Byways. In K. A. Case (Ed.), *Intersectional pedagogy: Complicating identity and social justice* (pp. 27–45). New York, NY: Routledge.

Grzanka, P. (this volume). Undoing the psychology of gender: Intersectional feminism and social science pedagogy. In K. A. Case (Ed.), *Intersectional pedagogy: Complicating identity and social justice* (pp. 63–81). New York, NY: Routledge.

Hall, N. (this volume). Quotes, blogs, diagrams, and counter-storytelling: Teaching intersectionality at a minority-serving institution. In K. A. Case (Ed.), *Intersectional pedagogy: Complicating identity and social justice* (pp. 150–170). New York, NY: Routledge.

Hughto, J. M. W., Reisner, S. L., & Pachankis, J. E. (2015). Transgender stigma and health: A critical review of stigma determinants, mechanisms, and interventions. *Social Science & Medicine, 147*, 222–231. doi:10.1016/j.socscimed.2015.11.010

Huston, T. A. (2006). Race and gender bias in higher education: Could faculty course evaluations impede further progress toward parity? *Seattle Journal for Social Justice, 4*(2), 591–611.

Jackson, L. C. (1999). Ethnocultural resistance to multicultural training: Students and faculty. *Cultural Diversity and Ethnic Minority Psychology, 5*(1), 27–36.

Jefferson, K. B., Neilands, T., & Sevelius, J. (2013). Transgender women of color: Discrimination and depression symptoms. *Ethnicity and Inequalities in Health and Social Care, 6*(4), 121–136. doi:10.1108/EIHSC-08-2013-0013

Killerman, S. (2015). *Comprehensive* list of LGBTQ+ term definitions* [Online resource]. Retrieved from itspronouncedmetrosexual.com/

Kurtis, T., & Adams, G. (this volume). Decolonial intersectionality: Implications for theory, research, and pedagogy. In K. A. Case (Ed.), *Toward an intersectional pedagogy model: Engaged learning for social justice* (pp. 46–59). New York, NY: Routledge.

Ladson-Billings, G. (1996). Silences as weapons: Challenges of a Black professor teaching White students. *Theory into Practice, 35*(2), 79–85.

Ladson-Billings, G., & Tate IV, W. (1995). Toward a critical race theory of education. *The Teachers College Record, 97*(1), 47–68. doi:10.1080/00405849609543706

Logan, E. (2014). Barack Obama, the new politics of race, and classed constructions of racial Blackness. *The Sociological Quarterly, 55*(4), 653–682. doi:10.1111/tsq.12071

Luhmann, S. (1998). Queering/querying pedagogy? Or, pedagogy is a pretty queer thing. In W. F. Pinar (Ed.), *Queer theory in education* (pp. 120–131). Mahwah, NJ: Lawrence Erlbaum Associates, Inc.

Malesky, K. (2014). *The journey from "colored" to "minorities" to "people of color"* [Online article]. Retrieved from www.npr.org/sections/codeswitch/

McCarty, M. (2016). *What's at stake in the 2016 legislative session* [Online article]. Retrieved from www.hrc.org/blog/

Merritt, D. J. (2008). Bias, the brain, and student evaluations of teaching. *St. John's Law Review, 82*(1), 235–287.

Nadal, K. L., Davidoff, K. C., Davis, L. S., Wong, Y., Marshall, D., & McKenzie, V. (2015). A qualitative approach to intersectional microaggressions: Understanding influences of race, ethnicity, gender, sexuality, and religion. *Qualitative Psychology, 2*(2), 147–163. doi:10.1037/qup0000026

Naples, N. A. (this volume). Pedagogical practice and teaching intersectionality intersectionally. In K. A. Case (Ed.), *Intersectional pedagogy: Complicating identity and social justice* (pp. 110–128). New York, NY: Routledge.

Nast, H. J. (1999). "Sex," "race," and multiculturalism: Critical consumption and the politics of course evaluations. *Journal of Geography in Higher Education, 23*(1), 102–115. doi:10.1080/03098269985650

Parent, M. C., DeBlaere, C., & Moradi, B. (2013). Approaches to research on intersectionality: Perspectives on gender, LGBT, and racial/ethnic identities. *Sex Roles, 68*(11–12), 639–645. doi:10.1007/s11199-013-0283-2

Racker, H. (1968). *Transference and countertransference*. London, UK: Karnac Books.

Randall, V., & Waylen, G. (Eds.). (1998). *Gender, politics, and the state*. New York, NY: Routledge.

Reynolds, A. L. (2011). Understanding the perceptions and experiences of faculty who teach multicultural counseling courses: An exploratory study. *Training and Education in Professional Psychology, 5*(3), 167–174. doi:10.1037/a0024613

Rios, D., Bowling, M., & Harris, J. (this volume). Decentering student "uniqueness" in lessons about intersectionality. In K. A. Case (Ed.), *Intersectional pedagogy: Complicating identity and social justice* (pp. 194–213). New York, NY: Routledge.

Roberts, D. E. (1995). Punishing drug addicts who have babies: Women of color, equality, and the right of privacy. In Crenshaw, K. (Ed.), *Critical race theory: The key writings that formed the movement* (pp. 384–425). New York, NY: The New Press.

Sensoy, Ö., & DiAngelo, R. (2014). Respect differences? Challenging the common guidelines in social justice education. *Democracy and Education, 22*(2), 1–10.

Shephard, K. (2008). Higher education for sustainability: Seeking affective learning outcomes. *International Journal of Sustainability in Higher Education, 9*(1), 87–98. doi:10.1108/14676370810842201

Solorzano, D. G., & Yosso, T. J. (2001). Critical race and LatCrit theory and method: Counter-storytelling. *International Journal of Qualitative Studies in Education, 14*(4), 471–495. doi:10.1080/09518390110063365

Solorzano, D. G., & Yosso, T. J. (2002). Critical race methodology: Counter-storytelling as an analytical framework for education research. *Qualitative Inquiry, 8*(1), 23–44. doi:10.1177/107780040200800103

Sorensen, G. (1989). The relationships among teachers' self-disclosive statements, students' perceptions, and affective learning. *Communication Education, 38*(3), 259–276. doi:10.1080/03634528909378762

Sue, D. W. (2010). *Microaggressions in everyday life: Race, gender, and sexual orientation*. New York, NY: John Wiley & Sons.

Sue, D. W. (2013). Race talk: the psychology of racial dialogues. *American Psychologist, 68*(8), 663–672. doi:10.1037/a0033681

Sue, D. W. (2015). *Race talk and the conspiracy of silence: Understanding and facilitating difficult dialogues on race*. New York, NY: John Wiley & Sons.

Sue, D. W., Lin, A. I., Torino, G. C., Capodilupo, C. M., & Rivera, D. P. (2009). Racial microaggressions and difficult dialogues on race in the classroom. *Cultural Diversity and Ethnic Minority Psychology, 15*(2), 183–190. doi:10.1037/a0014191

Sue, D. W., Rivera, D. P., Capodilupo, C. M., Lin, A. I., & Torino, G. C. (2010). Racial dialogues and White trainee fears: Implications for education and training. *Cultural Diversity and Ethnic Minority Psychology, 16*(2), 206–214. doi:10.1037/a0016112

Sue, D. W., Rivera, D. P., Watkins, N. L., Kim, R. H., Kim, S., & Williams, C. D. (2011). Racial dialogues: Challenges faculty of color face in the classroom. *Cultural Diversity and Ethnic Minority Psychology, 17*(3), 331–340. doi:10.1037/a0024190

Sue, D. W., Torino, G. C., Capodilupo, C. M., Rivera, D. P., & Lin, A. I. (2009). How White faculty perceive and react to difficult dialogues on race implications for education and training. *The Counseling Psychologist, 37*(8), 1090–1115. doi:10.1177/0011000009340443

Sullivan, N. (2003). *A critical introduction to queer theory.* New York, NY: New York University Press.

Turner, W. B. (2000). *A genealogy of queer theory.* Philadelphia, PA: Temple University Press.

Ukpokodu, O. N. (2007). Preparing socially conscious teachers: A social justice oriented teacher education. *Multicultural Education, 15*(1), 8–15.

Whisman, V. (1996). *Queer by choice: Lesbians, gay men, and the politics of identity.* New York, NY: Routledge.

Wise, T. (2013). *Colorblind: The rise of post-racial politics and the retreat from racial equity.* San Francisco, CA: City Lights Books.

10

DECENTERING STUDENT "UNIQUENESS" IN LESSONS ABOUT INTERSECTIONALITY

Desdamona Rios, Matthew J. Bowling, and Jacquelyn Harris

As a cognitive shortcut it is useful to categorize people into groups based on social identities (e.g., race or gender), however, real-life experiences do not fit neatly into categorized boundaries created by social institutions. The theory of intersectionality recognizes intragroup differences by highlighting how a person's lived experience may differ from others depending on where their intersecting social identities are located in a hegemonic structure (Cole, 2009). In the 1970s and 1980s, Women of Color, lesbian, bisexual, and transgender women developed the theory of intersectionality to challenge feminist theory that overlooked the impact of race, social class, sexual orientation, gender identity, and ability status on women's lives (Cole, 2009; Crenshaw, 1991; Fine & Asch, 1988; Hurtado, 1996; Morgan, 1970). As the concept of intersectionality becomes increasingly mainstreamed in American culture, key features of the theory are becoming diluted. In the context of higher education, students understand intersectionality simplistically as uniqueness at the junction of race, gender, and sexuality rather than differential amounts of power and privilege embedded in social identities. Thus, the task of teaching about intersectionality becomes especially challenging when addressing social justice issues and resisting ideals of unearned American exceptionalism and privilege (hooks, 2010).

We present our experiences with intersectionality pedagogy, as Case outlines in her intersectional pedagogy model (this volume), in a master's level course Psychology of Gender, Race, and Sexuality (GRS) where the focus is on complex intersections of gender, race, sexuality, class, and as noted in the syllabus, "other dimensions of difference within systems of oppression and privilege." Kim Case initially developed the course at the University of Houston-Clear Lake with a key component being social justice action via experiential learning (for overview see Case & Lewis, this volume). Building on this foundation, I (Desdamona) included key theoretical frameworks such as feminist, social constructivist, critical race, and queer theories as informed by psychological research. Students read foundational texts during the first three weeks of the course which introduced key analytic tools. The remainder of the course involved four books which served as canvases onto which students identified and applied key concepts. Additionally, as a class we practiced self-reflexivity (Hurtado, 2010) and experiential learning (Brookfield, 2012) to encourage a collaborative and challenging learning environment.

With this in mind, below we include both student and teacher reflections on teaching and learning the theory of intersectionality. In the tradition of liberation (Freire, 1970/2000) and feminist pedagogy (hooks, 2010), we are mindful of our positions as both teachers and learners and recognize our intersectional viewpoints as able-bodied U.S. citizens who also identify as:

- a middle-class, non-married, childfree Chicana professor who grew up in a working-class household headed by a single mother (Desdamona);
- a middle-class, single, childfree heterosexual African American female master's graduate raised by a single mother in a working-class home (Jackie); and
- a White heterosexual male master's student raised by a divorced, single mother, whose mother and father differed in terms of social economic status (low versus high), and who is partnered with a woman and raising a child (Matthew).

We focus our analysis on materials and exercises for learning about intersectionality. We also highlight intersections at which learning became challenging and liberating, such as resistance to acknowledging systems of privilege and oppression and our roles in maintaining them. Finally, we discuss positive outcomes of the course for recognizing how we unconsciously perpetuate inequality and what we are currently doing to change that (Case, 2012; Hurtado, 2010).

Uniqueness Is Not the Point: Goals for Teaching and Learning Intersectionality

A defining feature of intersectionality theory is that social identities are embedded in culturally specific systems of power and hierarchy (Crenshaw, 1991). Oftentimes students understand intersectionality to simply mean each person holds multiple social identities such as race, gender, and sexual orientation, and the intersection of these identities make each person unique (Case, this volume). Key learning goals for the course were based on Case's (this volume) intersectional pedagogy model and Cole's (2009) recommendations for studying groups of people:

- recognizing people have multiple social identities and each social identity has a differential amount of power and privilege (sometimes a lot, sometimes none) depending on context;
- understanding ways the intersection of social identities changes a person's experience in a particular situation and how privilege maintains systems of inequality;
- identifying key intersections where student discomfort may interfere with learning, such as White men feeling guilty or defensive of their privilege or Women of Color failing to identify privileged statuses or feeling defensive of marginalized identities; and
- highlighting key intersections of privileges students hold for the purpose of empowering them to use their privilege to challenge social inequality (Case & Lewis, this volume; Greenwood, this volume).

As a critical point of intersectionality (Case, this volume), pairing intersectionality with privilege is essential for understanding that differential levels of (often unearned) power and privilege embedded in each person's social identities change a person's lived experience in a given context. Additionally, Hurtado (2010) argued that self-reflexivity is integral when researching, teaching, and learning about how multiple social identities perpetuate and challenge social hierarchies. Haraway's (1988) term "god trick" captures the importance of self-reflexivity and refers to the assumption that all groups of people experience the world similarly including shared intentions and treatment as equal members of the community. Through the god trick, the most privileged members of a community imagine their perspectives to be complete and detached from their social context, allowing them to draw assumptions they believe to be objective and free of social influence (Haraway, 1988).

The god trick also facilitates denial of privileges held. For people who hold multiple marginalized identities, recognizing privilege may be especially difficult when drawing from master narratives of race, gender, or other singular identities that highlight oppression (Case, 2012; Hall, this volume; Rios & Stewart, 2013). Understanding when and how a person's vantage point is obscured from the experiences of others, as well as the process through which a person draws conclusions based on limited knowledge, opens a space for learning about intersectionality. Accordingly, recognizing each person's multiple social identities sheds light on the partial and subjective knowledge a person holds and the ways s/he uses that knowledge to draw conclusions about others (Haraway, 1988). Toward this goal, course assignments were designed to challenge students to identify their privileged and oppressed identities as well as reconceptualize their understanding of each in relation to specific contexts (local, national, and international) and other people who are more or less privileged and oppressed.

Tools for Learning: Key Concepts and Readings

The course provided students with multiple opportunities to identify, apply, and reapply key course concepts in their writing, class presentations, and activism. Students led the majority of class discussions with key features of Case's intersectional pedagogy model (this volume) identifiable throughout the course to guide students toward understanding the multifaceted nature of intersectional analysis. During the first three weeks of class, students read foundational texts about intersectionality, privilege, and oppression as follows:

- Intersectionality analyses and application:

  - Crenshaw (1991) - Structural, political, and representational intersectionality in context
  - Purdie-Vaughns and Eibach (2008) - Intersectional invisibility with close examination of marginalized identities and critical analysis of prototypicality
  - Cole (2009) - Introduction to how an intersectional lens can help psychology researchers identify differences and similarities between and within groups of people
  - Greenwood (2008) - Intersectional political consciousness within diverse groups and understanding oppression and privilege as systems.

- Privilege, oppression, and how they work:

  - McIntosh (1988) - Foundational definition with a focus on unearned privileges
  - Frye (1983) - Establishing oppression as a pattern of "forces or barriers which are so related to each other they jointly restrain, restrict, or prevent . . . motion or mobility" (p. 7)
  - Fryberg and Townsend (2008) - An overview of the psychological effects of invisibility (i.e., social representations) of one's group in American institutions (for an overview of teaching about invisibility see Rios & Stewart, 2013).

After reading foundational texts, students read four books including *Gay Dads* (Goldberg, 2012), *The Color of Privilege* (Hurtado, 1996), *Guyland* (Kimmel, 2008), and *Whistling Vivaldi* (Steele, 2010). Assigned books covered each topic in the title of the course (gender, race, sexuality) and were purposefully selected because they are situated in contexts amenable to intersectional analyses including parenthood (Goldberg, 2012), the civil rights era (Hurtado, 1996), higher education (Kimmel, 2008), and psychological consequences of prejudice and discrimination (Steele, 2010). For example, Goldberg's (2012) *Gay Dads* addressed the experiences of affluent, educated, and mostly White gay men and their processes for becoming parents via adoption or surrogacy. I assigned *Gay Dads* during the sexuality module to shed light on obstacles faced by sexual minorities who hope to become parents. Students noticed that adoption services typically do not consider the particular needs of a same-sex couple (absolute invisibility; Fryberg & Townsend, 2008). Additionally, students learned about prejudice same-sex parents experience, who often must argue against stereotypes (relative invisibility; Fryberg & Townsend, 2008) of gay men as disinterested in family life and only interested in the gay party scene (Goldberg, 2012). In the process of identifying the invisibility of same-sex couples in the social construction of parenthood, students inevitably understood how structural intersectionality works. For example, same-sex couples who can afford a private surrogate can circumvent traditional avenues of adoption. Students noticed the economic privilege of the men in Goldberg's (2012) study and pointed out that working class same-sex couples would not have access to the services these men could afford (i.e., surrogates) or the choice to have one parent stay home full time with their child. Students also began to recognize their own unearned privileges. Here, students reflected on the concerted planning same-sex couples must engage in to become parents, whereas heterosexuals may find themselves as "accidental" parents as in the case of unplanned pregnancy. Additionally, if heterosexuals choose adoption, assuming financial stability and no criminal record, they are likely to find ample support for doing so. Thus, students recognized how intersectionality works in perpetuating social inequality for sexual minorities in terms of social institutions (structural intersectionality) and media representations of sexual minorities (representational intersectionality), while securing unearned heterosexual privilege in the institution of the family.

Assignments: Apply, Review, and Repeat

Reflection Papers: Practice Makes Perfect

Students were encouraged to revisit foundational concepts by writing reflection papers on each book. Students wrote about two things they learned from each book, an example of how something from the readings applied to their lives, and one realistic example of how they could use the information to create social change in their lives today (Case, this volume). All papers required at least one reference to intersectionality as well as privilege or oppression (Pliner, Banks, & Tapscott, 2012). Although students initially reported the structure of these papers to be redundant, by the end of the semester they recognized the importance of revisiting material for a deeper, and often different, understanding of intersectionality. After writing several papers using these guidelines, students became increasingly proficient in analyzing and arguing their points using intersectionality to reflect on intragroup as well as intergroup differences (Cole, 2009; Crenshaw, 1991).

For example, Kimmel's (2008) *Guyland* offered insight into the privileged lives of middle-class White men in colleges and universities across the United States. Students expressed surprise in response to Kimmel's participants' sense of entitlement, as well as the systemic maintenance of white male privilege in colleges and universities. In her broader structural and representational intersectional analysis of rape culture, one student wrote about intragroup differences among White men and White women in college, as well as that of White women and Women of Color and the law:

> Laws defining rape and violence against women are simply another bar in the birdcage that is the oppression of women (Frye, 1983). Crenshaw (1991) states, "legal rules thus functioned to legitimize a good woman/bad woman dichotomy in which women who lead sexually autonomous lives were usually least likely to be vindicated if they were raped" (pp. 1266). This is similar to . . . Kimmel's *Guyland*, where women are punished whether or not they participate in sexual activity . . . Whereas Kimmel is discussing a period of life for American men that they will most likely leave [behind] as they mature, Crenshaw is discussing actual laws in the United States. It is not only the law that creates a barrier for women, but social constructions that are prevalent in the media. Crenshaw gives an example of a rape case in Florida where a man was acquitted on the charges because jurors believed the defendant "looked like she was asking for sex" (Crenshaw, 1991, p. 1267). Kimmel . . . paints a picture of young men that is similar to these jurors. Beautiful women surround young [college] men . . . Pornography shows women that love to have sex and maybe enjoy rough sex, so these young men . . . feel entitled to the sex that they see represented in pornography. These conditions are what creates the culture of entitlement that Kimmel argues exists in *Guyland* and that Crenshaw would argue shapes our laws in America.

In her reflection paper, the student described structural intersectionality for White men and White women in the same context, highlighting the differential treatment of survivors (women) and perpetrators (men) of sexual violence in colleges and universities. The student also identified representational intersectionality in portrayals of women in pornography which perpetuate male entitlement to women's bodies. Specifically, violent media depictions of Women of Color are more likely to be tolerated than those of White women, and historically "Black women who are raped are racially discriminated against because their rapists . . . are less likely to be charged with rape, and when charged and convicted, are less likely to receive significant jail time than the rapists of white women" (Crenshaw, 1991, p. 1277). Therefore, structural intersectionality illuminates intragroup differences among female survivors of sexual violence in judicial outcomes for Women of Color and White women (Crenshaw, 1991).

Student-Led Discussions: Making Connections between Theory and Real Life

Students led two class discussions which applied key concepts to one of the assigned books and completed the Intersectionality Project. As individuals, students signed up for small group student-led discussions for one of the assigned books and worked collaboratively to meet the following three goals:

- identification of key ideas presented by the author of each book;
- identification of key foundational concepts (e.g., structural intersectionality or privilege) in examples for each book; and
- original applications that combine book author examples and students' own examples identified in media, institutional practices, or other personal experiences.

In creating their student-led discussions, students learned to bridge ideas across materials and real-world scenarios. For example, *Whistling Vivaldi* (Steele, 2010) is superficially less about intersectionality than all the other assigned books and explicitly written from a psychological perspective. Steele introduces the theory of stereotype threat which refers to "being at risk of confirming, as self-characteristic, a negative stereotype about one's group" (Steele & Aronson, 1995, p. 797). Steele (2010) presents decades of research to support the existence of this phenomenon experienced by women (math performance), African Americans (general intelligence), Latina/os (general intelligence), and White men (athleticism). Students found making the connection between psychological processes and intersectionality quite challenging. As such, I introduced this particular book at the end of the semester when students have had sufficient time to practice applying intersectionality multiple times.

A poignant example of student mastery, a Latina student in the course described the psychological effects of structural and representational intersectionality on students she tutored in an after-school program. In the context of education, the student considered her own access to education to be a privilege because her working-class parents prioritized education as a goal for her. In her work as a tutor, she witnessed teachers conveying low expectations for low-income, Latina/o high school students as well as the subsequent negative effects on students. She argued that access to a quality education is differentially attainable (structural intersectionality), with Latina/o students representing one of the lowest academic achieving groups in the United States. Stereotypes about Latina/os include a lack of intellectual curiosity, as well as cultural values that do not endorse educational achievement and instead promote girls' teen pregnancy and boys dropping out of high school to work (representational intersectionality; Barreto, Manazano, & Segura, 2012). Thus, in the context of education, Latina/os may feel intellectually threatened. According to Steele (2010), one

way for a person to defend against threats to self-esteem is to devalue the importance of a domain or experience. To demonstrate what disidentification with a
domain looked like, the graduate student presented the following analysis of her
work with high school students in the tutoring program:

> Latina students would devalue the significance of earning a college degree
> and the importance of going to college in the first place. Through disiden-
> tification with this domain, they were attempting to preserve their sense of
> worth and would say things like "I don't care about going to college any-
> way" or even make fun of me by mimicking me in a taunting voice "I went
> to [liberal arts college name removed]." I was hoping they'd identify with
> me as a fellow Latina and see the possibility of themselves going to college.
> Instead, they mocked me in an attempt to feel better about themselves.

This graduate student also identified intragroup differences among Latino students including teachers, administrators, and academic counselors responding
differently to Latino boys versus Latina girls, and differing outcomes for male
and female students when they drop out of high school. In sum, she not only
identified intersectionality in Steele's (2010) book, she also explained psychological consequences of structural and representational intersectionality for
Latina/os who must navigate social structures that perpetuate inequality in the
United States.

The Intersectionality Project: When Theory Hits the Streets

The most powerful assignment for this course is the service-learning oriented
Intersectionality Project. According to Pliner et al. (2012), intersectional pedagogy should include the critical analysis of "structural and systemic inequalities
that exist within the cultural, political, social, and economic structure in everyday life" (p. 149). The Intersectionality Project was initially conceptualized for
the class as an experiential learning project (see Case & Lewis, this volume)
and has been modified for my course (Desdamona) to enact a collaborative
process. Paolo Freire (1970/2000) advocated that "for the truly humanist educator and the authentic revolutionary, the object of action is the reality to be
transformed by [people] together with other people" (p. 94). Therefore, as a
class we engaged in multiple collective projects. According to Bain (2004),
best teaching practices include experiential learning which occurs through a
"highly authentic, fascinating project that . . . challenge[s] students' thinking" (2004, p. 60). Good experiential projects have several features including
(a) collaboration, (b) a sense of ownership for students, (c) an authentic outlet
for students, and (d) teacher reminding students of the greater learning goals
(Bain, 2004). The field of psychology has many tools with great potential for
addressing social issues (e.g., feminist psychologists using traditional tools for

gender analysis), but it is through experiential learning that students observe psychological theory in action.

In the course, students carried out an activism project over the semester with multiple components and two main goals. First, the project explicitly focused on intersectionality, and second, students enacted real-life activism related to their chosen topic. Similar to Rivera's recursive funnel approach (this volume), the exercise facilitated students' consideration of how societal and institutional level issues affect people at the group and individual levels. As a group, the class selected one social issue to address such as same-sex marriage, addiction, or sexual violence. Students then identified specific intersections of identity to research in small groups of three or four (e.g., White stay-at-home fathers or undocumented immigrant lesbians). Therefore, the class identified one social issue together, thereby invoking the ownership component of experiential learning Bain outlined (2004). In smaller groups, students considered how the intersections of gender, race, and sexuality changed the ways different groups of people are affected by the issue. Next, in smaller groups students chose a type of intervention to carry out which may take the form of coordinating with a community organization, connecting to Bain's features of collaboration and authentic outlet, or the creation of products such as brochures for an organization or a social media outlet, enacting Bain's authentic outlet feature.

The final assignment for the course took the form of small group presentations where students presented an overview of their "intersection" (e.g., African American women), their activism, and connections made between their activism and course material. Groups presented their work to the larger class to illuminate differences and similarities of experiences at a particular intersection (e.g., White women compared to African American women), key lessons they learned during the process, and their previously held assumptions about the equality of laws, practices, institutions, or groups of people.

Learning Outcomes: Not Just About Getting the "Right" Answer

Teacher Reflections: Resistance, Resentment, and Remembering Not to Take It Personally

Asking adults to closely examine life-long held beliefs can be difficult and meaningful. In a sense, I asked students to hold a mirror to themselves and re-examine their beliefs about race, gender, sexual orientation, and other social identities in their process of learning about topics they are not expected to address in other classes. For example, in Jackie and Matthew's class, the privilege paper assignment required I create a space for students to discuss among themselves why it was important to think about their privilege rather than oppression. I separated students into small groups based on their most salient social identity as noted in their papers (see Dessel & Corvidae, this volume) which resulted in groups of African American women, Latina American women, White women, and a group of men that included one Latino-American and three White men. This small group exercise created space for them to identify their intragroup differences. For example, the White women discovered that one had grown up financially insecure in a single-parent household, whereas two had grown up in two-parent working-class households, and the fourth was raised in an upper-middle-class religious household. Among them, one was married to a man, while two identified as heterosexual and in relationships, and another identified as bisexual and not in a relationship. Although they recognized their racial privilege, they were able to discover on their own how they were similar but also different, and how these differences afforded some of them privileges others did not experience.

Not everyone appreciates the course content at first, and there is inevitably discussion among students about the futility of my pedagogy (e.g., why do we have to do activism?). However, I am reminded at the end of each semester that teaching about intersectionality as a tool for social justice is a process of planting seeds students will use in the future. Reflecting on the foundations of the course, I learned I must reiterate throughout the semester how intersectionality is not simply a listed description of a person (i.e., race, gender, sexual orientation, ability status, social class). Finally, encouraging students to lead the course meant students had to focus on different parts of themselves, and their analysis was therefore based on their own experiences. The student-led discussions along with my own reflections within the class allowed each of us to recognize the usefulness of intersectional analysis.

Jackie's Reflections: Race, Gender, Social Class, and The Cosby Show

I (Jackie) am a middle-class, single, childfree, heterosexual African American female raised in a single-parent household and who now holds a master's degree in psychology. I remember the first writing assignment was due the week following the readings on intersectionality, privilege, and oppression. I believe this paper set the tone for the course because the goal was to reflect on the privilege(s) one possesses. My first submission for this assignment did the exact opposite of the requirements and focused on my oppression via representational intersectionality, which is how social identities are represented in the media and pop culture (Crenshaw, 1991). I noted I had no role models in popular culture for academic success that fit my intersections (African American, female, working class) and recognized the relative invisibility in the misrepresentations of my group that dominates many contexts (Fryberg & Townsend, 2008). I wrote about the incongruence of my educational experience in a master's program compared to the only representation of a successful African American family in popular culture, *The Cosby Show* (well before the serial rape scandal came to light). Unlike my lived experience, this sitcom showcased an African American, two-parent, college-educated, upper-class household. Since I had not been exposed to intersectionality prior to this course, I focused on my experiences of combatting negative stereotypes and systemic racism associated with my race, an experience the characters on the show did not seem to share. I recalled the show teaching lessons about respectability and personal responsibility, but no storylines highlighted the social class privilege they enjoyed (Hall, this volume). Ignoring for the most part African Americans' experiences with racism, *The Cosby Show* exemplified intragroup differences within the African American community assumed to be based on personal (ir)responsibility such as intergenerational poverty and high incarceration rates of Black men.

Other students in the class had also focused on their oppression for this assignment (Case, Iuzzini, & Hopkins, 2012; McIntosh, 1988). As a collective, we had not met the requirements and were asked to rewrite the paper. Dr. Rios reiterated that these papers were only about our privilege and pointed out we all had some despite the oppression we might experience in different contexts. After the discussion about the rewrite, we formed groups based on race or gender. In the African American group, my group members and I agreed that Dr. Rios had a poor understanding of our oppression. In other words, we were defensive. As I listened to our small group discussion, I noticed the other African American women's perceptions of their oppression was sometimes different than mine, highlighting our intragroup differences. On the other hand, I also recognized privileges we each held. For instance, one student who identified as a lesbian and African American believed these identities additively increased her oppression. However, she also came from a middle-class, two-parent home which seemed quite privileged in contrast to my working-class single-parent home. This interaction with women I considered to be similar to me helped me grasp the oversights in my writing. When I rewrote the paper, I identified values my mother instilled in me like determination and working hard despite barriers I experienced as an African American woman. I became aware that having a parent who was able to encourage these values in me is a privilege because some people lack a stable family life such as those in the foster care system who are intersectionally invisible in most analyses of race, gender, and poverty (Purdie-Vaughns & Eibach, 2008).

Through this process, I realized I was subscribing to the god trick (Haraway, 1988), which was key to understanding intersectionality. Unlike many African Americans, my close family members who are high academic achievers served as social representations that higher education was a possibility for me (Fryberg & Townsend, 2008). This self-reexamination led to an analysis of structural intersectionality including how my familial role models partially facilitated my access to college and how my educational attainment will influence my future children's access to educational opportunities based on their intersectionality (Crenshaw, 1991; Hurtado, 1996). Thus, I was challenged to look beyond my understanding of oppression in the singular sense of being an African American and really see myself within a matrix of domination (Collins, 1990) that includes both privileged (heterosexual, college-educated) and oppressed (African American, woman) identities.

Matthew's Reflections: Initial Reactions and Victim Mentality

As with many profound experiences in my life, this course took me by surprise. From the perspective of a White heterosexual male raised by a single, divorced mother whose social economic status changed significantly post-divorce, my initial reaction to intersectionality was that while this made sense and surely fit other people, it simply did not apply to me. I reasoned that accepting intersectionality as a mechanism that shaped my day-to-day interactions was tantamount to adopting a victim mentality. Dr. Rios set the affecting tone of the course from the first time we were divided into groups to discuss our reflection papers. My group appeared on the surface to consist of other guys who were "just like me," but as we got to know each other, we noticed our similarities began to unravel. For instance, we initially assumed similarity based on educational goals and race (three of us being White and one a fair-skinned Latino). As we discussed our reflection papers in reference to McIntosh's (1988) privilege paper, I learned my group held comprehensively different intersections. For example, one member identified as gay, another as a middle-class conservative, and one as cognitively disabled. I realized Dr. Rios intentionally selected students into groups based on salient features, such as race or gender to facilitate experiential learning through recognizing how different we might be despite superficial characteristics.

Working in this small group of carefully orchestrated peers built upon the previous reflection paper experience and enhanced the course by demonstrating the concepts in Dr. Rios' lectures and required texts in a real-world interaction. Throughout this small group interaction, I identified the different intersections of each member and understood the various levels of privilege and oppression and specifically how divergent each intersection was from my own. An interesting component of working with this small group of men occurred via patriarchal comments that were exchanged during our interactions. Perhaps in an attempt to fraternize or to establish a rapport of camaraderie (Kimmel, 2008), one member of our "man group" referred to the course as a "fem class" and commented that he was probably going to drop the class. Another member remarked that Dr. Rios was "easy on the eyes." These subversive comments represented many of the conventions we were learning about in the course that keep in place systems of inequality, such as sexism, and the potential harmful effects produced at the intersection of gender, race, and other social identities. Through the pedagogical efforts of Dr. Rios, these same students became productive contributors to the course and adamant proponents of intersectional theory.

Growing up in a post-divorce, low-income, single-parent household, I experienced the struggles of financial insecurity that were shared by people of color who lived in my community. After reading Steele (2010), I identified with him when I realized I too had experienced a mix of privilege and oppression. However, unlike Steele's earned status as a scholar of psychology, I received benefits from my unearned White male privilege (Kimmel, 2008) while simultaneously experiencing the oppression of circumstance (poverty, fractured family structure). The inherent privileges of my gender differ in relation to race as evidenced in Steele's (2010) experience as a high achieving male scholar who also faced racial marginalization such as the insidious pressure of stereotype threat in his graduate program. Unlike Steele, being White means my potential has likely never been questioned in graduate school.

Understanding privilege and oppression was essential to my grasping intersectionality as an analytic tool because with closer examination of the intersections of my own identity, I was able to recognize the unique privileges I possess and the contexts in which these are most advantageous. Specifically, because of my impoverished upbringing I felt disenfranchised from the stereotypical White male experience of having a stable family life, adequate financial resources, and assured access to higher education (Kimmel, 2008). As a result, I assumed I shared a more similar lived experience with working-class racial minority Americans than White Americans. Of course, I overlooked privileges I enjoyed and continue to enjoy on a daily basis (McIntosh, 1988) as an able-bodied White heterosexual male living in the United States.

I also gained a deeper understanding of representational and structural intersectionality (Crenshaw, 1991) through recognizing my privileges at the intersection of race (Steele, 2010) and sexual orientation (Goldberg, 2012). For example, positive stereotypes about White, heterosexual males prevent my intelligence from being questioned in most settings (Steele, 2010) and having to prove myself as a good father (Goldberg, 2012). Higher education, employment, and adoption and other services related to parenting are not equally accessible to all people. Examining more closely my trifecta of privileged identities deepened my understanding of the differential treatment I experience. I recognized others view me as a person first, compared to racial minorities, women, and members of the LGBTQ community who are often reduced by others to their race, gender, or sexuality.

The Intersectionality Project: Sharing What We Know and Making Mistakes

In the spring of 2013, Jackie's and Matthew's class collectively chose the topic of marriage equality for their Intersectionality Project. At the time, same-sex couples were not able to legally marry in most of the United States including Texas. Students wanted to closely examine real-life implications of marriage laws relative to their own privilege, as well as intersections where oppression was invisible to them (Purdie-Vaughn & Eibach, 2008). Students selected intersections within the broader topic of marriage equality that included same-sex parenting and adoption, heterosexual Whites, African Americans, immigrants, Latina/o Americans, and polyamorous relationships. As such, Jackie and Matthew reflected on their process of applying intersectional theory to their activism and sharing their process and outcomes with peers.

Jackie's Reflection: Sharing Mistakes as a Tool for Learning

For the Intersectionality Project, I researched implications of marriage laws on same-sex couples who wish to adopt a child. In conducting our research on same-sex parenting, my group began to understand how representational intersectionality works in terms of media representation of the LGTBQ community. We felt it was important to emphasize the effects of heteronormativity (Warner, 1991), the belief that heterosexual relationships are the norm and the only acceptable form of romantic relationships, at the intersection of sexuality and parenthood that renders same-sex parents invisible in this context. As a group, we aimed to illuminate the challenges same-sex parents face at the intersection of sexual orientation, social class, gender, and race.

Our activism involved creating a Facebook page to advocate for Texas House Bill 201 which proposed a change to the Health and Safety Code of the supplementary birth certificate required in adoptions. The new bill would change the wording of the code to read "in the name of both adoptive parents" (H.B. 201, 2013) instead of the current statute wording which reads, "the names of the adoptive parents, one of whom must be a female, named as the mother, and the other of whom must be a male, named as the father" (Health and Safety Code, 1989). The wording of the code exemplifies structural and political intersectionality for same-sex couples in several ways. Prior to the 2015 Supreme Court ruling in favor of marriage equality, legal adoption in Texas for same-sex couples financially differed from heterosexual couples because of additional costs for supplementary birth certificates and legal fees associated with same-sex adoptions. Additionally, at the intersection of race, sexuality, and parenthood, activists in the LGBTQ community prioritized marriage equality and failed to take into account discrimination same-sex racial minority couples face, therefore dividing race and sexual orientation as separate issues (political intersectionality; Rosenblum, 1994).

Looking back on how my group worked together to complete the project helped me recognize the importance of an intersectional political consciousness. According to Greenwood (2008), an intersectional political consciousness includes "political beliefs and actions that are rooted in the importance of accounting for multiple identities when examining how the social world is constructed, in creating corrective goals, and in determining how to achieve these goals" (p. 38). My group included two White students, one African American, one member with a cognitive disability, and zero sexual minorities. Therefore, none of us had direct experience with the cause. I learned that activism goals can be realized when group members have an intersectional political consciousness and understand that among diverse group members, they may not all experience the same issue in the same way. In retrospect, I recognized that I had only started to develop my intersectional political consciousness. At the time, I was more focused on doing well in the course rather than understanding my group's similarities and differences in our individual perceptions of the topic, communication style, and contribution of ideas for activism. I could have been more patient and understanding of our differences if I was thinking intersectionally. In the end, I made accommodations to allow all of our points to be heard and appreciated, shared with my classmates the group's difficult process, and emphasized the importance of making room for allies with similar concerns to encourage coalition building (Greenwood, 2008).

Matthew's Reflection: Masculinity, Armor, and Self-Reflexivity

For the intersectionality project, I considered earlier material covered in the course. For the student-led discussion, my group presented our analysis of masculinity in the context of Kimmel's (2008) *Guyland*. Kimmel stated, "every man's armor is borrowed and ten sizes too big and beneath it he's naked and insecure and hoping you won't see" (p. 43). I shared this quote with the class to highlight Kimmel's insight of every man's armor being too big (in reference to masculinity), but for many the fit and comfort of their armor varies based on structural, political, and in some ways, representational intersectionality. Indeed, a gay African American man's armor will be inherently "looser" than a heterosexual White man because the armor is designed for the latter. An African American man's armor is looser from a structural intersectionality perspective because laws and procedures designed to protect citizens are not always extended to African American men (e.g., racial profiling). Likewise, a gay man's armor is looser than a heterosexual man's because matters of public policy based on political predilections, such as same-sex marriage, impact the rights of sexual minorities. Instead of being concrete and irrefutable, the rights of same-sex couples can be denied solely based on political inclinations. Heterosexual White men's armor protects them in terms of representational intersectionality by providing copious examples of socially acceptable, successful and admired White men in positions of power and authority. Teaching this section of Kimmel's (2008) book required reflection on my own intersectionality as well as intersectional invisibility (Purdie-Vaughns & Eibach, 2008) experienced by men who do not meet hegemonic standards of masculinity (e.g., White, affluent, heterosexual, athletic; Kimmel, 2008) and social structures based on maintaining privilege for some groups and oppression for others.

The activism portion of the course brought the material around "full circle," meaning I not only enriched my understanding of masculinity within systems of domination, but also applied what I had discovered to potentially affect change. For the Intersectionality Project, my group focused on heterosexual White Americans and created a "Marriage Equality" page on Facebook that provided material to highlight how marriage was, in 2013, a privilege not shared by all U.S. citizens. Initially, it was challenging to uncover instances where Whites as a group are systemically marginalized, but upon further inspection into marriage equality via prenuptial agreements I found instances of insidious inequality. One case study in particular demonstrated that even among the more privileged sector of society, at the intersection of race, gender, and social class, White women experience inequality. For example, in traditional marriages where men are the breadwinners and women the homemakers, prenuptial agreements can be written to benefit the person with the most economic power (Margulies, 2003). As such, the way the law works for White men and White women will vary greatly (structural intersectionality), thus maintaining systems of privilege and oppression that benefit one group over another based on gender (patriarchy) and social class (capitalism).

The discerning lectures that Dr. Rios administered coupled with the appropriate text assignments, small group work, in-class discussions, and student-led presentations worked harmoniously to create an environment not only of learning but deep understanding that became a pillar of my morality and worldview. I took away from both group projects that it is one thing to memorize course material and regurgitate it on an exam, yet another to use the material as analytic tools and present my analysis to my peers. This learning process was enlightening because I had to mine the material finely to ensure my confidence in endorsing the concept of intersectionality when explaining it to others, reflect on my own ideas about masculinity, race, and social class, and identify common interests at key intersections to promote coalition building among my peers (Greenwood, 2008).

Beyond the Psychology Horizon: Tips for Teaching Intersectionality across Disciplines

In getting to know Jackie and Matthew, I (Desdamona) learned about their interdisciplinary training with Jackie having taken courses in cultural studies and anthropology, and Matthew's interest in criminology. The assignments in the Psychology of Gender, Race and Sexuality course easily lend themselves to other disciplines at the undergraduate and graduate levels. The key for learning a complex theory like intersectionality is providing students with multiple opportunities to practice applying intersectionality across readings and examples (e.g., their own lived experiences or examples from their communities). For selection of texts, some creativity is needed to identify relevant materials for each discipline. For example, in the first three weeks of the course, I (Desdamona) introduced key foundational concepts from across disciplines to provide a context for students. Choosing materials from psychology, legal studies, and cultural studies (among others) helped contextualize how intersectionality is used in psychology as well as more broadly across disciplines. Choosing books for students to apply foundational key concepts (e.g., structural, political and representational intersectionality, intersectional political consciousness, intersectional invisibility, privilege) required a selection of texts that challenged students' assumptions about singular identities and oppression/privilege and allowed students to identify key concepts throughout the course.

Our goal here was to provide examples to illustrate the potential of each assigned book in the context of a course. Because I am a psychologist and this is a psychology course, most books I selected were written by psychologists. For pedagogues from other disciplines, choosing foundational texts from their discipline should complement Crenshaw's work (1991) on intersectionality. In addition to work presented in this collection (in particular, see Naples, this volume), legal scholars' recent work on colorblind intersectionality (Carbado, 2013), research methods (MacKinnon, 2013), political science and cross-movement politics (Verloo, 2013), transnational feminist perspectives on intersectionality (Mohanty, 2013; Patil, 2013), sociological intersectionality research methods (McCall, 2005), and social movement strategy (Chun, Lipsitz, & Shin, 2013) provide examples of scholarship available across disciplines to frame any course that seeks to infuse intersectional theory throughout the semester.

Conclusion: "Thank You for Pushing Me to Grow as a Person"

By the end of the semester, students gained a thorough understanding of how inequality affects different groups of people through public policies, social norms, and practices that reinforce existing systems of inequality. By using an intersectional perspective, students learned to become agents of change toward achieving positive institutional change and social justice as well as how the social constructions of gender, race, sexuality, and class impact a person's experiences. Finally, examination of intragroup differences as well as intergroup similarities moved us away from choosing a side (e.g., race or gender; Fine, Stewart, & Zucker, 2000) and toward solutions that consider both difference and similarity (Greenwood, 2008).

The theory of intersectionality looks closer at the lived experiences of people at critical intersections. Using intersectional theory allows for a richer understanding of a person's humanity within systems of oppression and privilege rather than a description (e.g., Latina, middle-class, heterosexual). Helping each other understand intersectionality as not simply a list of identifiable features that make us each unique allowed students in the course to consider more closely the lived experiences of dissimilar others, as well as differences among those they considered similar to themselves. End of semester student evaluations reflected the personal evolution and value of understanding the utility of an intersectional analysis in "a space that made you really evaluate your social standing and come [to] terms with your own oppression and privilege." Students also experienced the course to be "very important" and appreciated "this course being available . . . and wish it could be taught nationwide." They also reported having learned "a lot in class . . . thank you for challenging my point of view on education, [and] on the way I view myself and others." In our own ways, we now continue to use intersectionality to assess our environments, selves, and best solutions for social change with an understanding that our contributions to the world are what make us unique, not the list of our social identities.

References

Bain, K. (2004). *What the best college teachers do*. Cambridge, MA: Harvard University Press.

Barreto, M., Manazano, S., & Segura, G. (2012). *The impact of media stereotypes on opinions and attitudes towards Latinos*. Retrieved from National Hispanic Media Coalition website:www.nhmc.org/

Brookfield, S. D. (2012). *Teaching for critical thinking: Tools and techniques to help students question their assumptions*. San Francisco, CA: Jossey-Bass.

Carbado, D. W. (2013). Colorblind intersectionality. *Signs, 38*(4), 811–845. doi: 10.1086/669666

Case, K. (2012). Discovering the privilege of whiteness: White women's reflections on anti-racist identity and ally behavior. *Journal of Social Issues, 68*(1), 78–96. doi:10.1111/j.1540-4560.2011.01737.x

Case, K. A. (this volume). Toward an intersectional pedagogy model: Engaged learning for social justice. In K. A. Case (Ed.), *Intersectional pedagogy: Complicating identity and social justice* (pp. 1–24). New York, NY: Routledge.

Case, K. A., Iuzzini, J., & Hopkins, M. (2012). Systems of privilege: Intersections, awareness, and applications. *Journal of Social Issues, 68*(1), 1–10. doi:10.1111/j.1540-4560.2011.0173 2.x

Case, K. A., & Lewis, M. (this volume). Teaching intersectional psychology in racially diverse settings. In K. A. Case (Ed.), *Intersectional pedagogy: Complicating identity and social justice* (pp 129–149). New York, NY: Routledge.

Chun J. J., Lipsitz, G., & Shin, Y. (2013). Intersectionality as a social movement strategy: Asian immigrant women advocates. *Signs, 38*(4), 917–940. doi:10.1086/669575

Cole, E. (2009). Intersectionality and research in psychology. *American Psychologist, 64*(3), 170–180. doi:10.1037/a0014564

Collins, P. H. (1990). *Black feminist thought: Knowledge, consciousness, and the politics of power*. New York, NY: Routledge.

Crenshaw, K. (1991). Mapping the margins: Intersectionality, identity politics, and violence against women of color. *Stanford Law Review, 43*(6), 1241–1299. doi:10.1002/ir.395

Dessel, A., & Corvidae, T. (this volume). Experiential activities for engaging intersectionality in social justice pedagogy. In K. A. Case (Ed.), *Intersectional pedagogy: Complicating identity and social justice* (pp 214–231). New York, NY: Routledge.

Fine, M., & Asch, A. (1988). *Women with disabilities: Essays in psychology, culture, and politics*. Philadelphia, PA: Temple University Press.

Fine, M., Stewart, A. J., & Zucker, A. N. (2000). White girls and women in the contemporary United States: Supporting or subverting race and gender domination? In C. Squire (Ed.), *Culture in psychology* (pp. 59–72). Philadelphia, PA: Routledge.

Freire, P. (1970/2000). *Pedagogy of the oppressed*. New York, NY: Continuum.

Fryberg, S. A., & Townsend, S. M. (2008). The psychology of invisibility. In A. Glenn, M. Biernat, N. R. Branscombe, C. S. Crandall, & L. S. Wrightsman, (Eds.), *Commemorating Brown: The social psychology of racism and discrimination* (pp. 173–193). Washington, DC: American Psychological Association.

Frye, M. (1983). Oppression. *The politics of reality: Essays in feminist theory* (pp. 1–16). Trumansburg, NY: Crossing Press.

Goldberg, A. E. (2012). *Gay dads: Transitions to adoptive fatherhood*. New York, NY: New York University Press.

Greenwood, R. M. (2008). Intersectional political consciousness: Appreciation for intragroup differences and solidarity in diverse groups. *Psychology of Women Quarterly, 32*(1), 36–47. doi:10.1111/j.1471-6402.2007.00405.x

Greenwood, R. M. (this volume). Intersectionality foundations and disciplinary adaptations: Highways and byways. In K. A. Case (Ed.), *Intersectional pedagogy: Complicating identity and social justice* (pp 27–45). New York, NY: Routledge.

Hall, N. (this volume). Quotes, blogs, diagrams, and counter-storytelling: Teaching intersectionality at a minority-serving institution. In K. A. Case (Ed.), *Intersectional pedagogy: Complicating identity and social justice* (pp. 150–170). New York, NY: Routledge.

Haraway, D. (1988). Situated knowledges: The science question in feminism and the privilege of partial perspective. *Feminist Studies, 14*(3), 575–599. doi:10.2307/3178066

Health and Safety Code, Texas Statute. § 192.008 (1989).

hooks, b. (2010). *Teaching critical thinking: Practical wisdom*. New York: Routledge.

House Bill 201, 83rd Texas Legislature. (2013).

Hurtado, A. (1996). *The color of privilege: Three blasphemies on race and feminism*. Ann Arbor, MI: University of Michigan Press.

Hurtado, A. (2010). Multiple lenses: Multicultural feminist theory. In H. Landrine & N. F. Russo (Eds.), *Handbook of feminist psychology* (pp. 29–54). New York, NY: Springer.

Kimmel, M. (2008). *Guyland: The perilous world where boys become men*. New York, NY: Harper Collins.

MacKinnon, C. A. (2013). Intersectionality as method: A note. *Signs, 38*(4), 1019–1030. doi:10.1 086/669570

Margulies, S. (2003). The psychology of prenuptial agreements. *The Journal of Psychiatry Law, 31*(4), 415–432.

McCall, L. (2005). The complexity of intersectionality. *Signs, 30*(3), 1771–1800. doi:10.1086/42 6800

McIntosh, P. (1988). *White privilege and male privilege: A personal account of coming to see correspondences through work in women's studies*. Working Paper No. 189. Wellesley, MA: Wellesley Centers for Women.

Mohanty, C. T. (2013). Transnational feminist crossings: On neoliberalism and radical critique. *Signs, 38*(4), 967–991. doi:10.1086/669576

Morgan, R. (1970). *Sisterhood is powerful*. New York, NY: Random House.

Naples, N. A. (this volume). Pedagogical practice and teaching intersectionality intersectionally. In K. A. Case (Ed.), *Intersectional pedagogy: Complicating identity and social justice* (pp 110–128). New York, NY: Routledge.

Patil, V. (2013). From patriarchy to intersectionality: A transnational feminist assessment of how far we've really come. *Signs, 38*(4), 847–867. doi:10.1086/669560

Pliner, S. M., Banks, C. A., & Tapscott, A. M. (2012). Intersectional pedagogy and transformative learning. In S. M. Pliner & C. A. Banks (Eds.), *Teaching, learning, and intersecting identities in higher education* (pp. 148–161). New York, NY: Peter Lang.

Purdie-Vaughns, V., & Eibach, R. P. (2008). Intersectional invisibility: The distinctive advantages and disadvantages of multiple subordinate-group identities. *Sex Roles, 59*(5–6), 377–391. doi:10.1007/s11199-008-9424-4

Rios, D., & Stewart, A. J. (2013). Recognizing privilege by reducing invisibility: The Global Feminisms Project as a pedagogical tool. In K. A. Case (Ed.), *Deconstructing privilege: teaching and learning as allies in the classroom* (pp. 115–131). New York, NY: Routledge.

Rivera, D. P. (this volume). Revealing hidden intersections of gender identity, sexual orientation, race, and ethnicity: Teaching about multiple oppressed identities. In K. A. Case (Ed.), *Intersectional pedagogy: Complicating identity and social justice* (pp 173–193). New York, NY: Routledge.

Rosenblum, D. (1994). Queer intersectionality and the failure of recent lesbian and gay victories. *Law & Sexuality: Rev. Lesbian & Gay Legal Issues, 4*, 83–122.

Steele, C. M. (2010). *Whistling Vivaldi: How stereotypes affect us and what we can do*. New York, NY: W.W. Norton.

Steele, C. M., & Aronson, J. (1995). Stereotype threat and the intellectual test performance of African Americans. *Journal of Personality and Social Psychology, 69*(5), 797–811. doi:10.1037/0022-3514.69.5.797

Verloo, M. (2013). Intersectional and cross-movement politics and policies: Reflections on current practices and debates. *Signs, 38*(4), 893–915. doi:10.1086/669572

Warner, M. (1991). Introduction: Fear of a queer planet. *Social Text*, (29), 3–17.

11

EXPERIENTIAL ACTIVITIES FOR ENGAGING INTERSECTIONALITY IN SOCIAL JUSTICE PEDAGOGY

Adrienne Dessel and Timothy Corvidae

Social justice educators must be prepared to teach knowledge and skills about social diversity, inequality, conflict, and social justice issues (Adams, Bell, & Griffin, 2007; Dessel & Rodenborg, in press; Dessel, Rogge, & Garlington, 2006; Rodenborg & Boisen, 2013; Spencer, Martineau, & Warren, 2011). This preparation includes teaching students to negotiate the complexity of social identities that they will encounter in the world (Garran & Rozas, 2013; Jani, Pierce, Ortiz, & Sowbel, 2011). Intersectional theory contributes to an understanding of how multiple social identities intersect with each other and with systems of privilege and oppression (Case, this volume; Crenshaw, 1993; Marsiglia & Kulis, 2009). A focus on intersectionality supports students' critical examination of systems of oppression in order to promote social change (Garran & Rozas, 2013; Miller, VeneKlasen, Reilly, & Clark, 2006; Rios, Bowling, & Harris, this volume; Solórzano & Bernal, 2001) and aligns with many higher education accreditation standards for culturally appropriate diversity education.

Below, we provide a description of a graduate social work course, Dialogue Facilitation for Diversity and Social Justice, designed by Spencer et al. (2011) at the University of Michigan and taught by us for the last four years. We present classroom strategies for teaching and learning about intersectionality in the course, including readings, assignments, and experiential activities. We examine classroom activities, such as metaphor analysis, testimonials and personal narratives, privilege fishbowls, and other experiential pedagogies, and incorporate our instructor and student reflections throughout these descriptions. Our pedagogy follows the Case (this volume) model and promotes student reflection on:

- the intersection of privileged and oppressed social identities;
- multiple oppressions that students may experience (e.g., race and social class);
- the ways attention to intersectionality aids recognition of within-group diversity; and
- movement toward social change action.

While this course is taught at the graduate level and focuses on facilitation training, the pedagogies highlighted below would be useful in undergraduate courses with less practice-oriented foci.

Within the course, we incorporated intergroup dialogue theory and practice and social justice facilitation skills used to improve multicultural group interactions, address oppressive social dynamics, and resolve conflicts. Intergroup dialogue (IGD) is a social justice pedagogy that engages students across group conflict based on social identity (e.g., race, gender, social class, or sexual orientation) in a face-to-face, co-facilitated, and sustained group experience (Dessel & Rodenborg, in press; Nagda, Gurin, Sorensen, & Zúñiga, 2009; Zúñiga, Nagda, Chesler, & Cytron-Walker, 2007). Topics covered in the course included:

- social identity group development;
- prejudice and stereotyping and their effects on groups;
- difference and dominance and the nature of social oppression;
- individual and interpersonal connections to power, privilege, and oppression;
- understanding and resolving conflicts or resistance;
- methods of dialoguing and coalition building across differences; and
- basic group facilitation skills and their applications in multicultural settings.

Intergroup and other social justice pedagogies increasingly incorporate attention to intersectionality in order to encourage student reflection about the nuanced ways social identities overlap and shape their lives in relation to structural and systemic multiple oppressions and power dynamics (Case, this volume).

The course described below covers different models of dialogue and social justice facilitation used in higher education, community, and international settings and can be applied in many contexts (Maxwell, Nagda, & Thompson, 2011; Nagda & Maxwell, 2011; National Coalition for Dialogue and Deliberation, 2014; Search for Common Ground, 2015; Spencer et al., 2011). Students learn about the process-content model that focuses on both group process methods and social justice content (Beale & Schoem, 2001). We teach intercultural communication and conflict negotiation skills, and students learn to incorporate their own experiences into facilitating social justice dialogue. Students learn about their own social identities, methods of co-facilitation and multipartial facilitation, and promoting empowerment and commitment to socially just actions (Maxwell, Fisher, Thompson, & Behling, 2011; Nagda, Gurin, Sorensen, Gurin-Sands, & Osuna, 2009; Nagda & Maxwell, 2011). Multipartial (rather than neutral or impartial) facilitation is an approach to balancing social power that is particularly useful in affirming multiple perspectives, lifting up the narratives of marginalized groups, and challenging dominant narratives that create and uphold societal inequalities. This is done through attention to sharing of air time and silence, use of first person narratives, suspending judgment of privileged groups, not expecting marginalized groups to educate privileged groups, and naming dominant narratives (Routenberg & Sclafani, 2010).

Intersectionality refers to the concept of multiple and intersecting social identities that can compound the experiences of social oppression or create social privilege (Cole, 2009; Crenshaw, 1993, 1994; Hancock, 2007; Murphy, Hunt, Zajicek, Norris, & Hamilton, 2009). The concept of intersectionality is key in social justice education (Case & Lewis, this volume). These multiplicative negative effects can significantly compromise minority group members' psychological health and well-being (Cole, 2009; Szymanski & Gupta, 2009). An intersectional approach to social identity and intergroup relations provides an opportunity to more fully analyze each individual's overlapping and unique group identity experiences as well as understand within group differences based on other social identities (Cole, 2009; Crenshaw, 1993, 1994). Further, social justice organizing that fails to take intersectionality into account runs the risk of unintended exclusion of certain identity groups, thereby creating less effective coalitions (African American Policy Forum, n.d.).

Intersectionality is an important construct in social justice dialogue facilitation (Dessel, 2014; Dessel, Massé, & Walker, 2013; Dessel, Woodford, Routenberg, & Breijak, 2013; Rodenborg & Boisen, 2013; Sanders & Mahalingham, 2012; Walls, Roll, Sprague, & Griffin, 2010; Wernick, Dessel, Kulick, & Graham, 2013). As a key purpose, this type of small group facilitation aims to develop critical consciousness about power imbalances and group-based structural inequality (Nagda, Gurin, Sorensen, Gurin-Sands, et al., 2009; Sorensen, Nagda, Gurin, & Maxwell, 2009). This necessitates learning about the ways individual experiences of prejudice, oppression, or privilege based on social identity connect to larger social and institutional structures (Nagda & Maxwell, 2011). Our study of sexual orientation dialogue courses found students recognized the profound effects of multiple oppressions for people who hold both racial and sexual minority identities (Dessel, Woodford, et al., 2013). Learning about the intersectional nature of social identity in other dialogue courses also promoted increased empathy and perspective taking for women and people of color (Dessel, Massé, et al., 2013). Intergroup dialogues on social class as seen through an intersectional lens revealed the invisibility of social class discourse in that race and class are often conflated and students tended to focus more on their racial identity than their social class (Sanders & Mahalingam, 2012). Thus, a focus on intersectionality can contribute to awareness about social justice concepts.

Weaving Intersectionality into Social Justice Readings

In constructing our syllabus, we assembled readings each week that might appeal to a range of learning and cultural preferences and inform students' sense making of interpersonal, social, and structural dynamics they will encounter in their work. While other courses may have less direct connections to applied practice, we suspected that discussing with students the ways they might share or apply intersectional theory and related activities in their own future work would motivate their engagement with the concept of intersectionality. To support intersectional theory informing and interacting with practice, we wove multiple engagement modes together around the major ideas we introduced in the course.

This approach was exemplified in the way we introduced intersectionality in early weeks. We coupled readings on levels and forms of power, privilege, and oppression with several introductory pieces on intersectionality. These theoretical readings offered practical tips on developing intersectional awareness, provided a history of intersectional theory, countered strands of white feminism that neglect attention to multiple oppressions, and complicated intersectional theory by juxtaposing the concept of *simultaneity* (Collins, 2010; Holvino, 2012; Uwujaren & Utt, 2015). Simultaneity refers to the concurrent processes of identity, institutional, and social practices that contribute to experiences, privileges, and oppressions (Holvino, 2012). Additional readings tied intersectionality to contemporary issues such as the complicated interplay of gender identity and sexism (Garelick, 2015) and the intersection of gender and sport (Griffin, 2010). The readings provided a foundational approach to social justice education principles.

We also provided summary materials and activities to engage students with ideas of intersectionality and simultaneity and invited them to connect their reflections of personal experiences with structural-level analysis. The formats of these materials are versatile and allow instructors to change prompts and follow-up questions for different topics or learning goals. As we introduced these activities in class, we emphasized the importance of developing inquiry *within* ourselves (through reflection) and *between* ourselves (through facilitated dialogue). Although the course ran for 11 weeks, the curriculum for weeks 2, 4, and 5 represented the greatest intersectional focus.

Introduction to Intersectionality Handout (Week 2)

To inform students' dialogic inquiry with an intersectional lens, we created a handout that described some intersectional theories discussed in the literature. This presented a set of intersectional questions developed by a variety of theorists. Questions included:

- "When I see something that looks racist, I ask, 'Where is the patriarchy in this?' When I see something that looks sexist, I ask, 'Where is the heterosexism in this?'" (Matsuda, 1991, p. 1189);
- Whose experience frames the problem? (King, 1988);
- "Who is included within this category?" (Cole, 2009, p. 4);
- "How do debates across constituencies sound different when it is recognized that each community contains members of the other?" and "What is the broadest articulation of a problem that would embrace more than the interests of the most advantaged?" (African American Policy Forum, n.d., p. 6);
- "What forms of identity are critical organizing principles for this community/region (beyond gender, consider race, ethnicity, religion, citizenship, age, caste, ability)?
  - Who are the most marginalized women, girls, men and boys in the community and why?
  - What social and economic programs are available to different groups in the community?
  - Who does and does not have access or control over productive resources and why?
  - Which groups have the lowest and the highest levels of public representation and why?
  - What laws, policies and organizational practices limit opportunities of different groups?
  - What opportunities facilitate the advancement of different groups?
  - What initiatives would address the needs of the most marginalized or discriminated groups in society?" (Association for Women's Rights in Development, 2004, p. 7);
- Think of a situation where you found yourself claiming or not claiming your complex identities. What about the context made it so? (Holvino, 2012).

We encouraged students to keep this list handy in class, and these questions informed the dialogue guides we prepared for ourselves when facilitating these activities.

Metaphors of Intersectionality Activity (Week 2)

As we endeavored to introduce intersectionality as a key lens, we faced a dilemma of how to grapple with complexities and controversies around the concept of intersectionality itself as well as around framings of social identity and identity politics. I (Timothy) had past success employing explanatory metaphors. In considering which metaphor to use and how much to complicate intersectional theory, we put these questions into the students' hands. We developed a handout that positioned five metaphors side by side, suggesting the aspects of intersectionality that the metaphors emphasized and associated theorists (see Table 11.1). One example of a metaphor is a traffic cloverleaf where various roads intersect, representing different social identities and patterns of inequality and potential conflict. We first engaged students in a basic reflective activity about social identity categories in which they examined their many social identities in isolation from each other, called the social identity profile (Adams et al., 2007), and then we introduced the metaphor handout. We briefly discussed the implications of different metaphors with the students and broke them into groups of four with the task of coming up with an interactive activity that might help bring intersectionality alive. We encouraged them to continue to play with metaphor, using one from the handout or developing their own. We gave 30 minutes to plan and 30 minutes for reports and large group discussion. We provided them with large flip chart paper, markers, scissors, and smaller pieces of colored paper.

Metaphorical thinking as a design challenge facilitated creative engagement in the groups. Students even generated ideas that we might use in future teaching. One group devised an activity in which people would get a bucket to fill with paper water droplets that had social identities written on them. This game mechanism was meant to demonstrate the fluidity of identities. Social identities are represented as liquid water droplets that flow in and out of each other, can be contained within the bucket, and can be seen through the bucket or not depending on the opacity of the buckets used. Students suggested that droplets might be of different sizes and colors depending on their salience to the individual, and they might be put in the bucket or taped to the outside, depending on how private or public, personally held or socially ascribed the person felt the identity to be. As we discussed the activity, someone suggested that people could shape their own identities that feel more (or less) fluid to them in different ways. The class was excited by this playful and flexible metaphor. Students suggested that it was like a chemistry experiment, or mixing paint, layering on further metaphors to help people think about how society constructs and categorizes people based on group identity, often in a way that attributes privilege or imposes oppression.

Another student group proposed an activity in which identity would be treated as an abstract mural. Students invited each person to represent their identity by drawing on white paper with colorful markers. They discussed various media with which a mural might be made and suggested with the use of paint because the colors and shapes would change each other as they overlapped or mixed. One student chimed in that paint mixes differently if colors are added at the same time or after some drying time, which might represent how identities interact differently depending on when and how they develop. The group liked that the paint metaphor offered a way to think about resistance to oppressive power structures that often ascribe identity and gave them freedom to self-represent their identities as they mixed their own shades and tones of color.

A third student group created an activity in which people write on a two-sided poster the words "How do *you* see you?" and then the words "How do

TABLE 11.1 Metaphors of Intersectionality Handout

Metaphor	Traffic metaphor	Venn diagram	Baking metaphor	Pizza metaphor	Hologram (Simultaneity)
Metaphor Explained	Roads: patterns of inequality Traffic: contemporary issues Crossroads: position of people with membership in multiple oppressed groups Accidents: people in crossroads can get hit from one side, multiple sides, or hit from one side and thrown into nearby accidents on other roads		Ingredients: social identities Cupcake: individual person You can't take cupcake ingredients back apart after baking. Flour and eggs cannot be separated out from each other	Burgers: men Pizza: women, trans* people In a burger-centered world, working for pizza rights is too often done for and by cheese pizzas (straight, White women), ignoring the needs and strengths of deluxe pizzas (women of color and LGBTQ people)	Social identities are simultaneous processes (rather than locations) of individual, institutional and societal practice. The salience of specific differences changes by context
Critiques of the Metaphor	The intersections metaphor (and its Venn variation) imports the single-identity model it seeks to replace. It suggests a fixed location, ignoring fluidity of identity over time and in relational context		The baking metaphor can imply that identity is fixed and essentialized, and it focuses on individual experience	The pizza metaphor explains a critique of exclusion within feminist movement and theory, more than explaining intersectionality itself	Some argue simultaneity is the same as intersectionality, and its critiques focus on misinterpretations and misuses of intersectionality
Related Readings	Crenshaw (1994) Collins (2010)		Alsultany (2002) Anzaldua (1999)	Hughs (2015)	Holvino (2012)

* *Note:* *trans* is used to indicate the inclusion all identity terms that refer to trans women and trans men (e.g., transgender, non-binary, genderqueer).

others see you?" This group found the process of designing this simple activity to be consciousness-raising. They purposely started with the "how do *you* see you" side. They sketched an outline of a human figure that people might draw on to represent themselves, but then found themselves questioning what this physical figure would suggest. They erased the figure in order not to constrain people's imaginations with ableist or sizeist portrayals of bodies. The lesson continued as the class weighed the merits of seeing people's representations on big posters versus allowing more privacy with small paper. One student suggested they reconsider color choices to be more accessible for people who are colorblind or visually impaired. Students' reflections indicated a raised awareness about the ways societal views of people's social identities create power structures of inclusion or exclusion.

This activity was born out of our curiosity to see what students would create. Holding this activity during our second session set the class off on a foot of critical engagement and contemplation as students considered issues of representation, inclusivity, and accessibility in collaborative ways. Inviting students to develop their own metaphors helped them interact with intersectional theory to find their own way of making sense of it. The activity also gave us a window into which aspects of intersectional theory they were and were not focusing on in the course material. We noticed that students' attention most often got stuck at the individual level of identity (Rios et al., this volume). In the future, we might allow the individual focus to play out, and then invite some critical discussion about it. This occurred when one student shared that she was thinking of intersectionality like a thumbprint with a limitless number of different identities that form each unique individual. We validated that the thumbprint metaphor captured the individual experience of identity complexity while inviting students to consider how from a justice perspective, the thumbprint metaphor carries a different emphasis than the traffic intersections metaphor. In talking about a limitless number of identities, the thumbprint metaphor loses the focus on how discrimination and oppression targets people (e.g., women of color) based on their group memberships, not as unique individuals.

We recognize that these introductory activities were abstract and could feel distant from the seriousness of the systems of oppression that intersectional theory is meant to help us understand and dismantle. We did not want to get stuck in the abstract too long and moved on to invite more nuanced and personal explorations of students' lives and how those lived experiences connect to systems of power and oppression.

Testimonials Activity (Week 4)

We invited students to take time outside of class to prepare a 5-minute 'testimonial" or personal narrative in which they discussed two of their social identities: one of privilege in society and one of marginalization and oppression. They are asked to consider an intersectional lens around social identity when reflecting on and sharing their story.

The sharing of these narratives represents a pivotal moment in the course. This can be an opportunity for students to represent themselves with an intersectional complexity. When students do share complex and deep stories, they create an environment that supports nuanced conversations for the rest of the term. However, testimonials can be stressful and risky for some people. Students enter our class with previous socialization about how to appropriately represent their identities, especially their oppressed or marginalized identities. To mediate that pressure to perform cultural expectations, and also to demonstrate instructor self-reflection (Rivera, this volume), we model by sharing our own testimonials the week before when introducing the assignment. We each share from both privileged and marginalized identities (Adrienne as White and Jewish; Timothy as White, transgender, queer, and temporarily able-bodied) and how these identities afford social privilege or create experiences of oppression. Examples of student reflections on intersectionality in their own narratives included:

- how difficult it is to disentangle race and ethnicity from gender when considering the effect on one's social class;
- the influence of social class on eating disorders;
- how white privilege can overshadow the experiences of being from a lower social class and ethnic minority group; and
- that having U.S. citizenship privilege can be a very different experience depending on one's social class and race.

We reflected on the logic of limiting their focus to two identities in the assignment prompt. This focus aims to help them engage intersectionality with some specificity as they only get five minutes to share their narratives. We asked students to consider an intersectional lens when reflecting on and sharing their stories, but they needed more guidance for this assignment. In the future, we would offer more detailed reflective strategies to help students look at their own intersectional experiences. These strategies might include providing the examples above and instructing them to write a draft testimonial that included describing how each identity relates to the others.

Take a Position Activity (Week 4)

The above story-sharing activities helped students appreciate the complexity of each other's lives, notice differences as well as common threads, and connect individual experiences to larger systems and histories. We also used activities that exposed and explored students' opinions, motivations, and plans for taking social justice action. Early on, we introduced an activity called Take a Position in which we created a spectrum across the room (clearing away chairs) with the words "Strongly Agree" posted at one end, "Strongly Disagree" at the other, and a neutral line in the middle on which students are not allowed to position themselves. The instructors read statements and ask students to take a position along the spectrum that indicates to what degree they would engage in social justice advocacy or activism. Students are encouraged to follow their initial instincts in positioning themselves and to take risks. We asked students to "think about how intersectional theory influences your position." For example, we asked them to consider that interrupting sexual orientation prejudice may be easier for White people than people of color, or speaking out at a rally to support abortion rights may mean different things for people from different social classes.

This activity is sometimes called Take a Stand (adapted from the Crossing the Room activity by Bell, Love, & Roberts, 2007), but we take care to use the term *position* instead to be inclusive of students with physical disabilities and who might move or metaphorically position themselves, but not stand. We spread chairs along the line for students who need to sit during longer conversations. If there are participants for whom movement in the room is difficult, an instructor can offer to be positioned in their stead.

While this activity can be conducted in silence, we prefer to talk about why people position themselves where they are after each statement. Sample statements included:

- maintaining a healthy body weight is important for people in certain racial/ethnic groups;
- people of color can be racist;
- I would boycott a store or chain of stores when I find out they exploit workers who make their products;
- affirmative action based on class is a better way to ensure racial diversity on campus; and
- people who are more religious are less critical thinkers.

We designed statements as purposely ambiguous to allow for individual interpretation and then discussion. We invited students to generate additional statements to make responsibility for inquiry more collectively held. This ran the risk that students might pose statements that could offend or marginalize others in their wording or content, so we were prepared to rephrase or reframe statements. We also monitored students' body language, taking care to ask if people wanted to share when we saw notable reactions. If no one spoke up, we sometimes voiced possible concerns people might have to help make room for those with concerns to then speak up.

The impact of this activity lies in the dialogic conversations that occur throughout. The questions we asked shaped what the group takes away. It would be easy to experience the activity as polarizing. However, as we invited people to ask questions of each other and to consider how their own identity positionalities influence the positions they have taken, they began to see themselves in a complex constellation of stances. We also invited students to move themselves if, as they hear others speak, they realized where they have placed themselves is not accurate relative to others, or they find their opinions shifting and wanted to demonstrate this. This movement made physically visible the impact people have on each other in dialogue and encouraged constant reflection and re-evaluation of positions. We sometimes returned to this activity throughout the term in impromptu or planned ways, as the format gets everyone quickly involved in any given conversation.

Privilege Fishbowls Activity (Week 5)

Within social justice dialogues, students often raise concerns that those with more privilege expect to learn *from* those with less privilege (Walls et al., 2010) rather than educating themselves. In what might seem like a counterintuitive response, we addressed this in week 5 by spending a session focused entirely on privilege. Our goal is to develop a more complex awareness of our own privilege in order to be able to speak of privilege in ways that contribute to dialogic learning for all.

Given the opportunity to look intersectionally at identity, students often gravitate toward oppressed identities they hold, pivoting their focus off identities that give them access to privilege (Case, 2013; Case, Iuzzini, & Hopkins, 2012; McIntosh, 2012). In our work, we found that in examining intersections of Christian religious identity with racial and gender identities, students tended to focus more on their oppressed racial and gender identities than on their privileged Christian identity (Dessel, Massé, et al., 2013). In a dialogue in our class focused on heterosexism, heterosexual women spent over an hour discussing their experiences with sexism rather than discussing privileges they gain from heterosexuality. While we do encourage students to consider how their experiences with one identity might help them develop some understanding of the oppression faced by students with a different identity, we often find it necessary to ask students to suspend their attention to their more oppressed identities in order to more fully explore the privilege they do experience. This can be difficult, given the lack of awareness that the invisible nature of privilege has afforded them. Developing intersectional activities and assigning readings inclusive of privilege can help students unpack these dynamics and examine privilege as well as oppression. This privilege fishbowl activity is designed to facilitate this process.

We began the session with four "knapsacks" of privilege (McIntosh, 1988) drawn on flipchart paper posted on the walls of the room. The metaphorical knapsacks used were U.S. citizen, ability, Christian, and cisgender privileges. Students circulated silently and wrote in each knapsack the specific privileges they carry. We then held 20-minute rounds of dialogue about each privilege in a "fishbowl" format (Walls et al., 2010), with five to seven students who held privilege in that topic forming a circle in the middle of the room, while the rest of the class observed. We asked for a small number of volunteers, rather than inviting everyone who holds that privilege into the circle, to avoid "outing" any student as having or not having an identity. We had two students co-facilitate these fishbowls, although the fishbowls could also have been instructor facilitated or unfacilitated. The two student co-facilitators had 20 minutes to prepare at the beginning of the session while the rest of the class wrote reflectively about one of their areas of privilege. This reflective writing encouraged students to consider their own intersecting identities and what they may have learned from the activity (Case & Rios, this volume).

While caucusing based on one identity may seem counter to an intersectional treatment of identity, caucusing allows within-group differences to surface (including those based on how students' other identities intersect with the identity of focus). We ensured this happened by explicitly prompting the student co-facilitators to ask those in the fishbowl about the intersection of their other identities. We also found that privilege fishbowls countered the tendency of students with more privilege to turn to others with more marginalized identities to teach them. While it can be frustrating at times for people who hold less privilege in an identity to listen silently while people struggle through a conversation about that identity, this format removes the burden on more marginalized groups to be the educators of the privileged and gives them a window into those with privilege working on self-examination. During the debrief after the fishbowls, we invited observations or reactions from people without privilege, or who hold less relative privilege, in any of the identities discussed, and asked them to share what else they hoped people would think about. We then considered together how this session could inform future learning interactions across power differentials.

It became clear that this focused effort to discuss privilege was needed as the session continued. Even when invited to only speak of their privilege, students largely talked about what other people do not experience, such as racial oppression, and what rights people from marginalized groups do not have, such as pay equality for women (Case, 2013). For example, a White woman said she did not have to face racist hiring practices, yet avoided discussing her white privilege, and an African American woman spoke about her racial oppression rather than acknowledging her Christian privilege. After two rounds, we pointed this deficiency out. The dynamic did not improve tremendously in the third fishbowl, yet afterward students reported how this made them much more aware of their privileged thinking. Debriefing after such activities is critical, because often student learning comes as much from noticing group process as from the content that people share. Students became aware of their own and others' habits and/or lack of awareness of privilege by considering questions such as:

- How did thinking about intersectionality play out (or not play out) in these fishbowls?
- Were other identities considered?
- Were identities ever used to avoid facing privilege?
- Where did we see places of denial or resistance?
- How did these places of denial or resistance play out?

For example, we pointed out that when discussing U.S. citizenship privilege, students talked about a generalized "we" (U.S. Americans), but neglected to identify examples of their own specific life experiences. Noting this challenged students to notice how they participate in and benefit from dominant U.S. culture and laws.

They also explored the relative nature of privilege. In the U.S. citizen privilege knapsack, someone listed "not having to fear interactions with the police (because of deportation threats)." An African American student pointed out that not fearing police is not a privilege that all U.S. citizens experience. A Latina student pointed out that even with U.S. citizenship she may be targeted for police attention because of assumptions that she may be undocumented.

There is much to learn from the examination of the effects and mechanisms of privilege in our lives for those with and those without privilege (Walls et al., 2010), but these gains are often not realized in intergroup exchanges due to the invisible and denied nature of privilege. Dedicating a whole session to several, often less-examined, forms of privilege equips students to develop a more complex awareness of the interplay of privilege and oppression in their lives and the world. The use of experiential methods to raise awareness about intersectionality and privilege is also an important pedagogy (Rios et al., this volume). This awareness facilitates movement toward social justice actions (Gurin, Nagda, & Zúñiga, 2013).

Assignments

We infused intersectionality into the assignments in a number of ways. In the first essay assignment, where students reflect on their social identities, intergroup and facilitation experiences, and ideas about social change, we asked them: "What is your understanding of identity intersectionality? What is your understanding of how different social identities intersect with each other and the experience this provides for people? How do you think about and experience this in your own life?" Some students welcomed this opportunity that was inclusive of all of their identities. Others acknowledged the difficult intersection of multiple oppressions. In the final paper, we asked how students' stories changed over the semester with regard to these prompts. We also asked what specific course activities and materials enhanced their learning about intersectionality as well as ways to facilitate this awareness in others.

Bi-weekly online forums were an opportunity for us to prompt intersectionally informed reflective analysis. For example, one forum invited students to read Leondar-Wright's (2014) account of the ways noticing class culture differences and influences of gender, race, and movement histories can enable activists to strengthen their groups and cross-class alliances. The forum prompt was: "Tell about an incident or issue that you've understood and analyzed through one lens (racism, sexism, heterosexism, ableism, etc.) that changes for you if you add a class lens. How does it change?"

A number of different themes regarding student learning emerged in this forum. Students talked about being diverted from downward mobility by their families, as upon reflection they recognized that race is often used as a proxy for social class. As an example, students discussed how their parents talk to them about where to work or live or what careers to consider. Another theme involved students overlooking consideration of social class because of the inclination to focus on race, therefore not understanding the class dynamics involved in decision-making behaviors. This example included recognizing stereotypes they may hold, which are based on class assumptions, about the choices of customers in a coffee shop or retail store or behaviors of people in specific school systems. They recognized how these stereotypes based on class assumptions, or their lack of awareness about social class, leads to systems of structural inequality. Other themes involved new awareness about the intersection of gender and social class in family roles and dynamics and the ways social class contributes to conflicts that are assumed to be based on race. Through forums and journals, students indicated their learning that identity can be contextually determined as well as fluid and changeable throughout one's life. They also brought greater structural and cultural analysis to their thinking and showed increased awareness of how that might inform their participation in organizations and as professional social workers.

Reflections on Infusing Intersectionality into Our Teaching

In teaching this class, we found that raising awareness of intersectionality required intentional instructor incorporation into activities and discussions. Attending to the intersectional nature of social identity can help break through resistance some students exhibit to acknowledging the extent of identity-based oppression (Case & Cole, 2013; Wise & Case, 2013) and foster awareness of how differently people experience one identity based on their other identities. Throughout the many activities we used, students reported learning, for example, about how they have overlooked social class and instead focused solely on race, that heterosexism has often been defined as a "White" problem, and that research on certain social problems is often defined by those with educational and professional status. In these reflections, we see the increasingly complex ways our students begin to view their world and the worlds of others. This awareness clears the way to more socially just interactions and analysis and hopefully equips students to contribute to creating a more equitable society.

Instructors in social science and humanities disciplines, as well as in the arts, business, and law, can use the activities and materials discussed above to foster learning about the complexity of social identity and how the simultaneous nature of identities contribute to intersections among forms or systems of oppression, domination, or discrimination. These activities are relevant in all contexts that engage people in group interactions, for social identity dynamics are always at play (Adams et al., 2007) and careful instructor attention to them will create a more ideal learning environment for all students.

References

Adams, M., Bell, L. A., & Griffin, P. (Eds.). (2007). *Teaching for diversity and social justice.* New York, NY: Routledge.

African American Policy Forum. (n.d.). *A primer on intersectionality.* Retrieved from www.aapf.org

Alsultany, E. (2002). Los intersticios: Recasting moving selves. In G. Anzaldúa & A. Keating, (Eds.), *This bridge we call home: Radical visions for transformation* (pp.106–110). New York, NY: Routledge.

Anzaldúa, G. (1999). *Borderlands: La frontera* (2nd ed.). San Francisco, CA: Aunt Lute Books.

Association for Women's Rights in Development. (2004). *Intersectionality: A tool for gender and economic justice* (Primer). Retrieved from www.awid.org

Beale, R. L., & Schoem, D. (2001). The content/process balance in intergroup dialogue. In D. Schoem & S. Hurtado (Eds.), *Intergroup dialogue: Deliberative democracy in school, college, community, and workplace* (pp. 266–279). Ann Arbor, MI: University of Michigan Press.

Bell, L. A., Love, B. J., & Roberts, R. A. (2007). Racism and white privilege curriculum design. In M. Adams, L. A. Bell, & P. Griffin. (Eds.). (2007). *Teaching for diversity and social justice* (pp. 123–144). New York, NY: Routledge.

Case, K. (2013). *Deconstructing privilege: Teaching and learning as allies in the classroom.* New York, NY: Routledge.

Case, K. A. (this volume). Toward an intersectional pedagogy model: Engaged learning for social justice. In K. A. Case (Ed.), *Intersectional pedagogy: Complicating identity and social justice* (pp. 1–24). New York, NY: Routledge.

Case, K., & Cole, L. (2013). Deconstructing privilege when students resist: The journey back into the community of learners. In K. Case (Ed.), *Deconstructing privilege: Teaching and learning as allies in the classroom* (pp. 34–48). New York, NY: Routledge.

Case, K., Iuzzini, J., & Hopkins, M. (2012). Systems of privilege: Intersections, awareness, and applications. *Journal of Social Issues, 68*(1), 1–10. doi:10.1111/j.1540-4560.2011.01732. x

Case, K. A., & Lewis, M. (this volume). Teaching intersectional psychology in racially diverse settings. In K. A. Case (Ed.), *Intersectional pedagogy: Complicating identity and social justice* (pp. 129–149). New York, NY: Routledge.

Case, K. A., & Rios, D. (this volume). Infusing intersectionality: Complicating the Psychology of Women course. In K. A. Case (Ed.), *Intersectional pedagogy: Complicating identity and social justice* (pp. 82–109). New York, NY: Routledge.

Cole, E. R. (2009). Intersectionality and research in psychology. *American Psychologist, 64,* 120–180. doi:10.1037/a0014564

Collins, P. (2010). Toward a new vision: Race, class, and gender. In M. Adams, W. J. Blumenfeld, C. Castañeda, H. W. Hackman, M. L. Peters, & X. Zúñiga (Eds.), *Readings for diversity and social justice* (3rd ed., pp. 604–609). New York, NY: Routledge.

Crenshaw, K. (1993). Demarginalizing the intersection of race and sex: A Black feminist critique of antidiscrimination doctrine, feminist theory, and antiracist politics. In D. K. Weisbert (Ed.), *Feminist legal theory: Foundations* (pp. 383–395). Philadelphia, PA: Temple University Press.

Crenshaw, K. W. (1994). Mapping the margins: Intersectionality, identity politics, and violence against women of color. In M. A. Fineman & R. Mykitiuk (Eds.), *The public nature of private violence* (pp. 93–118). New York, NY: Routledge.

Dessel, A. (2014). Bridging the conservative Christianity and sexual orientation divide: A review of intergroup dialogue pedagogy and practice. In A. Dessel & R. Bolen (Eds.), *Conservative Christian beliefs and sexual orientation in social work: Privilege, oppression, and the pursuit of human rights* (pp. 313–344). Alexandria, VA: CSWE Press.

Dessel, A., Massé, J., & Walker, L. (2013). Intergroup dialogue pedagogy: Teaching about intersectional and under-examined privilege in heterosexual, Christian, and Jewish identities. In K. Case (Ed.), *Deconstructing privilege: Teaching and learning as allies in the classroom,* (pp. 132–148). New York, NY: Routledge.

Dessel, A., & Rodenborg, N. (in press). An evaluation of intergroup dialogue pedagogy: Addressing segregation and developing cultural competency. *Journal of Social Work Education.*

Dessel, A., Rogge, M., & Garlington, S. (2006) Using intergroup dialogue to promote social justice and change. *Social Work, 51* (4), 303–315. doi:10.1093/sw/51.4.303

Dessel, A., Woodford, M., Routenberg, R., & Breijak, D. (2013). Heterosexual students' experiences in sexual orientation intergroup dialogue courses. *Journal of Homosexuality, 60*(7), 1054–1080. doi:10.1080/00918369.2013.776413

Garelick, R. (2015, June 3). The price of Caitlyn Jenner's heroism. *The New York Times.* Retrieved from www.nytimes.com

Garran, A. M., & Rozas, L. W. (2013). Cultural competence revisited. *Journal of Ethnic & Cultural Diversity in Social Work, 22*(2), 97–111. doi:10.1080/ 15313204.2013.785337

Griffin, P. (2010). Sport: Where men are men and women are trespassers. In M. Adams, W. J. Blumenfeld, C. Castañeda, H. W. Hackman, M. L. Peters, & X. Zúñiga (Eds.), *Readings for diversity and social justice* (3rd ed., pp. 399–404). New York, NY: Routledge.

Gurin, P., Nagda, B. A., & Zúñiga, X. (2013). *Engaging race and gender: Intergroup dialogues in higher education.* New York, NY: Russell Sage Foundation.

Hancock, A. M. (2007). Intersectionality as a normative and empirical research paradigm. *Politics and Gender, 3,* 248–254.

Holvino, E. (2012). The "simultaneity" of identities: Models and skills for the twenty-first century. In C. L. Wijeyesinghe & B. W. Jackson III (Eds.), *New perspectives on racial identity development: Integrating emerging frameworks* (2nd ed., pp. 161–191). New York: NYU Press.

Hughs, A. (2015). *On intersectionality in feminism pizza* [Video]. Retrieved from www.youtube.com/watch?v=FgK3NFvGp58

Iani, J. S., Pierce, D., Ortiz, L., & Sowbel, L. (2011). Access to intersectionality, content to competence: Deconstructing social work education diversity standards. *Journal of Social Work Education, 47*(2), 283–301. doi:10.5175/JSWE.2011.200900118

King, D. K. (1988). Multiple jeopardy, multiple consciousnesses: The context of a Black feminist ideology. *Signs, 14,* 42–72. doi:10.1086/494491

Leondar-Wright, B. (2014) *Missing class: Strengthening social class movements by seeing class cultures.* Ithaca, NY: Cornell University/ILR Press

Marsiglia, F., & Kulis, S. (2009) *Culturally grounded social work: Diversity, oppression, and change.* Chicago, IL: Lyceum Books

Matsuda, M. (1991). Beside my sister, facing the enemy: Legal theory out of coalition. *Stanford Law Review, 43*(6), 1183–1192. doi:10.2307/1229035

Maxwell, K. E., Fisher, R., Thompson, M., & Behling, C. (2011). Training peer facilitators as social justice educators. In K. E. Maxwell, B. A. Nagda, & M. Thompson (Eds.), *Facilitating intergroup dialogues: Bridging differences, catalyzing change* (pp. 41–54). Sterling, VA: Stylus Publishing.

Maxwell, K. E., Nagda, B., & Thompson, M. (Eds.). (2011). *Facilitating intergroup dialogues: Bridging differences, catalyzing change.* Sterling, VA: Stylus Publishing.

McIntosh, P. (1988). *White privilege and male privilege: A personal account of coming to see correspondences through work in women's studies.* Working Paper No. 189. Wellesley, MA: Wellesley Centers for Women.

McIntosh, P. (2012). Reflections and future directions for privilege studies. *Journal of Social Issues, 68*(1), 194–206. doi:10.1111/j.1540-4560.2011.01744.x

Miller, V., VeneKlasen, L., Reilly, M., & Clark, C. (2006). *Making change happen: Power: Concepts for revisioning power for justice, equality, and peace.* Retrieved from www.justassociates.org

Murphy, Y., Hunt, V., Zajicek, A., Norris, A., & Hamilton, L. (2009). *Incorporating intersectionality in social work practice, research, policy, and education.* Washington, DC: NASW Press.

Nagda, B., Gurin, P., Sorensen, N., Gurin-Sands, C., & Osuna, S. (2009). From separate corners to dialogue and action. *Race and Social Problems, 1*(1), 45–55. doi:10.1007/s12552-009-9002-6

Nagda, B. A., Gurin, P., Sorensen, N., & Zúñiga, X. (2009). Evaluating intergroup dialogue: Engaging diversity for personal and social responsibility. *Diversity & Democracy, 12*(1), 4–6. doi:10.1007/s12552-009-9002-6

Nagda, B. A., & Maxwell, K. E. (2011). Deepening the layers of understanding and connection: A critical-dialogic approach to facilitating intergroup dialogues. In K. E. Maxwell, B. A. Nagda, & M. Thompson (Eds.), *Facilitating intergroup dialogues: Bridging differences, catalyzing change* (pp. 1–22). Sterling, VA: Stylus Publishing.

National Coalition for Dialogue and Deliberation. (2014). *Engagement streams framework* [Resource guide]. Retrieved from www.ncdd.org/

Rios, D., Bowling, M., & Harris, J. (this volume). Decentering student "uniqueness" in lessons about intersectionality. In K. A. Case (Ed.), *Intersectional pedagogy: Complicating identity and social justice* (pp. 194–213). New York, NY: Routledge.

Rivera, D. P. (this volume). Revealing hidden intersections of gender identity, sexual orientation, race, and ethnicity: Teaching about multiple oppressed identities. In K. A. Case (Ed.), *Intersectional pedagogy: Complicating identity and social justice* (pp 173–193). New York, NY: Routledge.

Rodenborg, N., & Boisen, L. (2013). Aversive racism and intergroup contact theories: Cultural competence in a segregated world. *Journal of Social Work Education, 49,* 564–579.

Routenberg, R., & Sclafani, T. (2010). Facilitating through "perfectly logical explanations (PLEs)" and other challenging participant comments. *Voices: ACPA's Commission for Social Justice Educators Newsletter, Fall & Winter,* 6.

Sanders, M., & Mahalingham, R. (2012). Under the radar: The role of invisible discourse in understanding class-based privilege. *Journal of Social Issues, 68*(1), 112–127. doi:10.1111/j.1540-4560.2011.01739.x

Search for Common Ground. (2015). Dialogue +. Retrieved from www.sfcg.org/tag/dialogue/

Solórzano, D., & Bernal, D. (2001). Examining transformational resistance through critical race theory and LatCRIT theory framework: Chicana and Chicano students in an urban context. *Urban Education, 36*, 308–342. doi:10.1177/0042085901363002

Sorensen, N., Nagda, B., Gurin, P., & Maxwell, K. (2009). Taking a "hands on" approach to diversity in higher education: A critical-dialogic model for effective intergroup interaction. *Analyses of Social Issues and Public Policy, 9*(1), 3–35. doi:10.1111/j.1530-2415.2009.01193.x

Spencer, M., Martineau, D., & Warren, N. (2011). Extending intergroup dialogue facilitation to multicultural social work practice. In K. E. Maxwell, B. A. Nagda, & M. Thompson (Eds.), *Facilitating intergroup dialogues: Bridging differences, catalyzing change* (pp. 147–159). Sterling, VA: Stylus Publishing.

Szymanski, D., & Gupta, A. (2009). Examining the relationship between multiple internalized oppressions and African American lesbian, gay, bisexual, and questioning persons' self-esteem and psychological distress. *Journal of Counseling Psychology, 56*(1), 110–118. doi:10.1037/a0012981

Uwujaren, J., & Utt, J. (2015, January 11). Why our feminism must be intersectional (and 3 ways to practice it) [Web log post]. Retrieved from everydayfeminism.com

Walls, E., Roll, S., Sprague, L., & Griffin, R. (2010). Teaching about privilege: A model combining intergroup dialogue and single identity caucusing. *Understanding and Dismantling Privilege, 1*(1), 1–32.

Wernick, L., Dessel, A., Kulick, A., & Graham, L. (2013). LGBTQQ youth creating change: Developing allies against bullying through performance and dialogue. *Children and Youth Services Review, 35*, 1576–1586. doi:10.1016/j.childyouth.2013.06.005

Wise, T., & Case, K. (2013). Pedagogy for the privileged: Addressing inequality and injustice without shame or blame. In K. Case (Ed.), *Deconstructing privilege: Teaching and learning as allies in the classroom* (pp. 17–33). New York, NY: Routledge.

Zúñiga, X., Nagda, B. A., Chesler, M., & Cytron-Walker, A. (2007). Intergroup dialogue in higher education: Meaningful learning about social justice. *ASHE Higher Education Report, 32*, 1–128.

CONTRIBUTORS

Glenn Adams, PhD, is Professor of Psychology, Director of the Cultural Psychology Research Group, and (until recently) Faculty Associate Director of the Kansas African Studies Center at the University of Kansas. He served as a Peace Corps Volunteer in Sierra Leone before completing his PhD at Stanford University. His graduate training included two years of field research in Ghana, which provided the empirical foundation for his research on cultural-psychological foundations of relationship. His current work builds on this foundation to decolonize knowledge production in psychological science and to articulate models of human development that promote sustainable ways of being and global justice.

Matthew J. Bowling is pursuing a master's degree in psychology from the University of Houston-Clear Lake. His thesis is focused on relationships between perceived morality of formerly incarcerated persons and knowledge of social structures that contribute to higher incarceration rates based on racial and social class stereotypes of some groups compared to other groups.

Kim A. Case, PhD, is Professor of Psychology at the University of Houston-Clear Lake, Faculty Mentoring Program Chair, Director of Undergraduate Psychology, and Director of the Applied Social Issues graduate program. Her mixed-methods research examines ally behavior when encountering bias and interventions to increase understanding of intersectionality and systemic privilege as well as reduce prejudice. Her pedagogical scholarship addresses diversity-course effectiveness, inclusive classroom practices, and teaching for social justice. Her previous edited book, *Deconstructing Privilege: Teaching and Learning* *as Allies in the Classroom* (2013), focuses on pedagogical strategies for teaching about privilege through an intersectional lens. As both Fellow of the American Psychological Association and Fellow of the Society for the Psychological Study of Social Issues (SPSSI), she serves on the APA Council of Representatives governing board and SPSSI Council.

Timothy Corvidae, LMSW, is a lecturer in the Program on Intergroup Relations (IGR), the Center for Global and Intercultural Study, and the School of Social Work at the University of Michigan. He is interested in experiential pedagogies that connect students to an awareness of positionality and that develop critical thinking, intercultural awareness and communications skills that will be useful beyond the classroom. He draws on a wide range of tools in his teaching, from Theatre of the Oppressed games to research on sense-making. Timothy is also a mediator, therapist, and facilitator using a Narrative approach.

Adrienne Dessel, PhD, LMSW, is Co-Associate Director of the Program on Intergroup Relations (IGR) at the University of Michigan. Her research and teaching focus on attitudes and prejudice reduction, intergroup relations, global conflict and co-existence, and processes and outcomes of intergroup dialogue pedagogy, most recently on topics of conservative Christianity and sexual orientation, Arab/Jewish conflict, and gender. Her recent edited book with Dr. Rebecca Bolen is *Conservative Christian Beliefs and Sexual Orientation in Social Work: Privilege, Oppression, and the Pursuit of Human Rights.* Her community consultations include social justice education and intergroup dialogue facilitation.

Ronni Michelle Greenwood, PhD, University of Limerick. Her research is concerned with social identity intersections and their influence on well-being, group processes, and intergroup relations. In her research on gender, she investigates the ways in which gender combines with other social identities, such as Muslim or immigrant, to shape women's social experiences and well-being. In her research on social justice, she investigates the ways in which white privilege shapes beliefs about minority groups and minority group concerns.

Patrick R. Grzanka, PhD, is Assistant Professor of Psychology at the University of Tennessee, Knoxville. His book *Intersectionality: A Foundations and Frontiers Reader* (2014) explores the history and future of intersectionality theory across the disciplines. His interdisciplinary research investigates the cultural politics of emotions and mental health, and his work has been funded by the National Science Foundation and published in leading journals, including the *Journal of Counseling Psychology*, *Sexualities*, *Sexuality Research and Social Policy*, and *American Journal of Bioethics: Neuroscience*. He holds a PhD in American Studies from the University of Maryland and formerly taught at Arizona State University.

Naomi M. Hall, PhD, MPH is Associate Professor in the Department of Psychological Sciences at Winston-Salem State University. She earned her MPH from San Diego State University, and her MA and PhD in Applied Social Psychology from Claremont Graduate University. Her primary research focus is on social and cultural factors associated with health disparities within the Black/African American community, particularly among young men and women attending Historically Black Colleges/Universities. She is an elected council member of the Society for the Psychological Study of Social Issues, Division 9 of the American Psychological Association.

Jacquelyn Harris, MA, earned her master's degree in psychology at the University of Houston-Clear Lake. Her master's thesis focused on the relationship between coping mechanisms, specifically John Henryism, used by racial/ethnic minorities and academic achievement in Latina/o Americans.

Tuğçe Kurtiş, PhD, is Assistant Professor of Psychology and Faculty Member of the Women's Studies Program at the University of West Georgia. She completed her doctorate in Social Psychology and a graduate certificate in African Studies at the University of Kansas. Drawing upon perspectives in cultural, feminist, and critical psychologies and interdisciplinary discussions in postcolonial studies and transnational feminisms, her research focuses on sociocultural constructions of subjectivity and relationality, which she examines through joint processes of voice and silence in interpersonal and collective experience. Her main objective as a social psychologist is to use psychological theory, pedagogy, and practice as resources for global social justice.

Michele K. Lewis, PhD, is Associate Professor of Psychology and Chair of the Department of Psychological Sciences at Winston Salem State University in North Carolina. She is the author of two books, *Multicultural Health Psychology: Special Topics Acknowledging Diversity* and *LGBT Psychology: Research Perspectives and People of African Descent.*

Nancy A. Naples, PhD, is Board of Trustees Distinguished Professor of Sociology and Women's, Gender, and Sexuality Studies at the University of Connecticut. Her research focuses on the intersection of gender, sexuality, race, political activism, and citizenship in comparative perspective. She is author of *Grassroots Warriors: Activist Mothering, Community Work, and the War on Poverty* and *Feminism and Method.* She is editor of *Community Activism and Feminist Politics* and co-editor of *Border Politics: Social Movements, Collective Identities, and Globalization, Women's Activism and Globalization: Linking Local Struggles and Transnational Politics,* and *Teaching Feminist Activism.* She is series editor for *Praxis: Theory in Action* published by SUNY Press.

Desdamona Rios, PhD, is Assistant Professor of Psychology and Women's Studies at the University of Houston-Clear Lake. She uses mixed research methods to study identity development in academic contexts. Her current projects include examining the role of culturally relevant curriculum in academic identity development among Latina/o American high school students, and narrative identity among diverse groups of gay, bisexual and queer college men.

David P. Rivera, PhD, is Associate Professor of Counselor Education at Queens College, City University of New York. A counseling psychologist by training, his practical work includes consultations and trainings on a variety of cultural competency issues. He holds degrees from Teachers College, Columbia University, Johns Hopkins University, and the University of Wyoming. His research focuses on cultural competency development and issues impacting the marginalization and well-being of people of color and oppressed sexual orientation and gender identity groups, with a focus on microaggressions. He is currently board co-chair of CLAGS: Center for LGBTQ Studies, on the executive committee of the APA's Society for the Psychological Study of Lesbian, Gay, Bisexual, and Transgender Issues, a consulting editor for the journal *Psychology of Sexual Orientation and Gender Diversity*, and an adviser to The Steve Fund. He has received multiple recognitions for his work, including national honors from the American Psychological Association, the American College Counseling Association, and the American College Personnel Association.

INDEX

West, C. 115
"We Wear the Mask" 138, 141
Whistling Vivaldi 197, 200
White male privilege 208
White men 156
whiteness, and intersectionality 49
White women, privilege of 2
Wiegman, R. 76–7, 111, 112
Wijeyesinghe, C. L. 2, 11, 153
Williams, P. 75
Winston Salem State University (WSSU)
  131–2
women: Black American 48, 67;
  health outcomes 30; loss of self 52;

objectification of 73; privilege of White
  women 2
Women, Race, and Class 114
Women's Lives: A Psychological Exploration
  84
women's movement 37, 113
women's studies, and intersectionality 111
word usage, revaluation of 179–80

Yuval-Davis, N. 114, 115

Zambrana, R. E. 14, 135, 142–3, 153–4,
  155
Zwier, E. 7–8

Taylor & Francis eBooks

Helping you to choose the right eBooks for your Library

Add Routledge titles to your library's digital collection today. Taylor and Francis ebooks contains over 50,000 titles in the Humanities, Social Sciences, Behavioural Sciences, Built Environment and Law.

Choose from a range of subject packages or create your own!

Benefits for you

- » Free MARC records
- » COUNTER-compliant usage statistics
- » Flexible purchase and pricing options
- » All titles DRM-free.

Benefits for your user

- » Off-site, anytime access via Athens or referring URL
- » Print or copy pages or chapters
- » Full content search
- » Bookmark, highlight and annotate text
- » Access to thousands of pages of quality research at the click of a button.

Free Trials Available
We offer free trials to qualifying academic, corporate and government customers.

eCollections – Choose from over 30 subject eCollections, including:

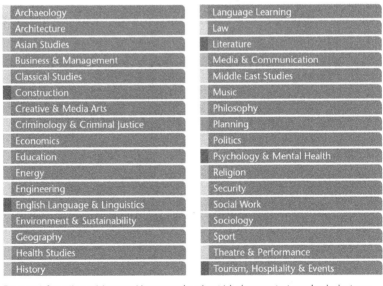

Archaeology	Language Learning
Architecture	Law
Asian Studies	Literature
Business & Management	Media & Communication
Classical Studies	Middle East Studies
Construction	Music
Creative & Media Arts	Philosophy
Criminology & Criminal Justice	Planning
Economics	Politics
Education	Psychology & Mental Health
Energy	Religion
Engineering	Security
English Language & Linguistics	Social Work
Environment & Sustainability	Sociology
Geography	Sport
Health Studies	Theatre & Performance
History	Tourism, Hospitality & Events

For more information, pricing enquiries or to order a free trial, please contact your local sales team:
www.tandfebooks.com/page/sales